THE CASE AGAINST SOCIALISM

ALSO BY RAND PAUL

The Tea Party Goes to Washington
Government Bullies
Taking a Stand
Our Presidents & Their Prayers

ALSO BY KELLEY ASHBY PAUL

True and Constant Friends

The

CASE
AGAINST
SOCIALISM

RAND PAUL

with

KELLEY ASHBY PAUL

BROADSIDE BOOKS
An Imprint of HarperCollins*Publishers*

THE CASE AGAINST SOCIALISM. Copyright © 2019 by Rand Paul. All rights reserved. Printed in the United States of America. No part of this book may be used or reproduced in any manner whatsoever without written permission except in the case of brief quotations embodied in critical articles and reviews. For information, address HarperCollins Publishers, 195 Broadway, New York, NY 10007.

HarperCollins books may be purchased for educational, business, or sales promotional use. For information, please email the Special Markets Department at SPsales@harpercollins.com.

Broadside Books™ and the Broadside logo are trademarks of HarperCollins Publishers.

FIRST EDITION

Library of Congress Cataloging-in-Publication Data has been applied for.

ISBN 978-0-06-295486-2

19 20 21 22 23   LSC   10 9 8 7 6 5 4 3 2 1

FOR KELLEY

In the dream you are gone
Every time
Not left
but mostly just erased
Your face flutters
Dances blurs
Approaches and recedes
I struggle
but can't bring you into focus

For whatever reason
I let you get away

one phone call
One bloody phone call
Why didn't I make that call?

you slip away

gravity pulls me under
Into an alternate universe
Where neither light nor love escape

A terrible what if
Consumes me
Till I wake beside you
And realize
I must have made that call

CONTENTS

Part VI: Never Let a Crisis Go to Waste: Socialism and Alarmism

THE CASE AGAINST SOCIALISM

INTRODUCTION

It was one of those long-winded speeches in front of thousands of goose-stepping soldiers that seem to be a signature performance in authoritarian regimes. The parade stands along Caracas's Avenida Bolivar are filled with posturing Venezuelan government officials and generals.

As President Nicolas Maduro steps to the podium, unbeknownst to him, two DJI M600 drones speed toward him. These drones are typically used by professional photographers and can carry about thirteen pounds but have a battery life of only sixteen minutes.[1]

The two drones speeding toward the dais each carry a payload of 2.2 pounds of plastic explosives. While they are not military drones, their intent is the same—assassination.[2]

As Maduro's speech plods on, his wife is the first to react. She glances quickly upward and her face registers horror at the six-rotor beast hovering above them in the sky before the first explosion occurs. It takes a second or two for Maduro to digest that the fire blast was meant for him.

All hell breaks loose. Seconds later, a second drone detonates down the street into the Don Eduardo apartment block. The parading soldiers break ranks and run helter-skelter. Maduro's security team screens him from the direction of the explosions with large cloth-covered shields.[3]

Though seven soldiers are injured, the socialist dictator of Venezuela is unharmed. Maduro later told reporters: "That drone was coming for me but there was a shield of love. I am sure I will live for many more years."[4]

Who would want to kill President Maduro, the leader of a socialist paradise that Hollywood star Sean Penn once claimed had alleviated 80 percent of the poverty in Venezuela?

Perhaps it was the sixteen-year-old girl who leads a gang that fights rival gangs for control of an operation that sifts through garbage for edible food. Or perhaps it is one of the young men from Chacao who hunt dogs and cats in the street and pigeons in the plaza to eat.

I'd like to know what Sean Penn would say to Lis Torrealba, nineteen, a Venezuelan refugee who fled to Colombia with her one-year-old daughter in a desperate attempt to escape starvation in Venezuela. She is one of more than a million Venezuelans who have done the same. Megan Janetsky, in an article for *USA Today*, wrote of the effects of lack of food and medicine, and of hyperinflation. She quoted Torrealba, "The money in our country, I couldn't even buy candy if I wanted to. . . . I can't buy anything, if there's something you need. You would need a stack of money to even pay for a tomato. You would need a big stack of money."[5]

Or maybe the attackers are related to one of the hundreds of political dissidents held without trial in Venezuelan jails. The attackers could be related to the thousands dying of curable infectious diseases in a country whose hospitals are filthy and crumbling. Nicholas Casey reported in the *New York Times*:

> *Hospital wards have become crucibles where the forces tearing Venezuela apart have converged. Gloves and soap have vanished from some hospitals. Often, cancer medicines are found only on the black market. There is so little electricity that the government works only two days a week to save what energy is left.*
>
> *At the University of the Andes Hospital in the mountain city of Mérida, there was not enough water to wash blood from the*

operating table. Doctors preparing for surgery cleaned their hands with bottles of seltzer water.

"It is like something from the 19th century," said Dr. Christian Pino, a surgeon at the hospital.[6]

The attackers really could be any one of Venezuela's citizenry who have lost on average almost twenty pounds from lack of food.

But this is not the story of who tried to kill Maduro with a homemade explosive drone. Rather, this is the story of an evil that inevitably and inexorably leads to poverty, starvation, and ultimately violence. This is a story of the continued false allure and sophistry of an evil that has killed millions of people and even today threatens a new generation of the naive.

This is the story of an evil well documented and yet still somehow enticing, even in America. This is the story of socialism in all its drab and dreary machinelike destruction of individual thought, creativity, and ambition. This is the story of socialism in all of its violence, bloodshed, and tyranny. It is a cautionary tale of how America has so far eluded the siren call of something for nothing, of an equality determined and enforced by the government—but also of how close we still are to succumbing to socialism.

President Trump in his January 2019 State of the Union address made it clear to the growing faction of socialists in Congress that "America will never become a socialist country!"

Republican members of Congress jumped to their feet with cheers of "USA. USA."

As the cameras panned in on the socialist senator from Vermont, though, he did not look pleased.

Trump explained that Maduro had taken the richest country in South America and inflicted socialist policies that brought "abject poverty and despair" to Venezuela.

The president explained to congressional socialists: "America was founded on liberty and independence and not government coercion, domination, and control. We are born free and we will stay free."

The most famous socialist in America, Bernie Sanders, pursed his lips and glowered at the president.

Later that night Sanders responded: "Trump says 'We are born free, and we will stay free.' I say to Trump: People are not truly free when they can't afford health care, prescription drugs, or a place to live. People are not free when they cannot retire with dignity or feed their families."

I guess Senator Sanders hasn't noticed that food and medicine are completely unaffordable and nearly unavailable in Venezuela. Sanders continues to assert that the democratic socialism he advocates for is somehow different, that his version of socialism will "reform a political system in America today which is not only grossly unfair but, in many respects, corrupt."

Sanders's socialism will make the world "fair." Yet, nowhere is the explanation of who gets to define "fair" and what weapons the "fairness police" will wield when they come.

President Trump is right to be concerned about socialism coming to America. A recent Gallup poll indicates that 57 percent of Democrats have a favorable view of socialism.[7]

What is it about socialism that casts such a spell that people refuse to acknowledge history? Time and time again socialism leads to the impoverishment of nations. Perhaps it is the allure of equality or fairness. Surveys in America alarmingly show about half of today's youth have a favorable opinion of socialism.[8] A Gallup poll found that 45 percent of young American adults (age 18–29) have a positive view of capitalism, while 51 percent of this same group see socialism positively.[9] These surveys link approval of socialism to a corresponding desire among young Americans to live in a "fair" world. Blasi and Kruse of Rutgers University write that "today's youth reject capitalism; what they really want is fairness."

They cite a "2016 Harvard University survey that found that 51 percent of American youth age 18 to 29 no longer support capitalism," and another 2015 poll by "conservative-leaning Reason-Rupe, [which] found that young adults age 18 to 24 have a slightly more favorable view of socialism than capitalism."

When asked to explain their answers in the Harvard Study, participants in a focus group reported feeling that "capitalism was unfair and left people out despite their hard work."[10] The mantra of fairness is one that is inculcated from a young age. The assumption is that in order for one person to become rich someone else must suffer. Leftists preach that the economy is a zero-sum game where the rich enrich themselves on the backs of the poor, a claim that is revealed to be false when you examine the facts.

The great industrialists of the nineteenth century are often tagged as robber barons. Yet as Andrew Carnegie's wealth grew so did the economy. Poverty declined from over 90 percent of people living in extreme poverty worldwide in 1820 to around 75 percent of people living in extreme poverty in 1910. By the time the industrial revolution was in full swing, wages were rising and the standard of living known previously only to kings was becoming far more accessible. From the time of Carnegie's death in 1919 until the present, the number of people living in extreme poverty declined to less than 10 percent.[11] As much of the world embraced capitalism in the twentieth century, childhood mortality plummeted from nearly a third of children dying before the age of five to less than 1 percent in wealthy countries and 4.3 percent worldwide.[12]

And still, American youth mistakenly are attracted to socialism.

Blasi and Kruse warn us that "the share of the overall population that questions capitalism's core precepts is around the highest in at least 80 years of polling on the topic." Gallup, in a 2016 poll, records 55 percent of millennials as favoring socialism.[13]

Yet, when millennials say they are for socialism, do they have any idea what socialism is in a historical sense? How many of them are even aware of the famines under Stalin, Mao, and Pol Pot? Reason Foundation asked millennials to define socialism and discovered that only 16 percent could identify socialism as government ownership of the means of production.[14]

The only good news about these surveys of young people is that they were overwhelmingly canceled out by the views of older people.

A study published in sciencemag.org concluded that although "children start off like Karl Marx, . . . they eventually become more like a member of the International Olympic Committee. The study 'finds that children's views on fairness change from egalitarian to merit-based as they grow older.'"[15]

The question is—will this next generation follow the path of previous generations? Will today's youth, when they leave their parents' basements and begin to earn a living, discover that their success depends on their merit and hard work, or will they succumb like Venezuela to the allure of something for nothing?

Part I

Because Eating Your Pets Is Overrated— Socialism Creates Poverty

Chapter 1

SOCIALISM DESTROYED VENEZUELA'S ONCE-VIBRANT ECONOMY

Socialism's great. Just ask Oliver Stone.

Oliver Stone has composed not one but two biopics glorifying the socialism of Hugo Chavez. Wonder if it'll become a trilogy with the finale showing images of Venezuelans eating their pets and burning their currency for warmth?

Doubt it. Remorse and honest regret are not found in any great quantity in Hollywood.

How did Oliver Stone, Michael Moore, and Sean Penn get it so wrong when observing the Venezuelan "miracle"?

Venezuela was so rich with oil that it took some time for socialism to completely destroy its once-vibrant economy. Even to this day Venezuela still has the largest oil reserves in the world, even greater than Saudi Arabia's. They just can't get it out of the ground because socialism has destroyed the pricing system, and endless government spending and debt caused hyperinflation that has destroyed its currency.

Some blame Chavez for this disaster. Some blame Maduro. But really, could any one man take a country with more oil reserves than Saudi Arabia and screw it up so badly that hundreds of thousands of citizens would flee the country? Could one man take the richest country in South America and turn it into a hellhole where citizens literally starve in the streets?

Chavez and Maduro alone didn't lay waste to Venezuela. Rather, it was the terrible constellation of ideas called socialism that reached its pinnacle under Chavez and Maduro that devastated Venezuela.

Some like to point to the Castro-loving Hugo Chavez as the beginning of socialism in Venezuela, but the roots of its government owning the means of production started decades before Chavez. State control over Venezuela's oil industry dates back to the 1970s.

According to José Niño, "in the 1950s, . . . Venezuela was at its peak, with a fourth-place ranking in terms of per capita GDP worldwide."[1] In the 1950s, when the Perez Jimenez government ruled, there were no extensive price controls. At that time, Venezuela was neither democratic nor a completely free market economy but rather a military regime with aspects of crony capitalism. For the most part, prices were not controlled and a limited marketplace allowed supply and demand to intersect and work their magic.

As Niño describes it: "A combination of a relatively free economy, an immigration system that attracted and assimilated laborers from Italy, Portugal, and Spain and a system of strong property rights, allowed Venezuela to experience unprecedented levels of economic development from the 1940s up until the 1970s."[2]

Daniel Lahoud is a professor at the Universidad Católica Andrés Bello, a Catholic university, and at the Universidad Central de Venezuela (UCV). Lahoud describes Venezuela's long path to socialism:

"Before 1973 our government did not own any companies and Venezuela grew 6.5 percent year-on-year. In contrast, between

1974 and 1998 we experimented with democratic socialism and brought GDP growth to 1.9 percent year-on-year. Since 1999 we are experimenting with scientific socialism and the rhythm is 0.0 percent or negative."[3] (Today, Venezuela's GDP is contracting at 10 percent.)

In contrast, consider another South American country, Chile, which abandoned its flirtation with socialism back in 1973. At that time, Chilean income was about 36 percent of Venezuela's. Operating under free markets and capitalism, Chilean incomes have increased by 228 percent, while Venezuelan incomes have declined by 21 percent. Capitalism has left Chileans 51 percent richer than their Venezuelan counterparts, who now starve despite the vast resources of their country.[4]

Lahoud thinks it is very important that people understand not only the enormity of Venezuela's disaster but the root cause:

"I have known the reality of the failure of socialism in my own flesh. And as I live in Venezuela, I want to show that this is an absolute failure always and everywhere. Socialism, whatever form it may take, only brings economic destruction and worsening of the conditions of human life."

Lahoud admits that "Venezuela was never a country of economic freedoms. But when we had less public spending, we grew more. . . ."[5]

In the late 1950s, military rule was replaced with "democracy." Romulo Betancourt (1959–64), an ex-communist, assumed the reins of power and made a significant turn away from a market economy. Niño describes Betancourt as adopting a "more gradualist approach of establishing socialism," as he was "part of a generation of intellectuals and student activists that aimed to fully nationalize Venezuela's petroleum sector and use petroleum rents to establish a welfare state. . . ." So, socialism in Venezuela was not a new program created by Chavez, but rather Chavez simply took socialism to another level.

Niño tells us that Betancourt's government tripled income taxes and generated massive fiscal deficits that "would become a fixture in Venezuelan public finance during the pre-Chávez era."[6]

Betancourt was succeeded by Carlos Andres Perez, who nationalized the entire petroleum sector in 1975.

As Niño puts it:

> *The nationalization of Venezuela's oil industry fundamentally altered the nature of the Venezuelan state. Venezuela morphed into a petrostate, in which the concept of the consent of the governed was effectively turned on its head.*
>
> *Instead of Venezuelans paying taxes to the government in exchange for the protection of property and similar freedoms, the Venezuelan state would play a patrimonial role by bribing its citizens with all sorts of handouts to maintain its dominion over them.*[7]

If socialism means that the state owns the means of production, then 1975 was a significant milestone in Venezuela's descent into socialism. With enormous oil reserves and a steady flow of cash, it would take a decade or two for socialist policies in the form of price controls and currency controls to completely ravage the economy.

Chavez didn't just arrive unannounced on the scene. He first came to prominence in a failed coup in 1992 against the Andres Perez regime. Chavez was imprisoned for two years. Upon his release, he decided this time to take power through the political process. He founded the Fifth Republic Movement and was ultimately elected president of Venezuela in 1998.

Leftists in America heralded Chavez's election. Bernie Sanders, Noam Chomsky, and others pointed with glee to data showing a decline in poverty. When socialism finally strangled the economy and Chavez resorted to violent means to quell protests, many on the left went radio silent on Venezuela.

Some leftists, however, stuck with Chavez and put an interesting spin on their defense of state violence against the people. George Ciccariello-Maher is a writer and activist who supported Venezuela's Bolivarian Revolution led by Chavez. He taught political science at Drexel University until being consumed by a Twitter storm over his tweet: "All I want for Christmas is White Genocide." When prompted to clarify his comments, he tweeted: "when the whites were massacred during the Haitian revolution, that was a good thing."[8]

Commenting on Chavez's crackdown on protesters, Ciccariello-Maher wrote: "If we are against unnecessary brutality, there is nevertheless a radically democratic form of brutality that we cannot disavow entirely. This is the same brutality that 'dragged the Bourbons off the throne' [. . .] This was not brutality for brutality's sake [. . .] It is instead a strange paradox: egalitarian brutality, the radically democratic dictatorship of the wretched of the earth. Those smeared today [. . .] are in fact the most direct and organic expression of the wretched of the Venezuelan earth."[9]

Oh my . . . "egalitarian brutality" . . . "democratic brutality"—so much for democratic elections restraining the excesses of socialism.

When Maduro took over from Chavez, some questioned whether the ensuing disaster should be blamed on Maduro. On the one hand, the country was already in a tailspin when Chavez died. Maduro, in many ways, was simply a continuation of the Chavez rule. Maduro was seen as Chavez without the charisma, and there was not enough distinction between the two to lay more blame on one than the other.

By the time Maduro came to power, Chavez had created a

massive socialist welfare state to transfer wealth with the goal of eliminating income inequality, all financed by the enormous cash flow from oil.

As Al Jazeera described it, "As Chavez strived to transform the nation with what he called 21st century socialism, his populist policies began to take a more radical turn. He nationalized industries and bloated state bureaucracy at great national expense, all funded by high oil prices and unchecked borrowing. Venezuela became saddled with record-high levels of debt."[10]

Yet, for several years Venezuela continued to plug along.

As CNN reported: "Hugo Chavez, the man who built his powerful persona on a populist platform of sharing Venezuela's vast oil wealth with the poor and disenfranchised, leaves his nation with a greater distribution of cash to the poor."[11]

Chavez's Hollywood supporters continued to crow about how income inequality was melting away in Venezuela. CNN reported that income inequality "dropped to among the lowest in the Americas during his tenure" and cited the World Bank reporting that "those living below the poverty line fell to 36.3% in 2006 from 50.4% in 1998 and infant mortality fell from 20.3 per thousand births when Chavez took over to 12.9 in 2011."[12]

And yet the dream of socialist paradise was always ephemeral. As Maduro came to power in 2013, the mirage of Venezuelan socialism vanished, only to reveal a disaster of immense proportion. The result was an economic catastrophe that included hyperinflation and mountains of debt and food shortages never before seen in modern Venezuela.

Margarita Lopez Maya, a professor at Central University of Venezuela, said, "Venezuelans today cannot eat. You see people eating from the garbage."[13]

When Chavez died in March 2013, Venezuela was already

poised to fail. As Al Jazeera reported, "Chavez handed over both the reins of power to his handpicked successor, Nicolas Maduro, as well as the poisoned chalice of an economy about to implode."[14] Within months of his death, Venezuela was forced to devalue the bolivar by 30 percent against the dollar. Despite having the world's largest oil reserves, oil production began to decline.

Venezuela's dependence on oil became its Achilles' heel. When oil prices hit the skids, the fragility of Venezuela's economy became apparent.

Ricardo Hausmann, a former Venezuelan government official, describes the economic collapse as "the largest recession in Western Hemisphere history—significantly larger, almost twice as large as the Great Depression of the US."[15]

How severe was the collapse? GDP contracted by more than 10 percent as inflation soared to 26,000 percent.[16]

Food became scarce as grocery store shelves emptied. The British newspaper *Independent* reported that "the economic crisis in Venezuela is so severe that 75 percent of the country's population has lost an average of 19 pounds in weight...."[17]

Peter Wilson at *USA Today* interviewed Roberto Sanchez, an unemployed construction worker in La Victoria, Venezuela, "as he waited in a line with 300 people outside a grocery store."

Sanchez: "We have no food. They are cutting power four hours a day. Crime is soaring. And Maduro blames everyone but himself...."

Wilson quotes the mayor of Chacao: "People are hunting dogs and cats in the street, and pigeons in the plaza to eat." Hyperinflation and currency controls limit the importation of food and medicine. Over the years, Venezuela, rather than grow its own food, purchased more than 70 percent from abroad, paying for it from oil sales.

Medicine shortages also plague Venezuela. You can hear the anguish in Luis Avila's voice: "My four year old daughter is dying of cancer, and there's no medicine here to treat her."[18]

Three Venezuelan universities conducted a "National Survey of Living Conditions."

About a third of Venezuelans were found to only have enough food for two meals or less each day. Whereas Sean Penn and others had lauded Chavez for eliminating 80 percent of poverty, this survey found that 87 percent of Venezuelan households had descended into poverty.[19]

The survey found that poverty had nearly doubled from 48 percent in 2014 to 87 percent in 2017. So much for socialism curing poverty. As poverty exploded under Maduro's socialism, more than a half-million people fled Venezuela into Colombia and Brazil.[20]

Socialism destroyed the economy of a country with vast natural resources. Despite the promises of leftist politicians and celebrities, the truth won't be denied: socialism poisons everything it touches.

Chapter 2

SOCIALISM
REWARDS CORRUPTION

Like most socialists, Chavez was elected on a promise to help the poor and equalize income, and yet like most socialists, he did not apply the theory of equality to himself.

Sympathetic international agencies reported that Chavez did partly succeed in reducing income inequality. But the result was less income inequality *and* less overall prosperity. Which goes to the heart of the question: would you rather be richer yourself—or make sure the rich get poorer?

And as the overall economy in Venezuela finally cratered, it became obvious that as Orwell warned, "some animals are more equal than others." As poverty and hunger became widespread across Venezuela, Chavez himself got richer and richer and fatter and fatter.

Famous for bloviating ad nauseam against the rich, Chavez was secretly enriching himself. As the *Washington Examiner* reported, "billions of dollars of public funds were diverted into secret Swiss bank accounts. The major beneficiaries of the Chavez regime appear to have been his family and friends. His daughter is reported to be a multibillionaire and the richest person in Venezuela. By contrast, Venezuelan doctors make an average of $2.20/day."[1]

What about Cuba? A refugee from Cuba tells of his father who as a doctor in Cuba had to "sell illegal meats out of his ambulance ... because Cuban doctors earn less than 1% of American doctors."[2]

Chavez and Maduro both worshipped at Castro's Cuban altar and visited Cuba often. In fact, Venezuela and Cuba were in many ways joined at the hip. For many years, Chavez then Maduro provided Cuba with oil below the market price.

It should surprise no one that Castro, like virtually every socialist leader before him, expressed nothing but love and concern for the proletariat while living like a king. Castro pretended to live in modest homes while shielding from the public his mansions and private islands. *Forbes* once estimated that Castro was worth nearly a billion dollars. As Keith Flamer comments: "That's a lot of socialist rationing for one person."[3]

Maduro, like Chavez, grew fatter and fatter as Venezuelans starved or took to scouring garbage for food. Like most men with money (in his case, someone else's money) he tried to disguise his enormous girth in supersized suits. (Think Ted Kennedy in his later years.) But his incessant need to be seen on television allowed the public to make up its own mind about whether Maduro subjected himself to the same "equal" lack of food as everyone else.

The public outcry hit a peak when Maduro was caught at a ritzy restaurant in Istanbul owned by the celebrity Nusret Gökçe ("Salt Bae"), stuffing his mouth with expensive steak personally cut into delectable morsels by the chef. Ironically, the celebrity chef had posted a photo of himself, cigar in hand, next to a poster of Castro to celebrate the opening of his luxury Miami restaurant. Only celebrity socialists can be so tone-deaf and obtuse.[4]

CNN recorded the response from exiled opposition leader Julio Borges: "while Venezuelans are suffering and dying of hunger, Nicolas Maduro and [his wife] Cilia enjoy one of the most expensive restaurants in the world, all at the expense of the money stolen from the Venezuelan people."[5]

Maduro had earlier singled out Borges as the mastermind of the failed drone assassination. Without any proof, of course. But proof is overrated in a dictatorship.[6]

The hypocrisy of yet another advocate of the people accumulating vast wealth is, unfortunately, the rule, not the exception. In fact, for all the incessant sop served up about equally distributing all goods and services, socialism and kleptocracy often seem indistinguishable.

Glenn Reynolds puts it this way: "Under capitalism, rich people become powerful. But under socialism, powerful people become rich."[7]

Power corrupts and as Lord Acton remarked: "absolute power corrupts absolutely." Unless you imagine a voluntary revolution where all owners of industry or commerce give up their wealth to the state, you have to acknowledge that state ownership of the means of production can only occur at the end of a truncheon.

Around the world, time and time again, strongmen have come to power promising the free stuff of socialism, only to succumb to the siren song of power. In the end, many of these authoritarians are remembered more for their kleptocracy than their socialism, but it is important to remember that most of these dictators came to power promising to use the apparatus of the state to redistribute the wealth.

Egypt's Hosni Mubarak is another prime example. While history does not remember Mubarak as a socialist, people forget that Mubarak's rule as an authoritarian directly descended from Gamal Abdel Nasser's Arab socialism. As Gerard Di Trolio writes at jacobinmag.com, Hosni Mubarak's National Democratic Party was a member of the Socialist International for decades.[8]

Mubarak, however, was, for the most part, seen less as a socialist and more as an authoritarian adept at corruption and personal aggrandizement. Nevertheless, Nasser's ideology bore the same fruit that did so many other schemes to accumulate centralized power. Even as Mubarak returned some industries to private ownership, he did so while replacing state ownership with his family's ownership, proving once again that once power is obtained, accumulating one's own wealth becomes more important than spreading the wealth.

ABC News estimated that the Mubarak family's personal wealth was probably between $40 billion and $70 billion, thanks to "military contracts during his days as an air force officer."[9]

Who said socialism doesn't pay? All economies ultimately distribute goods and wealth unequally. For those who can't stand a capitalist economy where income is largely based on merit, a big government–planned economy doesn't necessarily result in income parity. It often means that instead of being distributed on merit, income is distributed through the prism of party loyalty and cronyism.

Over and over again, history shows that socialism quickly devolves into kleptocracy. After all, despite the lofty rhetoric of socialist thinkers, they cannot ignore the fact that human nature is inherently self-interested and self-preserving. Socialism has failed humanity in every country where it has been tried, from the former Soviet Union to China, from North Korea to Venezuela, always with the same disastrous results.

Not all dictators came to power promising socialism, egalitarianism, and redistribution of the nation's wealth. Yet, even without an overt socialist agenda, many of these dictatorships share the central tenet of socialism: government ownership of the means of production.

Corruption is the one consistent theme of big governments with central ownership of resources. Equatorial Guinea is a prime example. A small, oil-rich city-state in Africa ruled by the Obiang family, Equatorial Guinea takes the cake when it comes to the mantra "some are more equal than others." President for life Teodoro Obiang Nguema Mbasogo is worth billions while 75 percent of the citizens live on less than a dollar a day.[10]

Not only does the autocrat Obiang use public money to fund his lavish lifestyle, he also brazenly diverts oil offshore and sells it off the books for cash. Some say he siphons off 40 million pounds a day in oil revenues. His son Teodoro "Teodorín," though, puts a capital *L* in lavish. A few years back he was arrested leaving Switzerland on his private jet loaded with eleven superluxury cars.

"Among them was reportedly a Porsche valued at more than $830,000 (£667,000) and a Bugatti Veyron which sells for $2m (£1.7m)." At home, dear leader Dad closes the freeways so Teodorín can race his sports cars without interference from the hoi polloi.

The BBC reports that "[p]rosecutors in Geneva say [Teodorín] has plundered his country's oil wealth to buy luxuries, including a private jet and Michael Jackson memorabilia."[11]

If President Obiang is the penultimate crook, his son Teodorín is the ultimate kleptocrat. According to the *Guardian*, "his official salary as minister of agriculture and forestry is about £5,000 a month, but in just three years he spent twice as much as the state's annual education budget on luxury goods. He was caught trying to buy a £234m super yacht earlier this year—and last month was reported to have lost a briefcase in Swaziland with £250,000 inside. 'He's an unstable, reckless idiot,' commented one US intelligence official."[12]

Like Saudi Arabia, Obiang spends millions to curry favor with the United States and obscure their terrible human rights record. What does that kind of money buy? Can money buy respectability for a kleptocrat?

Well, it seems to have bought him a great picture with Condoleezza Rice and other world leaders.

Chapter 3

INTERFERING
WITH FREE MARKETS
CAUSES SHORTAGES

C havez and later Maduro instituted widespread price controls that José Niño describes as the "main culprit in Venezuela's economic tragedy." Beginning in 2002, Chavez went beyond the oil industry to nationalize other sectors of industry. Currency exchange limits and price controls were added as well.

Within a few years, widespread shortages were apparent. The result, as Niño reports, was "images of citizens waiting in lines to get basic goods—toilet paper, flour, milk" plastered across the Internet.[1] A fundamental law of economics is that if government sets a price of a good below the market price there will be shortages and a thriving black market. Even in the United States, when we've experimented with price controls, shortages have arisen.

Rutgers professor Hugh Rockoff explains that the vast majority of economists are generally opposed to price controls. He paraphrases Milton Friedman to show the havoc price controls wreak:

. . . economists may not know much, but they do know how to produce a shortage or surplus.

Price ceilings, which prevent prices from exceeding a certain maximum, cause shortages. Price floors, which prohibit prices below a certain minimum, cause surpluses, at least for a time. Suppose that the supply and demand for wheat flour are balanced at the current price, and that the government then fixes a lower maximum price. The supply of flour will decrease, but the demand for it will increase. The result will be excess demand and empty shelves. Although some consumers will be lucky enough to purchase flour at the lower price, others will be forced to do without.[2]

Even in the United States, we have not been immune to the economic foolishness of price controls.

I'll never forget the gas shortages of the Carter era. I had just turned sixteen and was allowed the great "privilege" of driving my parents' red Vista Cruiser station wagon (with brown faux wood panel stripe, a real girl magnet). Carter put price controls on gas, and within weeks we had long lines at all the gas stations, while down at our local beach the talk was of full oil tankers floating offshore refusing to sell their oil below the market price. I remember being so angry. I had finally graduated from riding my bike everywhere to having my own wheels, only to be stymied by gas lines.

So, too, the havoc of price controls in Venezuela, only Chavez and Maduro refused to admit failure as Carter ultimately did.

By 2014, as inflation soared to several thousand percent, the Venezuelan government banned "profit margins over 30% and tightened price ceilings on basic goods."[3] With food shortages across Venezuela, the government set up committees to distribute what little food was available. And to no one's surprise, the Maduro supporters were granted front-of-the-line access.

With Venezuela dependent on foreign trade and multinational companies for much of its food and consumer items, companies chafed at price controls, and many shut down completely. Colgate-Palmolive and Nestlé plants shut down. Mexican bottler Femsa threatened to shut down. "Thousands of companies across the country have slowed production and at least 20 percent have stopped operating for lack of raw materials or customers."[4]

Are price controls socialism? Perhaps not precisely, but prices are a vital component of a market economy. Without prices consumers cannot judge how much to buy, and producers cannot judge how much to create. Without the feedback loop of prices, imbalances quickly arise, and only the outlet of the black market keeps complete collapse from occurring.

As Niño explains: "For producers, prices communicate whether it is a good time to enter or leave a certain market. Falling prices and the potential for losses signal to employers the need to leave a market. On the other hand, rising prices and potential for profit-making incentivize producers to enter a market."[5]

Some economists do argue, as George Reisman does, that price controls establish a "de facto socialism." The de facto socialism arises because price controls lead to shortages, which then lead to rationing, which is only enforceable with a price control police and ultimately a policing of production as well. While socialism is typically defined as government ownership of the means of production, Reisman argues that "socialism is not actually a positive economic system. It is merely the negation of capitalism and the price system." So, price controls that destroy freely fluctuating prices require centralization of power and essentially control also of the means of production.[6]

Reisman does a great job arguing that the enforcement of price controls inevitably "requires a government similar to that of Hitler's Germany or Stalin's Russia." Why? Because man's natural impulse to self-interest and self-preservation always leads to a

black market. As shortages and famine appear, the black marketers are not deterred by penalties alone or even the threat of jail.
Finally, because the people starve unless they purchase food on
the black market, it becomes difficult to get juries to convict black
marketers.

In turn, the state becomes desperate, and as Reisman concludes,
"in order to obtain convictions, the government must place the de-
cision of guilt or innocence in the case of black market transactions in the hands of an administrative tribunal or its police agents
on the spot. It cannot rely on jury trials."

Some will argue that that's far-fetched. Certainly, price controls
don't always lead to totalitarianism, yet, even in America, punitive
cigarette taxes created a black market in "loose cigarettes" in New
York, which resulted in tragic extrajudicial violence. The state, in
the form of at least one police officer, delivered a deadly choke hold
to Eric Garner, who on the day of his murder didn't even happen to
be in possession of any "loose cigarettes."[7]

Price controls and their disastrous effects are not new. The Ro-
mans tried price controls to thwart the state-created inflation.
Nixon tried price controls as well. (Although Milton Friedman
warned him that price controls would "end in utter failure and the
emergence into the open of the suppressed inflation."[8] And Friedman was proved right.) The Cato Institute's Gene Healy retells the
story of Secretary of the Treasury George Shultz telling Nixon in
1973, "at least the debacle had convinced everyone that wage-price
controls are not the answer." Of course, politicians are slow learn-
ers. So, even after Nixon's price controls failed, Carter tried them
again.[9]

Nixon's wage and price controls did, however, have a direct impact on my father's medical practice, his future, and ultimately, my
future. Three years after Nixon instituted wide-ranging wage and

price controls, in 1974, my father decided to run for Congress, in part because of his opposition to Nixon's wage and price controls and his severing the dollar's link to gold.

Nineteen seventy-four turned out to be a terrible year to run as a Republican and my father only garnered a little over 28 percent of the vote, but came back two years later and won a special election. My dad was in Congress when Carter resurrected Nixon's price controls, and he raised Cain about the terrible consequences to come. Dad was right, and ultimately saner minds prevailed as Reagan ended price controls during his first month in office.

In the Soviet Union and Eastern Europe, price controls and shortages were omnipresent.

One joke from communist Poland tells of a fellow who comes into a store and asks: "I guess you don't have any butter, do you?" To which the shopkeeper replied, "No, we're the store that doesn't have any toilet paper. The store across the street is the one that doesn't have butter."[10]

Venezuela is the country that doesn't have butter, toilet paper, or any consumer items and yet they persist with price controls that have trapped them in a historic disaster.

Girish Gupta describes the chaos of price controls.

"In Petare, a giant slum overlooking Caracas from the east, hustlers known as buhoneros sell their goods at a busy intersection. 'I've got milk, toilet paper, coffee, soap . . .' said 30-year-old Carmen Rodríguez, pointing to her wares by the side of a road busy with honking motorbikes, cars and buses."

Rodríguez admits, "Of course my goods cost more than the government says they should. We're helping people get the basics."

Gupta writes that the "scenes at Petare's intersection, 23 de enero's streets and Catia's supermarkets are manifestations of an economy in tatters: one in which people buy milk, toilet paper and shampoo at inflated prices because supermarkets, with long queues outside, are near empty; in which engineers and lawyers smuggle pasta and petrol across borders to earn many times more than they would carrying out their profession; and in which surgeons complain that people are dying on the operating table because they cannot import medicines and equipment."[11]

In Venezuela, price controls affect at least "fifty essential goods, from eggs to soap. . . . The products usually become unavailable within hours of the prices being fixed because they are bought up for resale on the black market."[12]

Those who might argue, "Oh, it's okay, it's democratic socialism," should realize that store owners who do not comply with price controls are imprisoned, and as the chaos empties store shelves across the country, Maduro has deployed the army to police prices.[13]

According to John Stossel, under Chavez's "democratic socialism," "30,000 businesses were confiscated."[14]

And yet Maduro persists and his socialist comrades around the world fail to wake up to the disastrous effects of price controls.

Marian Tupy describes his experience with price controls: "Say what you will about socialism, it always follows a predictable pattern. In an attempt to make something available to everyone, the socialists ensure that it is not available to anyone (except for the politically well-connected)."

Tupy writes: "As a child growing up behind the Iron Curtain, I recall constant shortages of basic foodstuffs. The price of meat, for instance, was kept artificially low due to political considerations. Low prices created an impression of affordability. On their trips abroad, communists would often boast that workers in the Soviet empire could buy and produce more meat than their Western counterparts. In reality, shops were often empty."[15]

Chapter 4

CAPITALISM IS THE
MORE MORAL SYSTEM

The inequality discussion became all the rage with the release of Thomas Piketty's 2015 book, *Capital in the Twenty-First Century*. America's admitted socialists, like Bernie Sanders, swooned while the Democratic Party's closet socialists chimed in with: "I told you so. I told you capitalism doesn't work." Piketty himself applauded Bernie's call for a progressive estate tax and for special new taxes on the wealthy. Piketty's book became a bestseller and brought the debate over inequality to the evening dinner table.

As David Harsanyi writes at the *Federalist*: "Piketty's book . . . [has] been deemed an 'important book' by a bunch of smart people. Why not? It validates many of the preconceived notions progressives have about capitalism: Inequality is growing. Mobility is shrinking. Meritocracy is dead. We all live in a sprawling zero-sum fallacy. And so on."

The central premise of Piketty's theory is that when the returns on capital grow faster than the returns for workers, income inequality between those who have capital and those who labor widens and does not self-correct.[1]

In reviewing Thomas Piketty's propositions on correcting income inequality, Daniel Shuchman writes at the *Wall Street Journal*:

"Piketty likes capitalism because it efficiently allocates resources. But he does not like how it allocates income."[2]

Piketty asserts that "when the rate of return on capital exceeds the rate of growth of output and income, as it did in the nineteenth century and seems quite likely to do again in the twenty-first, capitalism automatically generates arbitrary and unsustainable inequalities that radically undermine the meritocratic values on which democratic societies are based."[3]

How would Piketty fix these "unsustainable inequalities"? With massive income taxes on the wealthy. Piketty proposes an 80 percent bracket for incomes over $500,000 and a 60 percent rate for incomes over $200,000. Shuchman explains that Piketty is less concerned with raising tax revenue and more concerned with "putting an end to such incomes."[4]

Shuchman explains that Piketty believes that there is "a moral illegitimacy to virtually any accumulation of wealth, and it is a matter of justice that such inequality be eradicated in our economy. The way to do this is to eliminate high incomes and to reduce existing wealth through taxation."[5]

Adamsmith.org's Sam Bowman does a good job answering some of the standard accusations from the left on inequality. To those who, like Piketty, claim inequality slows growth, Bowman points out that studies that conclude that inequality slows growth are flawed and "end up comparing Sweden with Mexico, leaving out a lot of other factors that might be the cause of both Sweden's lower inequality *and* its lower crime and poverty rates, and assuming what they're trying to prove. But even though countries with lower inequality might have higher growth rates, that doesn't mean that cutting inequality will boost growth rates."

For example, while the Swedish population has longer average life spans, lower levels of violence, and higher overall education than the U.S. population, Swedish-Americans also have the same statistics while living in the United States.

Bowman cites a paper by Kristin Forbes that found the opposite of what liberals argue. She found that "an increase in a country's level of income inequality has a significant positive relationship with subsequent economic growth." So much for Piketty's argument that too much income inequality impedes economic growth.

Bowman concludes: "It's not inequality that matters, it's poverty and overall living standards." In other words, would you rather make $10,000 where the rich earn ten times that or make $30,000 where the rich earn 20 times that? What really matters is your standard of living, not your neighbors'. In reality, the poor are getting richer all the time, and the rich are also.[6]

HumanProgress.org does a good job analyzing the amazing leaps of prosperity over the past two hundred years. According to their website, in 1820 over 90 percent of the world lived in extreme poverty, measured as less than two dollars a day. In 1990, when I got married, the percentage of the world's population living in extreme poverty represented around 30 percent (in constant dollars). Fast-forward to today, where less than 10 percent of the world lives in extreme poverty.[7]

Dwelling on income inequality ignores the dramatic decrease in poverty that has occurred as capitalism and the division of labor have spread worldwide throughout the past two centuries.[8]

Perhaps part of the problem in examining unequal incomes is that we fail to acknowledge that it may be more important to analyze what you can buy with your income, rather than the actual dollar amount in your paycheck. Tim Worstall at *Forbes* writes that while we do "have widening inequality of cash or money incomes, . . . we're also seeing something of a shrinkage in inequality in terms of consumption."[9]

Before the industrial revolution, the poor lived a life of bare subsistence, lucky to have enough to eat. They lacked clean water and basic sanitation, resulting in epidemics of contagion, while the rich lived a pampered existence far removed from the vicissitudes of the street. Today, rich and poor alike enjoy the same basic necessities of food, clothing, housing, technology, antibiotics, etc.

As Worstall puts it: "Today's inequality might [peak with] the plutocrat with many mansions, jets and cars, but poverty on the bottom these days, absent mental or addiction problems, is about not having good food rather than having none, not having good housing rather than having none. We're all on the same spectrum now, not the poor falling off the bottom of the subsistence level altogether."[10]

Dalibor Rohac, at the *Washington Times*, explains how "despite greater numerical income inequality, cheaper consumable goods have really equalized the comforts available to people of all income levels." Because of trade and cheap consumer imports available at discount stores like Walmart, "low-income groups [have] access to goods that previously were enjoyed only by the rich," from flat-screen TVs to video games to cell phones and computers.

As I have noted on national television, much to my wife's chagrin, I buy shirts at Target for $7. Rohac writes that "[i]n terms of the actual material conditions of living, developed countries appear to be more equal than ever before." You can see this first-hand. Just go to Target or TJMaxx and you, too, can experience the equalizing effects of worldwide free trade and the division of labor.[11]

Deirdre McCloskey explains the equalizing effects of the worldwide economy. Despite income inequality, the poor have made incredible gains.

"In relative terms, the poorest people have been the biggest beneficiaries. The rich became richer, true. But millions more have gas heating, cars, smallpox vaccinations, indoor plumbing, cheap travel, rights for women, lower child mortality, adequate nutrition, taller bodies, doubled life expectancy, schooling for their kids, newspapers, a vote, a shot at university and respect."

McCloskey points out that at no other time in history have so few lived in poverty: "not in the glory of Greece or the grandeur of Rome, not in ancient Egypt or medieval China. What I call The Great Enrichment is the main fact and finding of economic history."[12]

Chapter 5

CAPITALISM BENEFITS
THE MIDDLE CLASS

Today's young socialists harangue on and on about income inequality. Deirdre McCloskey wants no part of it. "[Y]ou will have heard that our biggest problem is inequality, and that we must make all men and women equal," she writes. "No, we should not—at least, not if we want to lift up the poor. Ethically speaking, the true liberal should care only about whether the poorest among us are moving closer to having enough to live with dignity and to participate in a democracy. They are."[1]

Productivity gains have brought what were once considered luxuries to the masses, making income disparities less noticeable. Don Boudreaux, an economics professor at George Mason University, provides an excellent analysis of how each generation works far fewer hours to purchase goods like refrigerators, calculators, music gadgets, cell phones, dishwashers, washing machines, and clothes.

For example, in 1956 it took the average worker 116 hours of labor to earn enough to buy a Sears refrigerator. In 2013, the average worker could buy a similar refrigerator with only 15 hours of wages even though income inequality increased significantly over that time.[2]

These facts are unknown to Representative Alexandria Ocasio-

Cortez (AOC). She opined to an audience of millennials, "Capitalism, to me, it's an ideology of capital—the most important thing is the concentration of capital and to seek and prioritize profit. . . . And to me, that ideology is not sustainable and cannot be redeemed. . . . [W]e're reckoning with the consequences of putting profit above everything else in society. And what that means is people can't afford to live."[3]

Could that possibly, in any universe, be true? Does capitalism's profit motive somehow create wages that make it impossible to buy the basic staples of life?

Marian Tupy at HumanProgress.org examined this question and found the opposite. Tupy found that "for the same amount of work that allowed an unskilled laborer to purchase one basket of 42 commodities in 1919, he or she could buy 7.6 baskets [of consumables] in 2019." Instead of capitalism impoverishing workers, the free market actually allows workers to buy more than seven times as much stuff for the same amount of hours worked. No apologies for capitalism necessary—only accolades and amazement at the progress that comes with capitalism.[4]

Even the liberally biased *Washington Post* fact checker gave AOC three Pinocchios for her statement: "I think it's wrong that a vast majority of the country doesn't make a living wage."[5]

For the *WaPo* fact checker to even question AOC is extraordinary. It is an event worthy of my father-in-law's favorite wry observation that "even a blind squirrel sometimes finds the acorn!" For this particular *Washington Post* hack, "fact checking" actually means "I'm an apologist for the left who will infuse my bias with a feint at the truth."

For example, the same writer once gave me four Pinocchios for saying that I respected Eisenhower's warning that small wars could lead to big wars.[6] I have never quite understood how one could be caught "lying" about his own opinion. This supposed "fact checker" held the deluded belief that somehow Eisenhower belonged to the war crowd and was therefore indignant that I dared quote him to promote peace. No matter what the fake news tells you, Eisenhower was not some robotic cog in the war machine. He was a somber, reflective, and experienced hand at war. There is one Eisenhower quote that nation builders, regime changers, and other promoters of endless war should read and contemplate: "I hate war as only a soldier who has lived it can, only as one who has seen its brutality, its futility, its stupidity." Remember those words when you think of Eisenhower.

But back to AOC and her claim that the poor millennials are all in line at the workhouse waiting for "one more bit of porridge, sir."

Who could possibly be gullible enough to believe her claim that capitalism prevents workers from having a livable wage? Clearly she has an admirer in *Time* magazine's Charlotte Alter, who tweeted her agreement with the AOC bromide: "People our age have never experienced American prosperity in our adult lives— which is why so many millennials are embracing Democratic socialism."[7]

Never experienced prosperity? Where would they get such an idea?

Maybe from the government. Statistics from the Bureau of Labor have for years fed into this narrative that workers' real wages haven't risen in over forty years. By one measure, nominal wages have risen 483 percent since 1972, but inflation, as measured by CPI-W (the Consumer Price Index for Urban Wage Earners and Clerical Workers), has also risen 483 percent, which supports the democratic socialists' argument that workers' wages haven't risen while the rich have gotten richer.

Former senator Phil Gramm and John Early, however, point out that this statistic fails to reveal that "by virtually any definition of economic well-being, Americans are substantially better off today than they were a half-century ago." Gramm and Early explain that labor statistics make two big errors in asserting that wages have stagnated. First, the statistics fail to include employer benefits like health care, pension, and family leave in average hourly earnings. Second, labor statistics fail to account for consumer substitution and changes in how and what people spend their money on.

From bigger houses to more bathrooms to central air-conditioning to high-speed Internet (often for free, at the local coffee shop), not to mention virtually everyone on the planet owning a smartphone, everyone's standard of living has improved. Americans are living longer. Three times more millennials get college degrees as did their counterparts in 1972. You name it. It's almost impossible to find a standard of living measurement that hasn't improved dramatically in the past fifty years.

Statistics that argue wages are stagnant and the poor are getting poorer can't explain away the dramatic improvement in standard of living that comes from 224 million people with smartphones. It's nearly impossible to measure "inflation" in terms of the power of holding a mini computer in your hand that provides instant communication and access to unlimited information, education, and entertainment, and will even guide you to your destination anywhere on the planet. It replaces your need for a camera, a video camera, a physical music collection and stereo system, a calculator, a watch, a tape recorder, a flashlight; the list goes on and on. How do you compute the standard of living chasm between having that and a flip phone?

Frankly, anyone arguing that millennials are not the richest, most privileged young people ever is just not paying attention.[8]

David Harsanyi responds to the irresponsible AOC platitudes:

*The idea that millennials have toiled in uniquely grueling economic
conditions exhibits a delusional and extraordinarily narrow
understanding of history. Whether the majority of millennials
believes this myth or not, I don't know. I tend to doubt it. . . .
But, historically speaking, the only thing millennials have seen
is relative prosperity, most of it provided by free markets and
American political stability.*

    *. . . . since Ocasio-Cortez graduated from college—her
"adulthood"—she has only seen a single quarter of negative
growth, and 13 quarters of more than 3 percent growth. The
quarter she graduated, the United States economy grew by
4.7 percent. Her formative adult experience with the economy is
far better than most.*[9]

During AOC's adulthood, Jim Geraghty, at *National Review*, reports that "the U.S. economy has added jobs for 100 consecutive months, and there are seven million unfilled jobs in the country."[10]

Scott Lincicome points out that the American family has more disposable income because from 1980 to 2015, the average family spent 8 percent less of their household budget on food, clothing, shelter, and utilities.[11]

Just look at college. When I was born, fewer than six million Americans went to college. By the time Ocasio-Cortez came around that number had more than doubled. Today, more than 20 million kids are entering college.

Yet AOC complains, "millennials have lower earnings, fewer assets, and less wealth," to which Harsanyi responds, *yeah . . .* "because many of them are still young."[12]

It's virtually impossible to find statistical evidence that today is somehow worse for the beleaguered young. Derek Thompson writes at the *Atlantic*, "spending on food and clothing went from half the family budget in 1900 to less than one-fifth in 2000."

Thompson reports, "Over the next 100 years, the U.S. family got smaller, more reliant on working women and computers, less reliant on working children and farms, and, most importantly, much richer. About 68-times richer, in fact. Household income (unadjusted for inflation) doubled six times in the 20th century, or once every decade and a half, on average."[13]

Thank you, capitalism!

Ignoring the incredible gains that have occurred as consumer prices dropped dramatically and focusing just on income inequality leaves an incomplete and distorted picture of reality.

Historically, when income inequality was a consequence of a caste system or associated with hereditary nobility, complaints about inequality were valid. As Ben Domenech at the *Federalist* explains: "inequality of outcome was historically driven by hardened class systems—not so in a free market economy."[14] In America, our founders allowed us to escape the rigid class systems of Europe. Many historians, Barbara Tuchman among them, argue that what makes America unique is that for the first time an entire country based its economy on merit, not heredity.

Indeed, the history of America is distinguished by unprecedented income mobility. Domenech cites Kevin Williamson, who makes this point succinctly:

Far from having the 21st-century equivalent of an Edwardian class system, the United States is characterized by a great deal of variation in income: More than half of all adult Americans will be at or near the poverty line at some point over the course of their lives.[15]

Mark R. Rank and Thomas A. Hirschl looked at adult income distributions over a forty-four-year period among American adults and found that 73 percent will join the top 20 percent of wage earners for at least one year. Thirty-nine percent will achieve top 5 percent in income for at least one year. Perhaps most remarkable, 12 percent will actually make it to the top 1 percent in income.[16]

When you dig deep into the debate over income inequality, you discover that the preachiness of Piketty and others is really about a moral conclusion they've made that unequal outcomes are evil and should be regulated by government. Domenech points out that "the left continues to operate on an a priori assumption that income inequality/wealth concentration is a bad thing, because of those riches backstroking through their money. But that's just a jealousy trope. Upon closer inspection, you'll see that income inequality and wealth concentration don't inhibit economic mobility; they don't inhibit economic growth; and they are not detrimental to democracy or to human liberty."[17]

Chapter 6

INCOME INEQUALITY
DOES NOT RUIN
THE ECONOMY OR
CORRUPT GOVERNMENT

T
he argument that increasing income inequality hampers growth is a widespread belief with little evidence to support it. The economist Joseph Stiglitz, along with a string of liberal pundits from Paul Krugman to Alan Krueger, claims that with "inequality at its highest level since before the Depression, a robust recovery will be difficult in the short term, and the American dream—a good life in exchange for hard work—is slowly dying."[1] These same crepehangers chorused that economic growth would be stuck below 2 percent for the next decade.

The truth, however, is much different. The Republican tax cut of 2017 ushered in gross domestic product (GDP) growth above 3 percent in the midst of continued "income inequality." In fact, a study by Christopher Jencks, Dan Andrews, and Andrew Leigh found no correlation between inequality and economic growth among developed countries. Actually, for the period between 1960 and 2000, increased income inequality corresponded with increased economic growth.[2]

In examining income inequality and poverty, Alan Reynolds of Cato found the opposite of what the liberal choir is preaching, namely that the numbers of those living in poverty actually tend to decline even as the top 1 percent of income earners expand their share of income. And that poverty tends to increase when the top 1 percent lose their share of income.[3]

Scott Winship admits that "there is, of course, a rich literature on the relationship between inequality and growth. . . . Although there are many conflicting views, there is ample evidence that inequality can, in fact, hurt growth under many circumstances. But this literature focuses mostly on the experience of developing countries, and its applicability to the challenges currently facing the United States is not entirely clear."[4]

Even proponents of the theory that income inequality stifles economic growth, such as the Center for American Progress's Heather Boushey and Adam Hersh, admit that the empirical evidence is, in Winship's words, "inconclusive and largely inapplicable to America's circumstances." In fact, Winship goes even further to conclude that "there is simply no clear evidence that this slower growth is being caused by rising inequality."[5]

This whole liberal tale of a zero-sum economy where, when the rich get richer, the poor must get poorer is nothing more than fantasy. The deeper you look into the statistics the less believable the tale becomes. Winship points out that a study by "sociologist Lane Kenworthy also finds that, since 1979, higher growth in the share of income held by the top 1% of earners has been associated with stronger economic growth across several countries."

The argument that today's middle class is worse off than the same family in 1960 is frankly not true. According to Winship, "the median family today has nearly twice the purchasing power of its counterpart in 1960. The basic well-being of today's family is significantly better than that of a family living in the supposed golden age."[6]

Even when the left admits this truth, they still argue that today's middle-class family income is growing more slowly than in the past and that the incomes of the rich are growing more rapidly than in the past.

So, the middle class is better off now than in the past, but the left is dissatisfied because the rich are getting richer faster than the middle class is getting richer. Really? We're all getting richer, but the left is unhappy because some are getting richer faster? It seems that the Democrats' critique is more an exposé of envy than a valid scientific enterprise.

Winship points out that restraining income accumulation among the rich doesn't necessarily mean those riches wind up in the pockets of the poor. "The gains made by those at the top could not have accrued to people lower on the income ladder in any event," he writes. "For instance, had Chinese investors not enriched bankers in New York, their money would surely have gone to bankers in London or Frankfurt—not to workers in middle America."

The facts, if the left cares to consider them, are that everyone has gotten richer over the past few centuries. As Winship continues, "What has looked like gains for the wealthy coming at the expense of the poor and middle class turns out to be, in historical context, an enduring victory for workers in an 80-year tug of war with capital. The notion that inequality is stifling economic growth or suppressing the wages of the middle class is simply not supported by the available evidence."[7]

If you look at the historical data, the ability to ascend the income ladder is not getting harder. Winship found that men born in 1950 had about the same progress in ascending the income ladder as men born in the 1980s. "Among those raised in the bottom quarter of the family-income distribution, the fraction escaping the bottom fourth of earnings as adults fell from 63% to 60%, a decline too small to be reliably different from zero. They may have experienced greater mobility than men born in the early 1960s, when only 54% escaped the bottom fourth."

Piketty asserts that inequality is so pervasive that democracy itself is threatened. Starving Venezuelans might argue that lack of elections and dissolution of parliament are a more immediate threat to democracy. Socialism and capitalism both ultimately result in one percenters. But in capitalism, when uncorrupted by government cronyism, the one percent is, to a large degree, based on merit. In a true free market, you become rich only when you sell a service or a product at a price that people will voluntarily pay. Hence, you get legitimate and well-deserved billionaires like the Walton family, who founded Walmart, which offers quality goods at low prices.

For all the negative press Walmart has received for providing low-paying jobs, consider that in their 2019 Environmental, Social & Governance Report, Walmart reported that its average store manager salary was $175,000 annually. It also reported that 75 percent of its U.S. managers began working as hourly employees.

Admittedly, there are one percenters who gained their billions by using government cronyism to prevent competition, such as some in the drug industry. But that is not capitalism. It is government paternalism, which tilts toward the complete control of business that comes with socialism.

Under socialism, you still have one percenters, but they gain their lofty position not through merit but through party nepotism. In socialism, the one percenters are party members or bureaucrats or government planners who gain power *not* by giving the consumer what they want but by commanding the consumer to accept what they decree.

As Winship describes it, more than a few political scientists suggest "that growing income divides may reduce voting or other forms of participation that require time and money, and have expressed fear that these disparities will allow the rich to buy elections or make elected officials unduly responsive to those with deep pockets."[8]

The opposite argument is as likely to be true. Namely, that when lower-income folks are removed from the tax rolls, they still vote but they vote with particular abandon and unconcern for the punishment of taxes since they no longer suffer that punishment. The same can be said for spending. Why care about overspending or its corresponding debt if you know that you will not be sent the bill?

True, big money floods the political marketplace, but both sides seem to have their cash cows: George Soros, Howard Schultz, Bloomberg, big unions, and climate alarmist money on the left and Sheldon Adelson, the Koch brothers, the NRA, and the Chamber of Commerce on the right.

If you look objectively at our constitutional republic, we've actually held up pretty well considering that close to half of the electorate no longer pays any income tax.

Really, political science is ill-suited to prove or disprove sweeping statements that allege that income inequality is destroying democracy. Political science is not a field of mathematics, and twenty experts will give you twenty opinions looking at the same data.

Is income inequality destroying democracy? Winship concludes, "The truth is that political science has only begun to consider these questions and has yet to reach any consensus. Many in the field are well aware of this inconclusiveness."

Even the American Political Science Association Task Force on Inequality and American Democracy agrees: "We know little about the connections between changing economic inequality and changes in political behavior, governing institutions, and public policy."[9]

Chapter 7

UNDER CAPITALISM, THE 1 PERCENT IS ALWAYS CHANGING

When the left moans about the one percenters, realize that it's not one static group of rich people but an ever-changing group of individuals rising up the income ladder. Our liberal friends would like you to believe they are sticking it to one particular group of fat cats, but it turns out that new individuals join the ranks of the successful every year.

In fact, the chief groaner about millionaires and billionaires, Bernie Sanders, is himself a millionaire. When Martha Mac-Callum asked him at a Fox town hall why he didn't voluntarily give the government 52 percent of his wealth (as he has called for in his campaign), he responded by asking MacCallum why she didn't donate her salary. MacCallum answered, "I didn't suggest a wealth tax."

MacCallum pushed Sanders to respond. He muttered, "Come on. I paid the taxes that I owe."

"Do as I say, not as I do," seems to be Sanders's mantra.[1]

Bret Baier went on to ask Sanders, "When you wrote the book and you made the money, isn't that the definition of capitalism and the American dream?" Bernie, still red in the face from the previous question, hesitated and curtly answered, "No." John Phelan at the Foundation for Economic Education (FEE) doesn't let Bernie get away with this denial. Sanders, he writes, "is wrong. Having an idea, acting on it, and making a pile of money is the very definition of . . . entrepreneurial capitalism."

New millionaires like Bernie are proof positive that the wealthy class is not a static group.[2]

Before Thomas Piketty was even a twinkle in the eye of the new socialists, Thomas Sowell was making the point that when you evaluate income percentiles, "these abstract categories do not contain the same people over time." Moreover, sterile groupings ignore the "simple fact that people just starting out in their careers usually do not make as much money as they will later, after they have had years of experience." So young people almost always start in the lowest income groupings and work their way up the income ladder throughout their career. The same is true of wealth. Politicians rush to help senior citizens, yet senior citizens are the wealthiest category across all countries when wealth is examined by age group.

Ironically, the U.S. government subsidizes drug purchases for the richest group, senior citizens, and it is paid for by the poorest group—young adults.[3]

A Pew study confirms this age disparity in wealth. Net wealth increases the more years you have to accumulate wealth. That's simply common sense. Anyone who bemoans the fact that young people have less wealth needs to understand that, in every generation, as people move to middle-age and senior status, they naturally accumulate more wealth.

Income inequality is simply a misdirection campaign, an attempt to distract the public from the very real progress enriching all levels of income and to avoid a discussion of what economic systems foster the creation of wealth. The history of the past two to three hundred years in countries with market economies has seen the remarkable elimination of extreme poverty and an increase in income inequality. Instead of inequality being a problem, the data shows that poverty declines as income disparity grows.

Robert Carroll, a senior fellow at the Tax Foundation, studied income mobility from 1999 to 2007 and found that "60% of households in the bottom income quintile in 1999 were in a higher quintile in 2007." As far as those one percenters, half of the folks who made a million dollars in one year achieved millionaire status only once during the study period and only "6 percent of this group were millionaires in all nine years."[4]

In fact, according to a 2008 report by the Organisation for Economic Co-operation and Development there is a 27 percent turnover rate among the top one percenters. Indeed, income mobility exists up and down the economic ladder. A study from the University of Michigan showed that 95 percent of individuals in the bottom 20 percent category moved up and 29 percent even moved all the way to the top 20 percent of earners.[5]

Seems like America really is the land of opportunity and income mobility.

If unequal incomes are based on merit and occur as a consequence of voluntary transactions, there is no basis for complaint. Instead of being inherently evil, disparate outcomes based on merit encourage more merit and better decisions. One might argue that the possibility of gaining an "unequal" amount of income is precisely the incentive that invigorates capitalism.

When government intervenes in the name of fairness, you often get inequality of a different sort. Instead of inequality based on merit, skill, work ethic, and yes, luck, you get unequal outcomes based on party politics, nepotism, and cronyism.

Ben Domenech describes the inequality of incomes that government creates: "The real inequality problem is that of the Two Americas: not divided between one that is rich and one that is poor, but between one that is protected by government and another that is punished by it."

Instead of a class war between workers and owners as Marx described, Domenech writes that the real divisions in our society run "along the lines of the unprotected vs. the protected. The protected ruling class, thanks to its friends and cronies in government, gets the most lucrative opportunities with the least amount of risk, while the unprotected working class gets the opportunity to pay, via taxes, for the bailouts, subsidies, and rigging of the rules which largely run against their interests."[6]

Chapter 8

THE POOR ARE BETTER OFF UNDER CAPITALISM

S elwyn Duke makes an important point that socialists ignore: "The richest men hail primarily from nations providing economic freedom whereas the poorest live disproportionately in socialist countries. Even liberal NPR published a piece titled 'What the Stat About the 8 Richest Men Doesn't Tell Us About Inequality' and pointed out that income inequality has declined during the last 25 years; the statistic tells us only what people *own*, not what they *earn*, and that wealth alone doesn't determine quality of life. But then there's what neither NPR nor anyone else tells us about inequality: It's irrelevant."

Complaining about inequality is basically a variation of envy or coveting. Duke continues: "Equality tells us nothing about quality. You can have equality in poverty, equality in misery, or equality in incompetence, ignorance or stupidity."[1]

Yet, socialists like Bernie and liberals like Hillary Clinton still use equality as their measuring stick, and Scandinavia as their model. "Why can't we be like Sweden?" they protest. "That's the socialism America needs."

Economist and writer Walter Williams points out that it's important to know what choices you give up if you want the equality of Swedish socialized medicine. Williams tells the story of a patient with multiple sclerosis, which is an incurable disease that sometimes spirals downward. New medicines are becoming available, but they are expensive. Williams tells of how a Gothenburg, Sweden, multiple sclerosis patient's prescription for a new drug was denied because the drug was significantly more expensive than the older medicine. Not only was the patient denied government insurance payment for the drug, but he was also prevented from buying the drug himself. The Swedish equality police argued that "it would set a bad precedent and lead to unequal access to medicine."[2]

One might ask: Do high-ranking Swedish officials get the same denials?

Socialists say they want equality, but if you ask what people really want, they'll answer that what is important is the quality of their own standard of life.

Even if socialists admit that our standard of living is improving, they typically fail to understand why. For the socialist, economic progress is some quirk of history perhaps related to technology, but they deny that the voluntary exchanges of capitalism have anything to do with it. Williams, however, points out the undeniable correlation between capitalism and wealth.

Quoting Williams, Duke writes, "if you rank 'countries according to whether they are closer to being a free market economy or whether they're closer to having a socialist or planned economy' and based on 'per capita income,' you will find a general 'pattern whereby those having a larger measure of economic freedom find their citizens enjoying a higher standard of living.'"[3]

Thomas Sowell makes the point as well: "None of the Marxist regimes around the world has ever had as high a standard of living for working people as there is in many capitalist countries" dominated by the free market.[4]

Yet planners like Piketty think public policy should try to ameliorate income inequality. Reports of a handful of people owning nearly half the world's wealth incite calls to disallow such accumulation of wealth.[5]

In an article for the *Washington Times*, Dalibor Rohac illustrates how an obsession with income inequality can lead to ludicrous conclusions. He writes, "Liberal pundits are alarmed that income inequality in the United States is higher than in Pakistan or Ethiopia."[6] Which invites the question: Would anyone then choose to leave the United States and move to Pakistan or Ethiopia? Churchill famously explained the false allure of equality under socialism: "The inherent vice of capitalism is the unequal sharing of blessings. The inherent virtue of Socialism is the equal sharing of miseries."[7]

Every election we hear Hollywood celebrities, most with barely a high school diploma, threaten to leave America if Republicans win. They scold us from their Beverly Hills mansions and private jets. They lecture us through their Juvederm-plumped lips. Perhaps we should send them travel brochures on income equality in Pakistan and Ethiopia. Citizens in those countries enjoy much greater income equality, albeit less access to fine dining and Prada sunglasses.

These liberal actors can't separate themselves from the fiction of the big screen. If they could, they would look at the facts and argue for policies that actually help the poor. Rohac makes this point clearly: "If one cares about the welfare of the poorest and the most vulnerable, income inequality is not a useful measure. Measures of inequality tell us nothing about the living conditions of the poor, their health and their access to economic opportunity."[8]

Harry Frankfort, a professor at Princeton and the author of

On Inequality, makes a similar point. Like other critics of the obsession with income inequality, he's not buying the hysteria. He writes: "Economic equality is not, as such, of any particular moral importance, and economic inequality is not, in itself, morally objectionable."

Obsessing over income inequality misses the real debate. According to Frankfort, "Inequality of incomes might be eliminated, after all, just by arranging that all incomes be equally below the poverty line. Needless to say, that way of achieving equality of incomes—by making everyone equally poor—has very little to be said for it. From the point of view of morality, it is not important that everyone should have the same. What is important is that each should have enough."[9]

The mistake is believing that income inequality has anything to do with economic well-being. Stephen Pinker elaborates on this point: "the starting point for understanding inequality in the context of human progress is to recognize that income inequality is not a fundamental [measurement] of well-being. It is not like health, prosperity, knowledge, safety, peace, and the other areas of progress...."

To make his point, Pinker tells a Soviet-era joke.

> *Igor and Boris are dirt-poor peasants, barely scratching enough crops from their small plots of land to feed their families. The only difference between them is that Boris owns a scrawny goat. One day a fairy appears to Igor and grants him a wish. Igor says, "I wish that Boris's goat should die."*

Instead of wishing for greater wealth for himself, Igor, like today's equality zealots, would prefer to have equal misery.

Pinker argues that "the confusion of inequality with poverty comes straight out of the lump fallacy—the mindset in which wealth is a finite resource, like an antelope carcass, which has to be divvied up in zero-sum fashion, so that if some people end up with more, others must have less . . . wealth is not like that: since the Industrial Revolution, it has expanded exponentially. That means that when the rich get richer, the poor can get richer, too."

Pinker makes the case that Thomas Piketty is guilty of suc-cumbing to "the lump fallacy."

Piketty argues, "The poorer half of the population are as poor today as they were in the past, with barely 5 percent of total wealth in 2010, just as in 1910." But Pinker points out that "total wealth today is vastly greater than it was in 1910, so if the poorer half own the same proportion, they are far richer, not 'as poor.'"[10]

As usual, socialists (and their fellow travelers) get both the prob-lem and its solution all wrong. Rea Hederman and David Azerrad write at the Heritage Foundation, "Free-market economics is not about dividing up a dwindling pie, but expanding the pie to serve everyone. Those who succeed do not do so at the expense of oth-ers." The purveyors of the dwindling pie zero-sum world inspire the worst in us. If winning in the marketplace requires that some-one must suffer a corresponding loss, then the unhealthy tenden-cies of envy are stirred.

When policy is directed toward eliminating income inequality, the unintended consequence is to lessen the incentives that drive the wealth creation that has lifted millions of people out of pov-erty over the past few centuries. Hederman and Azerrad explain that "the Left's new American Dream is first and foremost about all that the federal government must do to create opportunity and ensure that incomes are distributed more equitably. Individual ef-fort takes a backseat to government spending and cradle-to-grave entitlements."

Despite the left's obsession with income inequality, Hederman and Azerrad argue: "Income disparities have not caused a decline in upward mobility. Standards of living have increased for everyone—as have incomes—and mobility, however one measures it, remains robust. Simply put, how much the top 1 percent of the population earns has no bearing on whether the bottom 20 percent can move up."[11]

Decades before the income inequality debate came into vogue, the great Austrian economist and writer Ludwig von Mises wrote: "Those who advocate equality of income distribution overlook the most important point, namely, that the total available for distribution, the annual product of social labor, is not independent of the manner in which it is divided. The fact that that product today is as great as it is, is not a natural or technological phenomenon independent of all social conditions, but entirely the result of our social institutions."

Mises's point is exactly what the left never gets, namely that wealth creation is not accidental, nor is it a guaranteed result. Wealth creation is dependent on the economic system. Capitalism creates wealth. Socialism does not.

Mises goes on to explain that the incentive of unequal returns is absolutely a necessary component of a successful economic system. Mises writes: "only because inequality of wealth is possible in our social order, only because it stimulates everyone to produce as much as he can and at the lowest cost, does mankind today have at its disposal the total annual wealth now available for consumption." If government destroys this incentive, it also destroys productivity and economic growth. On average, individuals are poorer when the incentive of "income inequality" is eliminated.[12]

Andy Puzder, the former CEO of Carl's Jr. and Hardee's, describes well socialism's inherent focus on greed.

"If you're in a capitalist economy, the only way you can succeed is by meeting the needs of other people," he said in a recent interview. "Socialism, on the other hand, focuses you inward. You're focused on what you can get."[13]

The technology revolution in the United States has also shown that the best outcomes for creating super wealth are often *not* the traditional paths to success. Who would have thought quitting college and tinkering in his garage would result in Bill Gates becoming the richest man in the world?

And Gates's success has inspired many more inventors to pursue their dreams. In America, the son of a car salesman and a teacher can invent a new virtual technology in his parents' garage and make millions. Palmer Luckey, a friend of mine, comes from a conservative, middle-class family. He was homeschooled. He spent one year at California State University, Long Beach but dropped out to work on his idea for a virtual reality headset. This invention became Oculus Rift, which was ultimately purchased by Facebook for $2 billion in 2014. Palmer's route to unfathomable success was possible only by having a society with equal opportunity but not equality of outcome.[14]

Friedrich Hayek argues that "from the fact that people are very different it follows that, if we treat them equally, the result must be inequality in their actual position, and that the only way to place them in an equal position would be to treat them differently."

His argument deserves restating. Since people have different and unequal talents, the only way you get equal outcomes is to treat them differently. In other words, to have an unequal application of the law. This should be anathema to both liberals and conservatives.

Hayek concludes: "Equality before the law and material equality are therefore not only different but are in conflict with each other; and we can achieve either the one or the other, but not both at the same time. How wonderfully put: Equal outcomes require the injustice of unequal treatment before the law. Love to hear the Bern respond to that one."[15]

Piketty, Sanders, and other crusaders for equality admit that they can't get rid of all inequality, but at the least, we should eliminate the extremes of income inequality. Socialists rarely speak of who it is that will have their wealth taken. They shy away from naming names. After all, Michelle and Barack Obama are one percenters who live in an enormous mansion and travel the world on luxury vacations. I certainly don't have a problem with that. They have made millions on book deals and speeches and can afford to celebrate their achievements. But I wonder if Representative Ocasio-Cortez does? How does Bernie feel about Michelle Obama's much-praised four-thousand-dollar Balenciaga boots? While Bernie and AOC might find the extravagant footwear of one percenters "unequal," I support the right of the rich to shine in glittery boots! After all, they are helping to support a luxury goods industry that employs creative people who craft fine materials into beautiful designs. If we didn't have rich people to buy such luxury items, those talents would be lost. Do today's socialists want a world without Balenciaga or Tom Ford?

The socialists argue that they'll leave just enough merit pay to incentivize the entrepreneurs. No harm, no foul. Perhaps, but I'm guessing that no one really knows how much incentive must remain to encourage the great breakthroughs of history. Shouldn't we at least worry that if enough "income inequality" is destroyed, perhaps the next Steve Jobs chooses to devote his time to surfing instead of entrepreneurship?

Selwyn Duke paints a scenario where, absent sufficient financial incentives, someone like Bill Gates never creates Microsoft: "[N]ot only would the 118,000 Microsoft jobs not have been created, but we wouldn't enjoy the more significant ancillary benefits: Countless millions of people use the company's products to help realize countless billions in increased productivity."[16]

Part II

Capitalism Makes Scandinavia Great

Chapter 9

BERNIE'S SOCIALISM ALSO INCLUDES PRAISE FOR DICTATORS

B ernie, for all his sincerity, also shows an abundance of misplaced admiration for states that ultimately no one supported, not even hardened socialists. Once upon a time, Bernie even had good things to say about Cuban, Nicaraguan, and Venezuelan socialism, until their failures became too glaring to overlook.

In 1985, Bernie praised Castro: "Everybody was totally convinced that Castro was the worst guy in the world . . . all the Cuban people were going to rise up in rebellion against Fidel Castro. They forgot that he educated their kids, gave them healthcare, totally transformed the society."[1]

Bernie famously honeymooned in Moscow under Soviet communism and had many good things to say about a host of communist regimes, from Nicaragua to El Salvador to Cuba.[2]

When Nicaraguan socialist Daniel Ortega came to the United States, he made sure to have time for a seventy-five-minute one-on-one visit with the mayor of Burlington, Vermont, Bernie Sanders.

David Unsworth reports that "so close was the relationship with Nicaragua that Sanders enthusiastically accepted an invitation by

Daniel Ortega's Sandinista government in July 1985. The visit was financed by the Nicaraguan government, except the airfare, which Sanders paid for."[3]

Even Bernie's rhetoric once sounded like a good Marxist. Decades ago, Bernie was quoted as saying "the basic truth of politics is primarily class struggle" and that "democracy means public ownership of the major means of production." It doesn't get much more orthodox Marx than that.

When the Sandinistas used violence to come to power in Nicaragua, Bernie was their most prominent American supporter. Michael Moynihan at the *Daily Beast* quotes a Sanders biographer as saying Sanders "probably has done more than any other elected politician in the country to actively support the Sandinistas and their revolution."[4]

Sanders himself describes with pride his visit to Nicaragua shortly after Ortega seized power, saying, "[B]elieve it or not, [I was] the highest ranking American official" at an event feting the Sandinista takeover.

Moynihan describes how Sanders, in 1985, "traveled to New York City to meet with Ortega just weeks after Nicaragua imposed a 'state of emergency' that resulted in mass arrests of regime critics and the shuttering of opposition newspapers and magazines." Sanders tried to deflect when asked if he supported Ortega's censorship. But, according to Moynihan, Sanders did finally acknowledge that "the Sandinistas' brutal crackdown 'makes sense to me.'"[5]

In 1988, Ortega was asked about his government's economic policy. "Apparently it is not yet understood that we Sandinistas are socialist, that Nicaragua has been socialist since July 19, 1979." When Ortega was asked about censoring the press, he responded: "They are more concerned when we temporarily close the newspaper La Prensa or Radio Catolica, or that we imprison those who break the law. This matters more to them than the life of a Nicaraguan child."[6]

To justify his support for Ortega's closing down opposition newspapers, Sanders responded: "If we look at our own history, I would ask American citizens to go back to World War II. Does anyone seriously think that President Roosevelt or the United States government [would have] allowed the American Nazi Party the right to demonstrate, or to get on radio and to say this is the way you should go about killing American citizens?"[7] Actually, what makes America unique is that our belief in freedom of speech is so strong that we tolerate even disturbing and hateful speech.

Now, to give Bernie his due, the Sandinistas got rid of Somoza, a U.S.-supported dictator. Like Castro, who overthrew Batista, another U.S.-supported dictator. Like the Ayatollah Khomeini, who overthrew the last shah of Iran, another U.S.-supported dictator. I get it. I sympathize with any nation that wants to throw off the yoke of any superpower arrogant enough to invoke its pleasure on a subjugated people. But time and time again, the revolutionaries end up just as bad as the folks they conspired to overthrow.

I sympathize to a degree with Bernie supporting self-determination for Nicaragua, but I can't abide a willful ignorance of the people's republic of socialism that the peasants installed. I lose my patience when Bernie insists on supporting the calamity and dysfunction of socialism.

Perhaps the most entertaining Bernie-ism that Moynihan uncovered was Bernie's response when asked about food lines in Ortega's Nicaragua: "Sanders claimed that bread lines were a sign of a *healthy* economy, suggesting an equitable distribution of wealth: 'It's funny, sometimes American journalists talk about how bad a country is, that people are lining up for food. That is a good thing! In other countries people don't line up for food: the rich get the food and the poor starve to death.'"[8] Wonder if Bernie has stood in any food lines in Venezuela lately?

His statement is false to the point of absurdity. In the United States, with all of our income inequality, the poorest segment of our population is the most overweight. Ironically our problem is too much inexpensive food. The left, of course, has an answer for that—if only poor people had more access to fresh fruits and vegetables, we could lower our obesity rates, they say. Federal and state government programs, championed by Michelle Obama, were instituted to remedy "food deserts" so people could make better choices. Seven years and hundreds of millions of dollars later, the USDA's report in its publication *Amber Waves* acknowledged the fact that being closer to grocery stores "has a limited impact on food choices" and "households and neighborhood resources, education and taste preferences may be more important determinants of food choice than store proximity." In other words, the veggies are rotting on the shelves, but the Coke and Doritos are still flying out the door.[9]

But back to Bernie. It wasn't just the Sandinistas in Nicaragua that drew Sanders's support. Moynihan reports that "in 1989 Sanders traveled to Cuba on a trip organized by the Center for Cuban Studies, a pro-Castro group based in New York, hoping to come away with a 'balanced' picture of the communist dictatorship. The late, legendary Vermont journalist Peter Freyne sighed that Sanders 'came back singing the praises of Fidel Castro.'"[10]

In 1985, Sanders complimented Castro because he "provided their children education, gave them health care, and totally transformed their society."[11]

Socialism, however, didn't work out for the Cubans or the Nicaraguans. By the late 1980s, Nicaragua's GDP per capita declined to nearly one-third its 1977 level. Even today nearly a third of Nicaraguans live in extreme poverty.[12]

Moynihan reports that Sanders told the *Burlington Free Press*:

> *"I think there is tremendous ignorance in this country as to what is going on in Cuba." [...] It's a country with "deficiencies," he acknowledged, but one that has made "enormous progress" in "improving the lives of poor people and working people." When he returned to Burlington, Sanders excitedly reported that Cuba had "solved some very important problems" like hunger and homelessness. "I did not see a hungry child. I did not see any homeless people," he told the Free Press. "Cuba today not only has free healthcare but very high quality healthcare."[13]*

I know many Cuban Americans who have seen the horrors of Cuban socialism firsthand and they find Bernie's words utterly repugnant. One of them, who did not want to be named for fear of repercussions to family members remaining in Cuba, becomes emotional when talking about today's socialists and their misplaced admiration for Castro.

> *When I hear of Bernie Sanders praising Castro, or see young people admiring Che Guevara, it makes me so angry. I think, how can you admire these criminals who killed thousands of people? People today are so uninformed about the horrors of socialism. I woke up one morning and the beautiful country I had known and loved was gone. The government had taken over all of the American and Cuban companies. Farmers were given twenty-four hours to leave their land.*
>
> *You have to be Cuban to know the truth. My family members still live in Cuba today and without the dollars I send they would not have enough to eat. Every week the Cuban people are given a*

ration book that tells them how much food and what type of food they can get. The ration coupons usually run out by Wednesday. There is no meat or fish available right now, only chicken. With dollars you can buy just about anything, but with Cuban money there is very little available.

You might get a "free" education, but you have to study what the government tells you to study. And even then there is no money to be made. Doctors make between $25 and $50 a month. There are many professionals who drive taxis in Cuba because they are tipped more in dollars from tourists than they can make at their professional job. The last time I visited Cuba our taxi driver was educated as a mechanical engineer.

The Cubans who do not have relatives that send dollars have a terrible time. And free health care? That is a joke! I know people in Cuba who have died from conditions that are completely treatable here in the United States. There is very little medicine available to the Cuban people so I send my family their prescription medications, even simple things like Band-Aids.

The idea that there is equality in Cuba is a lie—the people struggle for their basic needs while the government officials and those in the armed services live like kings! No ration books for them!

The infrastructure is crumbling and the streets are filled with potholes—except in the tourist areas. The government makes sure to present an attractive face to the rest of the world, but the regular neighborhoods are in terrible shape.

On every block, there is a house with people who spy and report back to the government—they know who visits you, how much money you have, everything. The government controls everything and there is no freedom of speech or opinion. The Cuban people don't know what is going on in Venezuela. They know only what the government wants them to know. Even the laws change from day to day, and something you can do today you might not be able to do tomorrow.

Chapter 10

TODAY'S AMERICAN SOCIALISTS DON'T KNOW WHAT SOCIALISM MEANS

Rashida Tlaib won an upset Democrat primary in Michigan and then won in November 2018 to become one of the first two Muslim women to serve in Congress. Tlaib gained instant notoriety with her foul-mouthed call to impeach Trump: "We need to impeach the mother-f***er." So much for civility on the left. I'm sure CNN, though, likely blames Trump for Tlaib's profanity.

The Democratic Socialists of America (DSA) endorsed Tlaib, but how does Tlaib define her ideology? Tlaib explains: "I'm a member of a lot of organizations; for me I've always pushed back on these socialist labels." Doesn't sound very definitive, does it?[1]

She continues: "Socialism, to me, means ensuring that our government policy puts human needs before corporate greed and that we build communities where everyone has a chance to thrive." Specific policy items include "a living wage for all people, abolishing ICE and securing universal health care." Sounds not too dissimilar to the progressive wing of the Democratic Party.[2]

Congress's newest and youngest socialist, Alexandria Ocasio-Cortez, tweeted her regret that "the restaurant I used to work at is closing its doors. I swung by today to say hi one last time, and kid around with friends like old times."

The restaurant in question, the Coffee Shop in Union Square, is where the women of *Sex and the City* frequently met. After twenty-eight years in business, owner Charles Milite announced that he was closing because "rents are very high and now the minimum wage is going up."

What AOC failed to acknowledge to her followers is that her 150 former coworkers didn't lose their jobs because of a failure in capitalism, but because of excessive government intervention.

An increased minimum wage is a big part of the democratic socialists' platform. The most discussed component of their platform is not promoting state ownership of the means of production, but rather a fifteen-dollars-per-hour minimum wage. Kshama Sawant, a democratic socialist, won a seat on the Seattle City Council with a fifteen-dollars-per-hour minimum wage as a main campaign theme.[3]

According to Fox News reporter Lukas Mikelionis, "Seattle is a troubling case, as research from the University of Washington's School of Public Policy and Governance found that the higher minimum wage led to significant job declines and actually left the poorest worst off in the city, the Washington Post reported."[4]

No wonder that despite Bernie's love for Scandinavian "socialism," Nordic countries generally don't have state-enforced minimum wages.

Not only are the Scandinavian countries largely free of consumer price controls, but they also largely lack governmental control of minimum wages. Those on America's left who clamor for fifteen-dollars-an-hour federal minimum wage laws might be somewhat embarrassed to discover that Scandinavian "socialism" has no minimum wage and yet workers seem to thrive.[5]

Scandinavian countries typically do have sky-high individual income tax rates on the middle class, but their corporate taxes have long been lower than American rates. Yet today's American socialists, who are enamored with Scandinavian "socialism," clamor for punitive taxes on "greedy" corporations.

Sawant, the Seattle City Council socialist, fought for a $48 million special tax on large corporations, which was apparently too much even for Jeff Bezos's Amazon to swallow and was ultimately rejected.

So, which is it? Is "socialism" a cry for hiking taxes on corporations or for emulating Scandinavia with its low taxation on corporations?[6]

Geoff Dembicki, at *Vice*, points out the disconnect between self-described socialists and historical socialism: "though 'socialism' is gaining in popularity, nobody can seem to agree on what it means."[7]

If you ask the new democratic socialists directly about socialism, you get gelatinous words intended to soothe and not scare unwitting youths. So, the Democratic Socialists of America (DSA) claim they "do not want to create an all-powerful government bureaucracy" . . . but they do "believe that the workers and consumers who are affected by economic institutions should own and control them."

Interesting. So, they seem to intuit big government's history of disastrous economic results, but they still want "worker ownership" of industry through cooperatives while also favoring "as much decentralization as possible." They do admit that some big industries like steel and the utilities may have to be owned and run by the central government but "that the whole economy should [not] be centrally planned." Of course, "major social investments like mass transit, housing, and energy" will need government planning. So, in other words, the new socialists are both for and against government owning the means of production. And to be clear, the new socialists are also both for and against central planning.[8]

Democratic Socialists of America weren't even a footnote in elections until Bernie came along. The DSA organized in 1982 and their membership was constant at a few thousand until recently, when membership jumped to over fifty thousand. Are they just excited progressives? Progressives, yes, but progressives on steroids. DSA's national director, Maria Svart, explains that the socialists she represents don't "see capitalism as compatible with freedom or justice or democracy."[9]

What separates these new socialists from traditional progressives is, according to Dembicki, that "they are less compromising, their rhetoric is more stark, and their demands are often more sweeping."[10]

Central to these young socialists is a generalized criticism of capitalism as an economic system or a culture. In socialist fashion, they do ultimately want to get rid of private ownership of corporations, but they seem happy, initially, to band together for a national minimum wage and other common progressive policies such as rejecting corporate donations. Refusing corporate donations or superPAC money is quickly becoming the new litmus test not just for uncloseted, proud socialists but also for progressives in general.

Income inequality and fairness are never far from the surface, though. Some analysts, like Dembicki, see the roots of these new socialists in the historical socialism of Eugene Debs. Debs received 6 percent of the vote in 1912, the high-water mark for socialists in American elections. Some DSA members point to the Occupy Wall Street movement as a recent momentum builder, but the new socialists are almost entirely an outgrowth of Bernie's presidential campaign.[11]

Ever since Alexandria Ocasio-Cortez's upset victory over Democrat leader Joe Crowley, conservatives have been pointing out her inconsistencies. But in our postmodern world facts are not what they used to be. Historical definitions or examples of socialism are immaterial to this new generation. To them it seems to be enough to stand up and proclaim, "I am a socialist!" And if asked to define its meaning, you will get some drivel about "I'm for fairness."

On a recent trip to Prague, I had the opportunity to talk with a true hero of liberty, Vaclav Klaus, the first prime minister of the Czech Republic after the fall of the Iron Curtain and the president of the Czech Republic from 2003 to 2013. President Klaus has been one of Europe's leading voices for free market capitalism since the Czechs gained their freedom in the Velvet Revolution.

As we were having lunch together, Klaus observed that the socialist dogma being preached to today's youth is actually worse than it was under Soviet rule, when teachers taught Marxism because they had no choice, but it was obvious that they did not accept its utopian propaganda as they were living every day under socialism's bleak reality. Klaus contrasted that with the academic climate in American universities today, where "intellectuals" who are true believers are zealously promoting socialism to young people. He laughed at the bitter irony that "there are more true believers of Marxism at the University of California Berkeley than we had in all of communist Czechoslovakia."

In a speech to the Victims of Communism Memorial Foundation in Washington, President Klaus warned, "We have to fight communism in its new disguises, in its new clothes, which are sometimes so chic and colorful that they camouflage their true content." Today's socialists use attractive disguises like income and lifestyle equality while providing zero specifics as to how they will bring it about. When pressed about the level of government control their plans would require, they obfuscate and demur.

Even Bernie, in the past few years, shies away from calling for outright state ownership of production. In fact, Bernie does not present his ideology as pure socialism, but rather dresses it up in its more palatable form: "fairness." In an interview with *Time* he now argues: "I don't believe government should own the means of production, but I do believe that the middle class and the working families who produce the wealth of America deserve a fair deal." Who knows exactly what a "fair deal" means, but I suspect that it's code for state-enforced redistribution of wealth.[12]

Today's new socialists have no clue what socialism means. Which makes them doubly dangerous, because they don't understand that, throughout history, enforced equality or enforced fairness starts out sounding "noble" but inevitably evolves into a society ruled by truncheon.

Marion Smith of the Victims of Communism Memorial Foundation decided that since today's youth seem infatuated with socialism, he'd survey them to find out what they thought socialism really was. Smith found that 69 percent of millennials couldn't really define socialism.[13]

Over time, Bernie's direct support for Russian, Venezuelan, and Cuban socialism has evolved into less specific calls for income equality and fairness and fewer specifics about how that jives with historical examples of socialism. Seems Bernie's socialism is now a "kinder, gentler socialism." You know. The kind without the gulag.

To date, though, Bernie has made no attempt to disavow his support for democratic "Scandinavian" socialism. So let's take a look at the Nordic form of socialism the left so loves.[14]

Typically, political scientists have defined socialism as a society in which the government owns the means of production. But the past century has given us example after example of governments that appear to have economies that function in the middle space between capitalism and socialism. In fact, even the U.S. economy is somewhere between capitalism and socialism.

Some economists argue convincingly that an economy with diffuse price controls inevitably leads to de facto control of production and a form of socialism.[15] Some also argue that when the state owns the main industries of a country but not all industry, that economy shares aspects of socialism.

Chapter 11

BERNIE SANDERS IS TOO LIBERAL TO GET ELECTED IN DENMARK

If socialist wannabes in America fail to look at the facts, the United States might finally succumb to socialism. The American left's love affair with Scandinavian socialism is dangerous because it holds the possibility of hoodwinking enough of the populace into voting to replace the capitalist system that made America great with the socialist system that made Stalin all powerful and the people all hungry. They say the republic dies when the majority discovers it can vote to take other people's stuff. Let's hope that day remains elusive.

How pervasive is the left's admiration for Scandinavian "socialism"? Well, it's definitely not limited to Bernie and his campaign followers. Hillary name-drops Sweden and Denmark as well. You can even go back twenty years and find Bill Clinton waxing poetic about Denmark. Bill even claimed that "Finland, Sweden and Norway offer more chances for individuals to out-earn their parents than the United States does." No news on Chelsea moving to Scandinavia anytime soon.[1]

But it is Bernie who is most enamored. In fact, according to CNN, "Bernie Sanders' American Dream is in Denmark" and "Bernie Sanders . . . won't stop talking about" the Danes.

Sanders is quoted as saying: "In Denmark, there is a very different understanding of what 'freedom' means . . . they have gone a long way to ending the enormous anxieties that comes with economic insecurity." Sanders plays the income inequality trope: "Instead of promoting a system which allows a few to have enormous wealth, they have developed a system which guarantees a strong minimal standard of living to all—including the children, the elderly and the disabled."[2]

The irony is that while American socialists want to become like Scandinavian socialists, Scandinavian socialists want to become more like American capitalists. I remember hearing a fellow senator put it this way: "The American left wants to become Western Europe. Western Europe wants to become Eastern Europe. Eastern Europe, sick of socialism and communism, wants to become American capitalists!" Indeed, the Danes seem a bit squeamish about all the attention from Bernie and want to make sure that the rest of the world knows they are not, in fact, socialist and are open for business.

It's not just the "socialist" label that might concern the Danes. Denmark's economic success is inseparable from free trade and low corporate income taxes. Bernie's policy decisions are the opposite of policies the Danes believe foster their success.

Indeed, before Republicans lowered the U.S. corporate tax in 2018, Denmark's corporate tax was significantly lower than ours. Bernie, on the other hand, has not been a fan of free trade or lower corporate income taxes.

In the MSNBC New Hampshire Democratic presidential debate, Bernie responded, "I do not believe in unfettered free trade. I believe in fair trade which works for the middle class and working families, not just large multinational corporations. I was on the picket line in opposition to NAFTA. We heard people tell us how many jobs would be created. I didn't believe that for a second because I understood what the function of NAFTA, CAFTA, PNTR with China, and the TPP is, it's to say to American workers, hey, you are now competing against people in Vietnam who make 56 cents an hour minimum wage."[3]

On corporate taxes, Bernie's opinion has been consistent: In the fall of 2018, on one of the Sunday shows, Bernie emphatically argued that if the Democrats retake the Senate, corporate taxes would "absolutely" go back up. However, the Scandinavian countries Bernie professes to admire believe the opposite. They support low, competitive corporate taxes and have embraced the free trade agreements.[4]

The Danes are vocal in distancing themselves from Bernie's policies and quite emphatically don't want to be known as a bad place to do business. The executive editor in chief for *Politiken*, a Danish newspaper, writes: "There is this idea that we are a heavily regulated society with a closed economy. The opposite is true."[5]

As Chris Moody of CNN writes, "In terms of pure semantics, few Danish politicians today would characterize themselves as 'socialist'—even a 'democratic socialist'—as Sanders does. The word has largely fallen out of fashion in recent decades."[6]

Lars Christensen, a Danish economist, writes: "When I hear Bernie Sanders talk about himself as a democratic socialist, it's a little bit 1970s. The major political parties on the center-left and the center-right would oppose many of the proposals of Bernie Sanders on the regulatory side as being too leftist."[7]

Chapter 12

NO, BERNIE, SCANDINAVIA IS NOT SOCIALIST

Ludwig von Mises, the famous Austrian economist, was once asked by his doctoral student Murray Rothbard if "he could single out one criterion according to which he could say that an economy was essentially 'socialist' or whether it was a market economy."

Rothbard recounts Mises's answer: "Somewhat to my surprise, he replied readily: 'Yes, the key is whether the economy has a stock market. That is, if the economy has a full-scale market in titles to land and capital goods. In short: Is the allocation of capital basically determined by government or by private owners?'"[1]

By that definition, let's look at Scandinavia. Sweden has had a continuous public stock exchange since 1819 and Norwegian companies are traded there. Finland has had a stock exchange since 1912. Iceland and Denmark have their own public stock exchanges. It seems that, by Mises's definition, Scandinavia may be less socialist than the left believes.

As far as private ownership, Giancarlo Sopo reports that even using Thomas Piketty's World Inequality Report (WIR) data, "90 percent of Scandinavia's combined wealth is privately owned."

Using Piketty's data, Sopo writes: "to put these numbers in perspective, Scandinavia has less state ownership of its national wealth today than the United States had under President Reagan (an average of 12.1 percent from 1981–1988). Perhaps even more striking is that a greater share of Scandinavia's wealth is in private hands (90.4 percent) than in the 17 other countries examined in the WIR study (86.8 percent)."

If government ownership of the means of production is the sine qua non of socialism, the facts argue quite convincingly that the Scandinavian economies simply are not socialist.[2]

Corey Iacono, a Thorpe fellow, writes at FEE: "In the Scandinavian countries, like all other developed nations, the means of production are primarily owned by private individuals, not the community or the government, and resources are allocated to their respective uses by the market, not government or community planning." Sounds more like capitalism than socialism.[3]

So when American socialists brag about Scandinavian "democratic" socialism, someone needs to ask—is Scandinavia really socialist at all? Jesse M. Plunkett describes the typical "conversation between a Republican and a Democrat about socialism" as ending "with the Republican asking, what about Venezuela, Nicaragua, and the Soviet Union?" And the Democrat responding, "What about Sweden, Denmark, and Norway?"

Conservatives point out the shortages, food lines, and outright famines in Venezuela, Stalin's Russia, and Mao's China, while American socialists stubbornly cling to the only "socialist" model left that has any claim to success—Scandinavia. Unfortunately for them, the so-called socialist success of Scandinavia is, in fact, due to good old-fashioned private property and capitalism!

Still, the argument from the American left persists. They continue to argue that it is Scandinavian socialism that is succeeding. Matt and Elizabeth Bruenig of the People's Policy Project make the argument that Norway is both socialist and a success. Norway

in recent history is, indeed, unique from her Scandinavian counterparts because of the discovery of oil in the late 1960s. Norway's
GDP rank climbed from 18th in the 1970s to 2nd by 2000 largely
because of its oil and gas production from the North Sea. Norway
is the number one oil producer in Europe and the 15th in the world.

The Bruenigs argue that Norway is a socialist nation because
the Norwegian government owns nearly 60 percent of the country's wealth. They use Piketty's World Inequality Report to argue
this point.

However, as Giancarlo Sopo reminds them, even the nationalized oil industry has a private component with a private board and
much of the government-owned assets in a sovereign wealth fund
valued at more than $1 trillion. The Norwegians invest that sover-
eign wealth fund in private companies like Microsoft and Apple in
capitalist countries. As Sopo describes it:

> To build a domestic energy industry, the Norwegian government
> created a partially private company that is run by wealthy oil
> industry executives. This company is publicly traded, operates on
> the profit motive, and deposits its surplus revenues into a trillion-
> dollar wealth fund that mostly invests abroad, including in the
> largest of American corporations. . . . [U]nlike in Venezuela,
> where the government used taxes on oil to fund social programs,
> the Norwegians use their sovereign wealth to accumulate more
> capital and cut taxes. Which of the two sounds more socialist
> to you?

Non-oil corporations in Norway pay low corporate rates and
individual income tax rates are among the lowest in Scandinavia.
While Norway did not institute as many of the market reforms as
other Scandinavian countries, its enormous oil revenue, for now,

has allowed the Norwegians to finance their exorbitant welfare state.

It's quite a stretch to argue that socialism created Norway's success rather than the fortuitous discovery of oil.[4]

Contrast Norway's behavior with the Chavez/Maduro model of spending the sovereign wealth rather than investing it.

The problem with interpreting Piketty's data to conclude that Norway is socialist is that, as Sopo points out, Piketty's data would also show Mexico or really any country with a large sovereign wealth fund to be socialist.

For that matter, using the Bruenig method of measuring socialism, the data actually argue that Scandinavia is less socialist than the United States, contradicting their thesis that Scandinavia is a socialist success story.[5]

Ever since American socialists' love fest with Scandinavia began, actual Scandinavians have been pushing back. A Swedish policy analyst named Nima Sanandaji recently published a book called *Debunking Utopia: Exposing the Myth of Nordic Socialism*.[6]

Sanandaji's research uncovered that much of Sweden's success occurred "before embracing its current welfare state. For the sixty some odd years before 1936, under a relatively low tax, low regulation capitalist market, Sweden's economy grew faster than the entire world." Sweden's taxes were lower than America's and Sweden led the world in individual income growth. When Sweden's welfare state grew in the 1970s, GDP began to slow. During this expansion of welfare, Sweden's GDP ranking dropped from 4th to 13th. As the welfare state grew, Sweden's economic growth shriveled.

Sanandaji presents copious evidence of Sweden's capitalist roots. As Jesse Plunkett summarizes him: "Between 1870 and 1950 Sweden had lower taxes than America and the highest per capita income growth in the world." As the welfare state grew from the 1950s through the 1990s economic growth declined until it "reached an average GDP growth of 0.2% from 1981 to 1993, among the very lowest among the 34 OECD countries."[7]

Even during the years that Sweden dabbled with outright socialism, capitalism was never banished. Despite the arguments of today's socialists, the means of production in Scandinavian countries has always been owned and controlled privately.[8]

The high taxes and anemic growth in the 1970s and 1980s did eventually lead Scandinavian voters to choose center-right governments that lowered taxes and lessened regulations, resulting in Nordic countries once again leading Europe in economic growth.[9]

To put it bluntly, today's American socialists disavow all historical examples of socialism from Stalin to Pol Pot to Hitler to Mussolini to Mao to current Venezuela. In the very same breath, they point to Denmark and Sweden and Norway as great socialist paradises. As we've seen, the facts do not support any "socialist" success in Scandinavia. Quite the opposite: it is clear that Scandinavian success came from capitalism and if anything, it has been impaired by big government and the welfare state.

Although today's socialists shy away from historical examples, it is imperative that we explore why and how socialism, even in its seemingly benign forms, always devolves into state-sponsored violence and why violence is an inevitable consequence of socialism, not merely a historical anomaly.

Chapter 13

SWEDEN'S RICHES ACTUALLY CAME FROM CAPITALISM

T he debate is not whether the Scandinavian economies are successful but what caused that success. Professor Jeffrey Dorfman of the University of Georgia accepts Bernie's assertion that the Nordic countries are economically successful. He writes, "It is certainly true that Sweden, Norway, Finland, and Denmark are notable economic successes. What is false is that these countries are particularly socialist."

Dorfman explains: "Socialism can take the form of government controlling or interfering with free markets, nationalizing industries, and subsidizing favored ones. The Nordic countries don't actually do much of those things."

This debate is essentially, which came first: the chicken or the egg? Which came first: socialism or success? Because today's socialists hang their collective hats on the great success of Nordic socialism, it is important to determine the roots of that economic prosperity.

Close examination of the "Nordic success story" shows that the only way Scandinavia can afford such generous welfare benefits is that enough capitalism remains to create the necessary tax revenue.[1]

Once it is clear that most industries are privately owned, prices are not regulated, and a free and open stock market exists, the mirage of "socialist" success evaporates.

Evidence for a capitalist Scandinavia abounds. The Fraser Institute ranks countries based on their fidelity to the free market and the "limited government ideal." It publishes a worldwide economic freedom index that scores Denmark, Finland, Norway, and Sweden all in the top twenty-seven freest economies.[2]

Fraser's economic freedom index also maintains that for corporate taxes Scandinavia is actually more business friendly than the United States.[3]

In fact, the Scandinavian countries all score higher than South Korea and Japan, which many would consider to be friendly to free markets.[4]

World Bank statistics actually rank Denmark the third-easiest country with which to do business worldwide. In this ranking, Denmark ranks ahead of the United States and just behind Singapore and New Zealand.[5]

The Heritage Foundation also compiles an index of economic freedom. Heritage ranks Denmark eleventh freest in the world, also ahead of the United States.[6]

Iceland, Sweden, Norway, and Finland all rank among the top twenty-six freest economies.[7]

The *Economist* reports that the Nordic nations are "stout free-traders who resist the temptation to intervene even to protect iconic companies." Denmark, Norway, and Sweden "all rank in the top 10 easiest countries to do business in."[8]

The Nordic countries do indeed have large welfare states and extensively socialized medicine, as well as free tuition for college financed by extremely high taxes at all income levels. But the Nordic countries have never gone so far as to attempt to take over the means of production. As Professor Dorfman describes it: "The

Nordic countries are smart enough not to kill the goose that lays the golden egg."[9]

Most debates over Scandinavian socialism or socialism in general begin and end with misinformation. Witness the dustup between Joy Behar and Meghan McCain on *The View*.

McCain commented on the primary victory of self-proclaimed socialist Alexandria Ocasio-Cortez by pointing out that socialism had virtually destroyed the once-rich nation of Venezuela. Behar directed the conversation away from Venezuela: "I think [Ocasio-Cortez] is talking more about Scandinavia." When McCain challenged Behar to name one country where socialism has ever been successful, Behar responded, "Sweden, Denmark, Finland, Iceland." The gullible audience roared. Unfortunately, no one had time to discuss whether Nordic countries actually owe their success to socialism.

From the liberals at *The View* to Hillary Clinton to this new wave of young Democrat socialists, the drum they beat always plays the tune of Scandinavia and its socialist success.

Chris Matthews, at *Fortune*, writes that "Vermont Senator and Democratic presidential hopeful Bernie Sanders has been at the forefront of this new Nordophilia. He has repeatedly name-checked countries like Denmark and Sweden in interviews and debates, arguing that we should copy policies like mandatory paid leave for new parents and free healthcare and college education to improve the economic lives of ordinary Americans."[10]

As he told George Stephanopoulos one Sunday morning, Bernie believes that "[i]n those countries, by and large, government works for ordinary people and the middle class, rather than, as is the case right now in our country, for the billionaire class."

Bernie and others continue to ignore the inconvenient truth that Scandinavia is in many ways as capitalist as the United States.

In the Democratic presidential debates, Bernie tried to let his love for Denmark shine brighter than Hillary's. Bernie proclaimed: "I think we should look to countries like Denmark, like Sweden, and Norway and learn from what they have accomplished for their working people."[11]

Hillary's initial response was "We are not Denmark," but she quickly followed up with: "I love Denmark. We are the United States of America and it's our job to rein in the excesses of capitalism so it doesn't run amok."[12]

But perhaps we should listen to the Scandinavians themselves. Denmark's prime minister chided Sanders and asked him to stop insulting his country as "socialist." Perhaps the prime minister didn't want potential investors or foreign corporations looking at Denmark and getting the wrong idea.[13]

"You have nothing but capitalism in Denmark," says Annegrethe Rasmussen, a Danish journalist. "We have one of the lowest corporate tax rates in the world. But once the capitalists have done their work, we just tax the hell out of our people!"

As Jesse Plunkett wrote in the *Orlando Sentinel*, "Scandinavian countries truly are exceptionally wealthy, but 'democratic socialists' are being dishonest about their policies. Far from socialist, the Nordic countries are actually closer to true laissez-faire capitalism than the U.S., as reflected in the Heritage Foundation's Economic Freedom Index, year after year."[14]

The economist David Lacalle writes, "Private property [in Scandinavia] is guaranteed by law and citizens' savings are fully private and free of government control." In fact, according to Lacalle, Scandinavian countries in recent years have become more capitalistic. As Lacalle writes: "All Nordic countries have been lowering the tax wedge and—until the recent US tax cuts under President Trump—had lower corporate tax rates than the US."[15]

Despite the facts, American socialists continue to point enviously and approvingly to the large welfare systems in Scandinavian countries as "successful socialism." On *60 Minutes*, Ocasio-Cortez said, "My policies most closely resemble what we see in the U.K., in Norway, in Finland, in Sweden."

She fails to understand, though, that the story of Scandinavia is one of success before socialism, economic stagnation under the socialist policies of the 1970s and '80s, and finally a return to economic growth in the 1990s as center-right governments instituted market reforms and lowered taxes.

During its socialist era, Sweden grew 1 percent slower than Europe and 2 percent slower than the United States. Sweden's government grew to consume 70 percent of GDP and their debt exploded to 80 percent of GDP, and more than 400,000 jobs were lost.

When the center-right government was elected in 1991, they partially privatized health care and allowed private schools and school choice vouchers. Welfare benefits were reined in. New spending proposals could only be considered if they were offset by corresponding spending cuts.

Debt as a percent of GDP was cut in half. In reality, Sweden is hardly the "socialist miracle" Sanders and Ocasio-Cortez believe they are extolling.[16]

In a 2015 speech at Harvard, Denmark's prime minister was quite explicit in responding to those on the American left who refer to his country as socialist. He said, "I know that some people in the US associate the Nordic model with some sort of socialism. Therefore, I would like to make one thing clear. Denmark is far from a socialist planned economy. Denmark is a market economy."

Plunkett notes, "Unsurprisingly, Sen. Bernie Sanders has refused to stop using Denmark as an example of a 'democratic socialist' economy."[17]

It is politically expedient for Bernie to ignore the fact that Nordic success owes more to its capitalist origins than to any semblance of socialism.

As Iacono, a Thorpe Fellow with the Foundation for Economic Education, summarized, "Sanders has convinced a great deal of people that socialism is something that it is not, and he has used the Scandinavian countries to prove its efficacy while ignoring the many ways they deviate, sometimes dramatically, from what Sanders himself advocates."[18]

Sanandaji, who is of Kurdish-Iranian ancestry, migrated to Sweden as a child and grew up in a welfare-supported family. Sanandaji received his Ph.D. degree from the Royal Institute of Technology in Sweden and has become a well-known author who has spent much time researching the reasons for Nordic success.[19]

Sanandaji points out that rather than socialism, it is "the affluence and cultural norms upon which Scandinavia's social-democratic policies" rely that created their success. Sanandaji writes in *Scandinavian Unexceptionalism* that the success of Scandinavia "developed during periods characterized by free-market policies, low or moderate taxes, and limited state involvement in the economy."

Sweden began the nineteenth century as a poor nation. During this period there was a surge of Swedes fleeing to the United States. Sweden's prospects improved later in the century. As Sanandaji explains, "around 1870, [Sweden] turned to free-enterprise reforms. Robust capitalism replaced the formerly agrarian system, and Sweden grew rich. Property rights, free markets, and the rule of law combined with large numbers of well-educated engineers and entrepreneurs [allowed for] an unprecedented period of sustained and rapid economic development." Over the next fifty-six years, Sweden had the highest economic growth in the world.[20]

Sanandaji maintains that not only is Nordic success not a result of socialism but actually it is a result of Scandinavia's embrace of capitalism.[21]

He writes that "a closer look shows that what the left admires about Nordic societies is not due to socialism, and that the true lesson from Nordic countries is the importance of free markets and a vibrant work ethic," reminding us that for most of the past century and more, Scandinavia was not socialist but "relied on free markets and protection of private property." [22] Author Stefan Karlsson agrees that "Sweden's history is actually one dominated by capitalism."

Ignoring Sweden's history allows today's socialists to argue that high taxes and an enormous welfare state are not detrimental to economic growth.

But Karlsson reminds us that "far-reaching free market reforms in the 1860s allowed Sweden to benefit from the spreading Industrial Revolution." Also, Sweden was fortunate to be the home of many great creators, from Alfred Nobel, the inventor of dynamite and the founder of the Nobel Prize, to Sven Wingquist, who invented the self-aligning ball bearing, to Baltzar von Platen, who invented the gas absorption refrigerator.[23]

Wingquist's SKF became the world's largest bearing company and ultimately created another successful Swedish company, Volvo, all during Sweden's capitalist heyday. Before the era of big government, the car manufacturer SAAB and the telecommunications giant Ericsson originated.

As Karlsson puts it: "with just a few exceptions, nearly all large Swedish companies were started during the late 19th and early 20th centuries, which was not only a period of strong growth, but also the time when the foundation for later economic growth was laid."[24]

John Larabell agrees that much of Sweden's success can be traced to the capitalist era at the beginning of the twentieth century when IKEA, Tetra Pak, and other Swedish powerhouses were founded and "Sweden . . . saw phenomenal growth."[25]

Even today, the majority of Swedish industrial success stories actually originated during the capitalist era. Sanandaji points out that "of 38 [current] privately owned businesses in Sweden 21 were founded before 1913. 15 were founded between 1914 and 1970. Only two had been formed after 1970."

If you examine the one hundred largest firms ranked by how many people they employ, you find that none of Sweden's large employers were founded after 1970. It is clear that Sweden's economic success predates the 1970s expansion of the welfare state.[26]

In addition to its capitalist roots, Sweden has also been fortunate to avoid war. Sweden was not involved in either of the twentieth century world wars. In fact, Karlsson notes that "Sweden is, in fact, the country with the longest consecutive period of peace, having fought no war since 1809. . . ."[27]

Contrary to the myth espoused by today's new socialists, Sweden boomed for nearly a century as a capitalist mecca. During this era, Sweden was famous for defending property rights and free markets and enjoyed unprecedented economic growth. Basically, the capital formed in this era allowed Sweden to afford the ensuing welfare state.

As Sanandaji recounts: "Sweden's economic development can be divided up in four eras. A free-market era lasted between 1870 (when capitalism was introduced) and 1936 (where the social democrats came to power). During this time the economic policies of the country were characterized by minimal government involvement, and the Swedish economy grew more rapidly than any other Western European country."

As Karlsson points out: "Sweden had the highest per-capita income growth in the world between 1870 and 1950, by which time Sweden had become one of the world's richest countries, behind only the United States, Switzerland, and Denmark (who have since also fallen behind because of high taxes)."[28]

Even when the social democrats ruled, between 1936 and 1970, Sanandaji points out, "they were careful not to disturb the free-market." As taxes and government grew during this period, Sweden continued to grow but went from leading Europe in economic growth to a growth rate closer to the European average.[29]

That is not to say that the social democrats didn't begin to muck up the capitalism of the previous era. As Karlsson puts it: "like FDR in America and Adolf Hitler in Germany, they started to expand government power over the economy. Until 1932, government spending had been kept below 10% of GDP in Sweden. . . . Even in the early 1950s, Sweden was still one of the freest economies in the world, and government spending relative to GDP was in fact below the American level."[30]

From the 1950s through the mid-1970s, however, Sweden's government spending grew from about 20 percent of GDP to more than 50 percent of GDP in 1975. Taxes spiraled upward and the size of government exploded. Sweden's massive welfare state came into being during this period.[31]

Chapter 14

THE NORDIC MODEL
IS WELFARISM,
NOT SOCIALISM

C orey Iacono writes at the Foundation for Economic Education that "while it is true that the Scandinavian countries provide things like a generous social safety net and universal health care, an extensive welfare state is not the same thing as socialism. What Sanders and his supporters confuse as socialism is actually social democracy, a system in which the government aims to promote the public welfare through heavy taxation and spending, within the framework of a capitalist economy."

There is a name for this mix of capitalism and welfarism—economists refer to these mixed economies as the "Nordic model." This mixture of big government and private ownership is not, however, free. It comes with the heaviest middle-class tax burden in the world.[1]

It's worth noting that one of the reasons that this type of welfarism is accepted in Denmark, for example, is the high degree of cohesion in both racial and cultural identity among its 5.7 million citizens, unlike the diversity in America's 350 million. Hillary Clinton was right when she flatly refuted Bernie's Denmark dreams with the withering retort, "We aren't Denmark."

Historically, people in Denmark and other Scandinavian countries have embraced 60 percent taxation of middle-class earnings because they are actually utilizing all of the services that they get in exchange. The free tuition and health care are not a safety net for the poor, but used by all. This system has been challenged by the recent wave of immigrants from Syria, Afghanistan, and other Muslim countries, which illustrates the difficulties such a system would face in a country as culturally and racially diverse as the United States.

"In Denmark, both parents work full time and everyone utilizes the high quality state run day care. Being a 'stay at home' mom is virtually unheard of among native Danes. Due to cultural and religious differences, many immigrant families have the mother staying at home with the young children, and therefore drawing more in benefits than they are paying in taxes," explains Danish journalist Annegrethe Rasmussen. "This has caused resentment among some Danish who believe they are not contributing fairly to the social welfare system, and is one of the many reasons why the last four elections have been all about immigration." In other words, the Danish welfare system only works when every citizen pays equally high taxes. As reported in the *New York Times*, Kristian Madsen of the Danish newspaper *Politiken* said, "The Social Democrats lost four out of five elections this century because of the immigration issue." It is noteworthy that in 2018, Denmark stopped accepting UN quota refugees.

And yet American socialists persist in their belief that the "free stuff" that is offered in Scandinavia can somehow be paid for by high taxes only on "the rich." As Matt Palumbo writes, Scandinavian "countries offer much of what Bernie wants for America—free college, socialized medicine, paid year-long maternity leave, among other generous welfare state benefits."

How do they pay for it? Well, high taxes for sure. Higher rates than most Americans can imagine or likely will tolerate. And not just on the rich; the Scandinavian middle class is taxed at a significantly higher rate than in America.

Johan Norberg, a Cato fellow from Sweden, comments, "Yes, we have a bigger welfare state with more public services than the U.S. but it's not paid for by 'the rich'; they are too few and too important for the economy. The dirty little secret of the Swedish tax system is that we don't squeeze the rich, we squeeze the poor."

Norberg references an OECD study to make his point, saying, "the top 10% of earners in the United States paid more than 45% of all income taxes . . . whereas the Swedish top 10% paid less than 27%." Remember that the next time you hear Elizabeth Warren or Bernie accuse the rich of "not paying their fair share" in the United States.[2]

American socialists look at the giant welfare states and relative economic success of Scandinavia and conclude that you can have big government and economic growth. American socialists forget that Scandinavia didn't become wealthy at the same time they created a giant welfare state. As Palumbo puts it: "Scandinavia's economic success predates the era of high taxes and big government. Scandinavia is rich today—but in spite of their generous government policies, not because of them."[3]

American socialists who bandy about the success of Nordic socialism are crowing about welfarism within the context of and paid for by capitalism.

As Dorfman writes, "in reality the Nordic countries practice mostly free market economics paired with high taxes exchanged for generous government entitlement programs."[4]

While most left-wing Democrats once hid their socialist banner, now many progressives flaunt it. Actress Cynthia Nixon got raucous applause at a New York Democrat convention when she said, "Since Republicans are going to call us socialists no matter what we do, we might as well give them the real thing."[5]

Yet when today's socialists point to Scandinavian welfare states and trumpet their economic success, they fail to understand that, as Dorfman puts it: "It was not the government benefits that created wealth, but wealth that allowed the luxury of such generous government programs."[6]

The *Economist* points out the irony: "Indeed, the 'socialist' part of those countries that Mr. Sanders's fans like would be unaffordable without the dynamic capitalist part they dislike."[7]

Barack Obama joined the chorus on a 2013 pilgrimage to Sweden when he said: "Sweden also has been able to have a robust market economy while recognizing that there are some investments in education or infrastructure or research that are important, and there's no contradiction between making public investments and being a firm believer in free markets."[8]

At least President Obama admitted that Sweden had both capitalism and a welfare state and not socialism. Obama did, however, argue that "Nordic countries have some of the least income inequality in the world, which may explain one of the reasons that they're some of the happiest people in the world."[9]

Pakistan and Ethiopia are right up there with Nordic countries with the least income inequality. Wonder how they are doing on the happiness scale?

Despite tax reductions over the past few decades, Scandinavians today still pay very high taxes. CNN reports that "Danes pay some of the highest taxes in the world, including a 25% tax on all goods and services, and a top marginal tax rate hovering near 60%." Sweden's top rate is 56.4 percent while "the top tax rate in the U.S., by comparison, is less than 40%." However, when combined with our state and local taxes, the wealthy in the United States also pay more than half of their income in taxes.[10]

Danish taxes still approximate nearly 50 percent of their GDP. In America, as much as we complain about our tax burden, taxes here are about 20 percent of GDP.

If they want us to become Denmark, Bernie and the new socialists should at least be honest and inform everyone that the overall tax burden would have to more than double and a significant part of that burden would be placed squarely on the middle class and working poor if we adopted their 25 percent national sales tax.[11]

In America, though, the top income tax rate is limited to the upper class while in Scandinavia the top rate hits a huge swath of the middle class. According to Palumbo, "If America had Denmark's tax brackets, someone earning $60,000 a year would be subject to the top 60% tax rate." Whereas, in the United States, that person would likely pay an income tax rate of less than 15 percent.

Denmark also imposes some of the highest car taxes in the world. Until last year's tax cuts, new cars were taxed at nearly 200 percent of the car price. It is now down to a "reasonable" 100 percent. So if you want to buy a $30,000 car, you now only have to come up with an additional $30,000 for the government. Yes, you read that correctly. According to Rasmussen, "You take a loan almost like a mortgage to buy a car. No students have cars. It's insanely expensive." No wonder the Danes are always shown riding their bicycles and looking so fit and ruddy-cheeked! I suspect most Americans, however, would balk at having to rely on bike transportation in frigid weather.[12]

In addition to those punitively high income and car taxes, everyone, the poor, the middle class—everyone—in Denmark, Sweden, and Norway pays a 25 percent national sales tax on virtually everything they buy, including food.[13]

This national sales tax is a consumption tax known as a value-added tax, or VAT, and is much hated. This sales tax is applied up and down the production chain rather than just at the point of sale. No one escapes the VAT. Rich or poor or middle-class, the VAT is omnipresent and ensures that the Scandinavian welfare state gets a healthy bite of everyone's paycheck.[14]

Since consumption is a higher percentage of your income the less income you have, a 25 percent sales tax translates to low- and middle-income families paying taxes at a higher rate than the rich. The Scandinavian tax system is the very definition of regressive taxation.[15]

To summarize, today's socialists say they want socialism but are vague on the details of which industries the government should own and when. Today's socialists want Scandinavian socialism except it's not socialism because the state doesn't own or control most of the means of production. Today's socialists want to emulate Scandinavia's welfare state except for their high taxes on the middle class, their regressive 25 percent VAT, and the absence of punitive taxes on their top one percent.

Confused?

Well, maybe today's socialists don't know what socialism is and haven't read enough history to understand the horrors that occur whenever complete socialism is attempted. Perhaps today's socialists are simply welfarists who utilize envy to incite the majority to pay the bill.

After all, today's socialists clap the hardest for free health care and free tuition. Since we already have a certain degree of welfarism, perhaps they just want more.

What today's socialists really want is free health care, lunch, tuition, and someone to pay for really, really long maternity and paternity leave.

Most progressives, the ones who don't willingly self-identify as socialists, at least, understand that the argument for welfarism is much easier than the argument for socialism. No need to defend Stalin, Hitler, Mao, Pol Pot, Hugo Chavez, etc. But can one promote an economy that's a happy medium between capitalism and socialism, thus sidestepping the need to defend the indefensible attempts at real socialism?

This argument is only legitimate for the progressives who don't argue they are socialists. For Bernie, Ocasio-Cortez, and the other proud socialists it is incumbent upon them to explain why their socialism won't ultimately require totalitarian methods to enforce.

But what of the welfarists who promote big-government social programs and high taxes but would leave protections for private property and a stock exchange in place? Can these advocates of a mixed economy argue that the Enforcement Police will be a compassionate presence?

Let's take a look. In America, we have a mixed economy. The government owns the old-age pension program, Social Security. It is mandatory and paid for by taxes. Your forced savings don't go into an account. The money goes into the general budget and is spent. The government technically borrows the money and gives the Social Security Administration a promise to pay later—a nonnegotiable Treasury bill that is not redeemable in the marketplace. These Treasury bills are only redeemable with new taxes on the next generation. When you retire, you don't receive the money the government took from you. You receive money the government taxes from the next generation. The problem is, as family sizes diminish, there are not enough young people to pay for the old people. Social Security now pays out more than it brings in. Consequently, as of 2017, there is approximately an $11 trillion shortfall in funds necessary to keep Social Security afloat.

There is a "gotcha" question that reporters love to ask conservatives and libertarians who criticize Social Security. They ask: "Do you think Social Security is socialism?" Most critics of Social Security squirm and evade the question. But it is a good question—Is Social Security a socialist program? Social Security is mandatory and involves the force of taxation. So, what is it?

Before we answer that question, perhaps we should visualize government control and welfarism as a spectrum, ranging from no government—anarchy—to complete government—totalitarianism. The spectrum can stretch from complete freedom (no government) to complete lack of freedom (totalitarianism). Thomas Paine and most of our founders viewed government as such. They argued that government was a necessary evil, necessary to prevent the chaos of no government but evil in that government always requires force to implement its policies.

As we've seen, the more complete the socialism, the more complete the confiscation of property, the more force that is necessary. Force, ultimately in the form of government brutality, is an essential companion to complete equality. The more "equality" you want, the more force necessary to bring it about.

Social Security, government health care, free tuition, and the rest can all be seen in the same way. In a free society, people will voluntarily decide how much they will save. In a completely socialist society, all decisions about retirement would be controlled and dictated by the government. After all, you can't be trusted to do it yourself!

Where on the spectrum is America? Social Security taxes are 7.5 percent of everyone's income plus the 7.5 percent your employer "contributes." Realize, however, that your "employer's contribution" is put down in his or her accounting as a wage expense; therefore, it is part of your salary, just not received. Social Security taxes are only applied to the first $100,000 or so of income.

So, is Social Security socialism? A better question is what policies go toward more socialism and what policies go toward more freedom. Policies that promote more state control of your pension would include raising your Social Security taxes or increasing the income limits subject to the payroll tax. Both policies are supported by most of today's progressive Democrats, and both are more socialist.

Alternatively, policies that promote more freedom by making the Social Security tax completely voluntary, allowing workers to choose individual accounts to store their "contribution," and lowering the Social Security tax would take the pension system in the direction of capitalism.

The same goes for health care. Under complete socialized health care, the state would own all the hospitals, doctors, and nurses. No private options would be allowed. Actually, even under Mao's China they never got that far, although it was certainly their goal. In the United States, we have the hospitals and doctors and nurses in private hands, but about half of the health care in America is paid for with public funds.

Obamacare took us closer to socialism. Obamacare continued our hybrid system but increased taxes to have more of health care paid for by the taxpayer.

Alternatively, if we want to go in the direction of more capitalism, we would allow people to save more of their money tax-free for health care. We would allow patients to organize and buy their insurance through associations. We would remove obstacles to buying insurance across state lines, and we would legalize the sale of all forms of insurance, including high-deductible, low-premium insurance, which is a reasonable lower-cost alternative for young, healthy people.

If we chose more capitalism in the distribution of prescription drugs, we would legalize discount prices for wholesale buyers.

Currently, the courts prevent transparent discounts for larger purchasers of prescription drugs. A complicated rebate system arose to get around this government impediment, but the rebate system allows middlemen to carve out part of the profit without really letting the consumer in on the transaction.

Less socialism in legal drug distribution would mean less government protection of Big Pharma's legal patent monopoly. Drugs would still have patent protection, but it would expire at a certain date and generic competition would seamlessly follow without the millions of dollars in legal impediments that Big Pharma places in the way. Less socialism in pharmaceuticals would mean no banning of international drug sales.

More socialism in pharma could mean having the government assume ownership of Big Pharma, a disaster I hope we never choose, or it could mean keeping private ownership of the drug companies and increasing taxes to pay for the drugs. Drug companies would be all for it; Big Pharma's profits expanded greatly under Obamacare, something progressives hate to admit. Or we could allow more tax-free saving to purchase prescription drugs, legalize co-ops to have leverage to bring drug prices down, and prevent Big Pharma from gaming the system to extend their patents forever.

As Democrats call for a government-run "Medicare for All" system, it is interesting to note that in the last twenty-five to thirty years the wealthy in Denmark have increasingly opted out of the public health system for private health care and hospitals, while still paying the full taxes to support the public system, of course. According to Annegrethe Rasmussen, this has created "a parallel system that did not exist in my childhood."

And it's not just the wealthy who are opting out of the public health system. Often Danish companies offer private health care to their executives. For example, if a COO needs a medical procedure and his company doesn't want him to wait for two months to have the surgery because they need him back at work faster, they will pay for care at a private hospital.

Ms. Rasmussen elaborated that "you cannot choose, completely freely, your health care in the public system. There are waiting lists. You have to wait. I think the waiting list for a hip replacement is 3 to 6 months. But you know, if you want it in America you can have it in a week. So there is obviously a difference. While the care is generally quite good, you have to choose a doctor nearby. You cannot, for example, choose to go to the best doctor in Copenhagen if you live out in the countryside."

When asked her opinion on the increasing number of Danes opting out of the public health care system, Ms. Rasmussen responded, "In general, I think this trend is because Denmark has become less uniform and more classically liberal, or as you Americans call it, capitalist."

Chapter 15

SWEDEN IS SHRINKING TAXES AND WELFARE

The liberal love fest with Scandinavia has been going on since the 1970s. Jeff Jacoby remembers for us a 1976 story in *Time* that described Sweden as "a country whose very name has become a synonym for a materialist paradise. Its citizens enjoy one of the world's highest living standards. Neither ill-health, unemployment nor old age pose the terror of financial hardship. [Sweden's] cradle-to-grave benefits are unmatched in any other free society outside Scandinavia."[1]

Unfortunately the long-term results of soaring taxes and incipient socialism were not so utopian. As Jacoby reports, "taxes soared, welfare payments expanded, and entrepreneurship was discouraged. . . . Sweden's world-beating growth rate dried up. . . . By then, Swedes had begun to regard their experiment with socialism as, in Sanandaji's phrase, 'a colossal failure.'"

Across Scandinavia, the results were similar. The flirtation with socialism led to decreased economic growth and a flight of wealth.[2]

When Sweden embraced socialism in the 1970s, the laws of economics finally caught up. Economic growth slowed dramatically, and unemployment rose. The facts demonstrate that Sweden grew dramatically and led Europe in growth as a relatively low-tax, capitalist economy, and when Sweden's welfare state grew, its economy slowed and stagnated.

Sanandaji relentlessly debunks the myth that Nordic countries became rich by relying on socialism. He reminds us that "as late as the 1960s, taxes in Scandinavia were still comparable to the US. Denmark had a rate of 25%. Sweden's rate was 29% compared with 29% in the US."[3]

Before entering the high-tax era of the 1970s, taxes across Scandinavia competed with or even outcompeted the tax rates of America. During this low-tax era, there was an economic boom.[4]

Stefan Karlsson writes, "This changed in the 1970s after Olaf Palme, from the left wing of the Social Democratic party, became Prime Minister. Palme stepped up the socialist transformation in Sweden, rapidly increasing anti-business regulations, and sharply increased payroll taxes."[5]

During the 1970s and '80s, Sweden drifted toward socialism and became one of the highest-taxed nations in the world. Tax revenues rose dramatically to consume 50 percent of Sweden's GDP. Denmark also saw taxes rise to consume more and more of their GDP, eventually also reaching 50 percent. Economic growth suffered and ever since that time, Swedish governments have been turning away from socialism. [6]

Swedish voters' unhappiness with their government was no state secret. As Karlsson recounts: "Popular discontent from the economic woes created by the global economic downturn, the massive tax increases, the increased regulations, and the increasing inflation enabled the center right to come into power in 1976, breaking 44 years of uninterrupted Social Democratic rule."[7]

In 1970, Sweden was the fourth-wealthiest country in the world. Over time the ill effects of high taxes and increased regulation consumed a significant share of Sweden's wealth until they fell to fourteenth in the world in 1993.[8]

As taxes rose and economic growth stalled, Sanandaji reminds us that during this time, "Sweden's growth rate fell to the second lowest among western European countries." Even as Sweden's growth rate fell, though, the great wealth created in the previous era allowed the illusion of socialist success.[9]

All across Scandinavia, as the Nordic countries embraced higher taxation, economic growth stalled. By the 1980s, politicians across Scandinavia began to debate whether they'd gone too far in raising taxes. It became impossible to ignore the economic stagnation.[10]

As the welfare state grew by leaps and bounds and the taxes ate an ever-bigger chunk of everyone's paycheck, Denmark's GDP per capita went from seventh to tenth and Sweden's went from fourth to eleventh.[11]

But the flight of successful Scandinavians and the slowing of economic growth ultimately led to a change of heart in the populace and a change in direction for government.[12]

Swedish taxes got so high in the 1970s that the effective marginal rate sometimes exceeded 100 percent. As Rich Lowry comments at the *New York Post*: "There is a reason that IKEA founder Ingvar Kamprad fled the country in 1973. Sweden instituted a scheme to confiscate corporate profits and hand them over to labor unions. The idea was, in the words of a Swedish economist, to have 'a market economy without individualist capitalists and entrepreneurs.'"[13]

Other famous Swedes who fled include Alpine skier Anja Paerson, high jumper Kajsa Bergqvist, and triple jumper Christian Olsson.[14]

During the 1980s, Scandinavian governments began to wake up to the economic effects of their crushing taxes. Denmark, Norway, and Sweden all cut their corporate taxes in half until their rates reached the mid-20s—more than ten percentage points lower than that of the United States.[15]

Jeff Jacoby writes in the *Boston Globe*, "That 1976 story in *Time*, for example, went on to report that Sweden found itself struggling with crime, drug addiction, welfare dependency, and a plague of red tape. Successful Swedes—most famously, Ingmar Bergman—were fleeing the country to avoid its killing taxes. 'Growing numbers are plagued by a persistent, gnawing question: Is their Utopia going sour?'"[16]

Prime Minister Palme was assassinated in 1986 and Ingvar Carlsson took his place. Stefan Karlsson, at Mises.org, describes this period: "Worried that Swedish growth had trailed most other countries, Carlsson's government implemented a number of free-market reforms. Among these were the lifting of all currency controls in 1989 and a tax reform that dramatically reduced marginal tax rates."[17]

Despite lowering taxes in the 1980s, Swedes were still contemplating fleeing the country in the early 1990s. Daniel J. Mitchell writes, "Stefan Persson, the main owner of fashion retailer H&M, threatened to leave the country in the 1990s because of the wealth tax. The Social Democratic government at the time changed the law, giving him an exemption."[18]

As Jordan Drischler points out: "Following overhauls once again in the early 90s and again with the election of the Moderate Party as the majority in 2006, Sweden returned to a free market economy. But some aspects, including universal health care and high tax rates, remained. These lingering effects of Sweden's socialist era has led to individuals incorrectly labeling their current, largely free market economy as socialist."[19]

As far back as 2007, writers were noting that instead of moving toward more socialism, Sweden was becoming more capitalist by lowering its taxes. Mitchell from Cato wrote, "Maybe the next Bjorn Borg won't feel compelled to move to Monaco now that

Sweden plans to scrap a decades-old 'wealth' tax that imposes lev-
ies on assets—not just on income. . . . The move . . . underscores
the country's efforts to keep successful Swedes and their capital at
home by changing its fabled but costly welfare state."[20]

But a small country like Sweden doesn't get a Bjorn Borg every
generation. Tennis player Borg did return home for a while in the
mid-1980s. It was reported that the Swedish government under
Palme allowed him to recover about $500,000 tax-free.[21]

While taxes remain high according to U.S. standards, lower top
rates did ultimately encourage IKEA's Kamprad to return home.
But to this day, Scandinavians still suffer from high individual tax
rates even though the overall burden has come down.[22]

Finally, in 1991, the Swedish electorate voted out the socialist
government and elected a center-right government. From 1991 to
the present, taxes have come down, regulations have abated, and
as a consequence, Sweden now has "the second highest growth
rate in western Europe during its new free-market era, between
1991 and 2014," writes Nima Sanandaji.[23]

Karlsson reminds us that during this period marginal tax rates
were lowered and currency controls eliminated, banks were deregulated, and several state-owned companies were privatized.

The Swedes also deregulated the retail and telecommunications
sectors and the airline industry. Deficits were brought down and
an attempt was even made to control spending. Sounds more like
the policies of Reagan and Thatcher than it does the policies of
Bernie Sanders and Elizabeth Warren.

Although American socialists point to the economic growth of
the last twenty years as successful socialism, Karlsson concludes:
"the relative improvement of performance is due not to high taxes
(lower now than previously), but to free-market reforms."[24]

Per Bylund writes that the economic depression of the 1990s

finally motivated the populace to choose a new government. "The social democratic government resigned, government lost control (to the extent it ever had any), and politicians from all parties got together to enforce strict budget discipline (no deficits) and consistently cut back on the state's generous welfare benefits. At the same time, pseudo-market forces were reintroduced through Friedmanite voucher systems, private health care was no longer prohibited, and the national pharmacy monopoly was privatized. Even Sweden's railway traffic is now carried out largely by private companies."[25]

In short, as American socialists clamor to increase American corporate and individual taxes, Sweden's taxes have come down. As Chris Matthews at *Fortune* reports: "since the 1990s, the total taxation of the Swedish economy as a percentage of GDP has fallen more than 5%, while labor market reforms, such as Denmark's cutting of unemployment benefits have helped Scandinavian economies rocket up measures of economic freedom . . . as Sanandaji puts it, Scandinavia is slowly 'returning to its free market roots.'"[26]

Chapter 16

WELFARISM
REQUIRES HIGH
MIDDLE-CLASS TAXES

American socialists who look to Scandinavia might reconsider once they learn that the middle-class tax burden there is significantly higher than in the United States. Contrary to what Bernie would have you think, it's not just millionaires and billionaires paying the price. In fact, one could argue that the United States has a significantly more progressive tax structure than Scandinavia, considering that Americans making above $400,000 are already paying more than half of their income in taxes when state and local taxes are added.

Yet the socialist Ocasio-Cortez thinks the rich are getting off scot-free. She's proposing a new 70 percent tax rate for people making $10 million or more. Brian Riedl of the Manhattan Institute makes several points about this ridiculous proposal:

He writes, "A 70 percent tax bracket would raise very little (if any) revenue, while damaging the economy and sending income and jobs overseas." Riedl calculates that such a tax would bring in .25% of our GDP while the socialists are proposing to approximately double government spending as a function of GDP.

Today's socialists, Riedl estimates, want to spend about "$7–

$10 trillion over the decade" on the Green New Deal and another $32 trillion on Medicare for All and another $6.8 trillion on a federal jobs guarantee and another $1.4 trillion on student loan forgiveness and $800 billion on free college tuition, a trillion on infrastructure, $270 billion on mandatory paid leave, and $188 billion on Social Security expansion. That comes to a total of over $50 trillion in new spending proposals.

Ocasio-Cortez's tax on people making over $10 million, Riedl judges, would only bring in $50 billion—that is, if it didn't chase all the wealthy out of the United States, as happened in Sweden during the 1980s. That's $50 billion with a *b* in revenue against $50 trillion with a capital *T* in expenditures. Sounds like a significant amount of red ink for a country already borrowing about a trillion dollars each year.

The unavoidable truth is that the socialist Christmas list of welfare programs can only be paid for by massive taxes on everyone, including the middle class and the working class, just like the taxes in Europe and Scandinavia.[1]

Today's socialists falsely promote that they will pay for their laundry list of new federal spending by taxing the millionaires and billionaires, but it's a lie.

It isn't enough to point out that Ocasio-Cortez's tax brings in $50 billion and her spending proposals cost $50 trillion. Basic math is not enough to win the hearts and votes of today's voters. Don't get me wrong, facts are still important but somehow, we must get today's voters, particularly the youth, to love the liberty of voluntary transactions between consenting adults—capitalism—and to fear the coercion of regulated, controlled exchanges that come only when the government consents or gives you permission.

To millennials who may not care about the numbers or the debt or the taxes, we must impress upon them that socialism also inevitably robs them of choice. A government that owns or controls the means of production can only exert that control by limiting the freedom of choice.[2]

Most millennials, however, are blissfully unaware of the punishing taxes necessary for socialism or its stepchild welfarism. Millennials are shielded from the burden of taxes because most of them are part of the approximately half of the U.S. population that pays no income tax at all.

In the United States, the top 1 percent of income earners pays nearly 40 percent of the total income tax revenue, and the top 10 percent pays almost 70 percent. Meanwhile the bottom 50 percent of taxpayers paid only 3 percent of federal income tax in 2016. When today's socialists claim the rich aren't paying their fair share they are ignoring the facts. The upper middle class and the rich pay virtually all of the income tax in America and our tax code is already more progressive than that of Scandinavia.

Endlessly, the left in America decries any tax cuts, and they utilize mathematical fallacies to argue their points. You hear progressives say the tax cut will disproportionately benefit the rich. Well, if taxes are disproportionately paid by the rich, it stands to reason that tax cuts would always benefit more the people who pay taxes.

It bears repeating, since 50 percent of Americans pay no income tax, tax cuts typically only affect the 50 percent of Americans who actually do pay an income tax.[3]

Modern socialists, and virtually all Democrats (and their mouthpieces in the media), endlessly and breathlessly broadcast the message that tax cuts are for the millionaires and billionaires. This lie needs to be debunked, rebuked, and explained again and again. It is impossible to design a tax cut that does not disproportionately affect the wealthy because the wealthy pay the vast majority of the income tax under our existing, heavily progressive taxation system.[4]

Socialists also argue for keeping America's corporate taxes high. However, the Scandinavians have taken the opposite approach. In a sea of high taxation, the Scandinavians do have one exception. Their corporate taxes have long been below U.S. rates. As Kai Weiss reports at the Austrian Center: "Corporate income tax rates are in the 20 percent range in all Nordic countries and thus, in stark—positive—contrast to countries like Germany and France, which can boast rates up to 35."

If you look at Tax Freedom Day, the calendar day that each individual has paid government its due and begins to earn money for themselves and their family, you discover that it comes earlier for the Nordic countries than it does for Germany, Austria, France, and Belgium.[5]

It's amazing that the American left continues to showcase "Scandinavian socialism" as these same countries have steadily reduced taxes and strengthened their capitalist roots. As José Niño reports, "countries like Sweden implemented a number of sensible reforms during the 1990s and 2000s like tax cuts and school choice, while others like Denmark liberalized their labor market to make it more competitive and flexible." The resulting economic success extolled by American socialists today is a reversing of the high-tax trends of several decades.[6]

In 2007, thirty years after Sweden's flirtation with socialism, the government eliminated its estate tax. Their foreign minister Anders Borg explained that it was unsustainable to have wealth taxes that exceeded other European countries. As Dan Mitchell from Cato reports: "Several European countries have dropped taxes on wealth in the last decade, including Denmark, the Netherlands, and Finland."

Swedish authorities admitted that there was a great deal of Swedish capital outside the country that could create jobs if brought home to be invested. Eliminating the wealth tax was a very direct way of trying to get wealthy Swedes to bring their capital home. What does Ocasio-Cortez say about that? Do any of today's socialists want to join Sweden in eliminating the estate (wealth) tax? Absolutely not! Rather, Bernie wants to make the estate tax more progressive.[7]

In fact, for American socialists touting Sweden's high taxes, they need to realize that Sweden no longer has the highest worldwide tax rate. They're still number four, but they've recognized the problem and have headed in the right direction. Their spending still consumes more than 50 percent of their nation's GDP, but as Bylund reminds us, "the national debt as a fraction of GDP, not including pensions and other liabilities, has halved over the course of the last two decades. Twenty years of reform, away from the extensive welfare state and socialist experiment, explains Sweden's relatively strong finances in the present financial crisis." It isn't so much socialism that explains Scandinavian success but rather Sweden's turn away from socialism.[8]

Scandinavia's retreat from socialism continues to this day. In recent elections, four out of five Nordic nations chose center-right governments. Wonder if someone should tell America's young socialists that not only is Scandinavia not socialist, but they seem to be heading back toward American capitalism.[9]

Are taxes still high in Scandinavia? Absolutely. In Sweden, the top rate is over 60 percent and that rate applies to incomes beginning at $75,000. According to John Larabell, that 60 percent includes a 34 percent municipal tax that everyone pays.

Norway, with its vast oil wealth, has a top rate of only 38.7 percent, which was lower than the U.S. top rate of 39.6 percent until the 2018 Trump cut lowered the top rate to 37 percent. Like most of Scandinavia, the top rate in Norway starts at a much lower level of income so their top rate actually captures a significant swath of the middle class.

As Larabell puts it, "While the rich do get soaked in Scandinavian countries, the middle class gets soaked even more. Even working-class people with relatively low-wage jobs get hit with tax rates that would be considered high in America."

Once you add up the national sales taxes, old-age pension taxes, and income taxes, it is not uncommon for folks in the middle class in Scandinavian countries to pay 70 to 80 percent of their income in taxes.[10]

So, really, today's new American socialists must come clean. They love, love, love Scandinavian "socialism" but they ignore the fact that the Scandinavian welfare state is actually financed by extraordinarily high middle-class taxes.

In America, these socialists claim they will finance their dreams of "Medicare for All" by sticking it to the rich and leaving the middle class alone. Which is it? Come on, socialists international, which is it? Do you want the Scandinavian welfare state financed by the world's highest taxes on the middle class? Or are you making the argument that you can tax the rich at 200 percent of their income?

Bernie and his merry band of socialists inform us that they only want to punish the top 1 percent. What they won't admit is that the top 1 percent already pays more than a third of all U.S. income tax revenue and the top 10 percent pays two-thirds of our income taxes. The question is: At what point do the producers finally flee to Galt's Gulch?

To get an idea of how ferociously the Scandinavians tax the middle class, consider this analysis from Jesse Plunkett: "In Denmark, any family earning over 1.2 times the average income pays the top rate of 60 percent; this is the equivalent of the 40 percent of American families earning over $70,000 paying the top tax rate." Even Democrats understand there would be a revolution in America if they proposed an income tax rate of 60 percent on income over $70,000.

In Norway also, the middle class is heavily taxed. All incomes over $94,000 are taxed at 40 percent, whereas in America the top rate applies only to incomes over $426,000.

While Bernie calls for a special tax on billionaires, in Denmark and Norway there are no special tax brackets for the superrich. Rather, the top U.S. income and payroll tax rate is already greater than that of Norway and Germany and England as well.

So, American socialists really don't want Scandinavian "socialism." They want all the free stuff of the Scandinavian welfare state, but they want only the superrich to pay for it. American socialists never seem to advocate for the astronomical middle-class taxes and high value-added sales taxes that pay for the cradle-to-grave Scandinavian welfare.[11]

Chapter 17

AMERICAN SCANDINAVIANS HAVE IT BETTER HERE THAN IN SCANDINAVIA

I t's not just the left-wing politicians who drool over the Scandinavian welfare state. The partisan, left-of-left economist Paul
Krugman seems to have his own personal love affair with the
Nordic Nation. He writes: "Danes get a lot of things right, and in
doing so refute just about everything US conservatives say about
economics."

Krugman gushes that the Danish welfare state is "beyond the
wildest dreams of American liberals."

Like Bernie, Krugman extols the "free" health care, college tuition, and day care. He admits the taxes are high but doesn't bother
explaining how high or how extensively those high taxes reach
into the middle and lower classes.

The takeaway message for Krugman, who never met a tax or
government program he didn't like, is that "taxes and benefits just
aren't the job killers right-wing legend asserts."[1]

I remember debating him on one of the Sunday morning shows
and making the point that government had grown tremendously

under President Obama's watch. He responded that I was misinformed and that government employment had shrunk under the Obama administration.

When questioned further, though, it became obvious that Krugman was slyly referring to both state and federal government together. Of course, state government shrinkage had absolutely nothing to do with Obama and his merry band of Democrats. State government size began to shrink only after the Tea Party tidal wave of 2010 swept in a net of six new GOP governors, and all governors faced decreased revenues during the recession.[2]

Like Krugman, Joseph Stiglitz seems to have forgotten any sense of academic neutrality to become more of a partisan than an economist. A few years back at a Time 100 event, I just happened to be seated next to Stiglitz. It was a cocktail hour, and I was feeling a bit mischievous, so I asked the Nobel laureate: "I understand you believe that free markets are 'inefficient' because information is asymmetrically distributed . . . what do you think is the most important bit of information that needs to be transmitted in the marketplace?"

He didn't answer immediately. I decided to follow up with my answer, so he didn't think I had the audacity to quiz him. (Which, I guess, I sort of was . . .) My answer: prices. Nothing is more important than prices in transmitting information throughout an economy and perhaps the disfunction Stiglitz sees in the free market might be explained by government's manipulation of the most important price of all: interest rates. I think at this point he became more interested in the person seated to the opposite side of me.

My short interaction, though, makes me unsurprised that Stiglitz has argued that "American policymakers should use Scandinavia as a model for promoting more balanced growth."[3]

The Austrian economist William L. Anderson describes "Stiglitz [as] a one-man advocacy band for growth of the state." Stiglitz's admiration for big government extends not only to Scandinavia but to Venezuela as well. Stiglitz thought that Chavez was successful "in bringing health and education to the people in the poor neighborhoods of Caracas, to those who previously saw few benefits of the country's oil wealth." Stiglitz also extolled Chavez for distributing income more equally. Like so many others who were infatuated with Chavez, Stiglitz is keeping mum now that Venezuelans are eating their pets and burning their currency for warmth.[4]

A useful question to ask if you are an American socialist: If Scandinavia is such a great place to live, are Scandinavians as an ethnic group doing better in Scandinavia or here in low-tax America?

The answer is intriguing. Scandinavians in the United States earn more than the average American and more than their counterparts in Scandinavia. Something is special about Scandinavia, but it turns out it isn't their economic system at all. Sanandaji maintains that Scandinavian success is not about socialism, welfarism, or high taxes—but about Scandinavian work ethic and culture.[5]

The American left crows about long life spans and low infant mortality among Scandinavians as if these statistics are a result of socialism. The facts argue otherwise. As Sanandaji points out, "the admirable social outcomes pre-date the welfare state." Not only do their quality-of-life statistics predate the growth of the welfare state, but these same quality-of-life numbers follow the Nordic people wherever in the world they migrate.

Indeed, Sanandaji empirically shows that historical "tables . . . show the global rankings of life span and child mortality—before the introduction of large welfare states in the Nordics"—were actually higher than the statistics under the welfare era. Sanandaji argues that the "good outcomes" have more to do with "the healthy diets and lifestyles of Nordic people" than socialism.

Sanandaji points out that life expectancy in Denmark today is 1.5 years longer than in America. However, the Danish lived 2.4 years longer than Americans well before they chose high taxes and a welfare state.[6]

In fact, before the advent of Scandinavian universal health care back in the early 1960s, Plunkett reports that "Norwegian men already lived to be 71 and Swedish men 72, compared to less healthy American men living only to 67."

When universal health care was initiated in 1961, Scandinavians were already living several years longer than Americans. Maybe the correlation of welfare state and a long life is not what we thought.

Errors in assessing cause and effect lie at the root of the American left's infatuation with the Scandinavian welfare state.

One of the strongest arguments against the Nordic model of a giant welfare state and high taxes being responsible for success is that Scandinavians seem to have the same success whether they are in Scandinavia or elsewhere.

Sanandaji writes that Scandinavian success here in America extends to "exponentially lower high-school dropout rates, much lower unemployment rates and even lower poverty rates." So, if Swedish-Americans, Danish-Americans, and all other Nordic-Americans are better off both financially and in quality-of-life measures, maybe it's time once and for all to dismiss with prejudice the phony argument of the left that Scandinavian success stems from socialism.

In fact, if you look at immigrants who migrate to Nordic countries, who do not share the cultural values of Scandinavia, they "fare worse than [immigrants] to the U.S. in regards to employment, self-reported health and the school result of their children."

Which would further argue that it is Scandinavian culture, not the welfare state, that is responsible for their success.[7]

A Scandinavian scholar once supposedly said to Milton Friedman, "In Scandinavia, we have no poverty." Friedman quipped back, "That's interesting, because in America, among Scandinavians, we have no poverty, either."[8]

As Rich Lowry summarizes Sanandaji, "The descendants of Scandinavian immigrants have median incomes 20 percent higher than the US average, and their poverty rate is half the average." In addition, Danish- and Swedish-Americans, according to Sanandaji, earn "50% more than their counterparts back at home,"[9] and that's not even accounting for the fact that Nordic-Americans also get to keep a much larger percentage of their income as our taxes are so much lower. Think about that. Danes who've come to America not only have higher incomes than the average American but have higher incomes than Danes who remain in Denmark. The same goes for Swedish-Americans (53 percent higher than native Swedes) and Finnish-Americans (59 percent higher incomes than native Finns).

We can learn from Scandinavian success. It just doesn't appear to have anything to do with socialism or the welfare state.[10]

Only for Norway is the advantage of living in America small. Perhaps because of the massive oil wealth of Norway, the living standard of American Norwegians is only 3 percent higher than in Norway.

If you compare poverty and unemployment rates you also find that Scandinavians in America have lower poverty and unemployment than Scandinavians who remain in Scandinavia.

And it's not just income success that separates Nordic-Americans from average Americans. This group of immigrants also graduates from high school at 14 percent above the American average.[11]

As Jeff Jacoby lays it out:

The real key to Scandinavia's unique successes isn't socialism,
it's culture. Social trust and cohesion, a broad egalitarian ethic,
a strong emphasis on work and responsibility, commitment to
the rule of law—these are healthy attributes of a Nordic culture
that was ingrained over centuries. In the region's small and
homogeneous countries (overwhelmingly white, Protestant, and
native-born), those norms took deep root. The good outcomes
and high living standards they produced antedated the socialist
nostrums of the 1970s. Scandinavia's quality of life didn't spring
from leftist policies. It survived them.[12]

Sanandaji maintains that the Scandinavian success story stems from the fact that "Nordic societies have for hundreds of years benefited from sound institutions, a strong Lutheran work ethic and high levels of trust and civic participation."[13]

For those who might want to discount Scandinavian culture as a cause for their success, José Niño responds: "These social [cultural] characteristics were more than random idiosyncrasies, they were part and parcel of a robust social fabric that facilitated Scandinavia's initial economic success."[14]

From all of this incredible data, it is impossible to argue that socialism or welfarism explains Scandinavian success. But it is also impossible and a mistake not to try to understand the cultural and capitalistic reasons for Scandinavia's success.

After compiling this data and writing two books about it, Sanandaji concludes that Scandinavian success at home and upon emigrating is the result of cultural values such as work ethic and honesty.[15]

Chapter 18

SWEDISH COLLEGE IS FREE, BUT IT'S NOT CHEAP OR UNIVERSAL

W hat about socializing college tuition? In Scandinavia tuition is free and today's socialists love free. But nothing in life is truly free. As we've seen, citizens of the Nordic countries pay for "free" college tuition with the highest middle-class taxes in the world.

And before socialists go all wobbly in the knees for the Scandinavian system, realize that not everyone gets to go to college. If anything, Scandinavia and most of the world are a much harsher meritocracy than America when it comes to college admittance.

Take China, for example. College is "free" but to get there, you have to take perhaps the most difficult college entrance exam in the world: the Gaokao, a nine-hour exam taken over two days. Ten million Chinese high school seniors take the test each year, but only 0.2 percent score high enough to be admitted to a top college.[1]

In Denmark, there are strict limits on degrees. The state and the university system together regulate the number of degrees in each field. "Let's say you want to be a political scientist, or a midwife, or a doctor, those are the most difficult educations to get into, and you would have to be in the top 10% to get into those fields. If your grades aren't good enough, you will have to choose a field that is less competitive or else in high demand by the state," says Anne-grethe Rasmussen.

In fact, despite "free" tuition, the percentage of Scandinavians who matriculate into college is not any higher than in the United States. In Norway, for example, there are disparities in who goes to college. About 14 percent of children from the least educated families attend university compared with 58 percent of children from the most educated families. Statistics on admissions to American colleges is similar. Income statistics also largely follow the degree of education, so even in Norway there are still more college students from wealthier families than poor families.

John Larabell summarizes the situation well: "the problem isn't just money, it's about familial and cultural values. Also, since many blue-collar jobs pay quite well in Scandinavian countries, and the welfare state is almost paternal in its scope, there's not as much incentive to actually go to college and pursue a degree."

Larabell makes another point that is worth pondering: "If everyone gets a college education, such an education essentially becomes worthless, no better than a high-school diploma is now. Plus, under a tax-funded system, those who choose not to go to college, for any number of reasons, would still be paying for it, much the same way parents who put their kids in private schools in America still pay for the public schools via property taxes."[2]

Many American students who are laden with enormous college debt and either no degree because they flunked out, or a worthless degree because they chose a worthless degree, would not be saddled with that debt anywhere else in the world. Not because of a lack of "free" tuition but because of stringent test scores that most of the rest of the world requires.

Interestingly, while tuition is free in Sweden, students still wind up with nearly as much debt as their American counterparts. The average Swede ends up with about $19,000 in debt while the average American has about $24,800 in debt. While the debt burden is less, more Swedes have debt than Americans. Eighty-five percent of Swedes finish college with debt, while about 50 percent of Americans graduate with debt.

How does that happen? Well, while tuition is "free," rent, food, and entertainment are not. Sweden also has one of the highest costs of living in the world. Another reason that the Swedes graduate with so much debt is that in Sweden college students are expected to pay for their daily expenses.

So, if today's socialists want to import Scandinavian "free" tuition, they must realize it comes with a price: extremely high middle-class taxes, the state gaining much more control over who gets to go to college and their academic field of study, and college debt not markedly dissimilar from American college debt.[3] Nothing is free.

Part III

A Boot Stamping on the Human Face Forever— Socialism and Authoritarianism

Chapter 19

SOCIALISM BECOMES AUTHORITARIANISM

One of the greatest ironies of modern political history is that as socialists around the world rose up to overthrow authoritarian regimes, they ultimately replaced them (despite their promises to establish free democracies) with authoritarian regimes of their own.

The overthrow of Batista in Cuba gave us Castro. The overthrow of Somoza in Nicaragua gave us the Sandinistas. The overthrow of the czars gave us Stalin, and on and on. Each time a revolt of the "people" promised the manna of socialism and justice. And each time the result was rule by an elite that degenerated into rule by the few or even rule by one, often with the democratic title of president but with the ominous subtitle—"for life."

Socialists want to argue that each case from Zimbabwe to Nigeria to Equatorial Guinea to North Korea is an anomaly or that none of these historical examples are "real" socialism. And yet the "liberators" time and time again call themselves socialists.

So, before we sign on with any of the new American socialists' campaigns, it would behoove us all to reexamine the legacy of historical socialism. Despite popular belief to the contrary, violence and authoritarianism are an inevitable part of socialism.

The only way to avoid confronting this reality is to dress social-ism up in promises of prosperity and safety, counting on the pub-lic's ignorance to pave the way. There's a great deal of irony that two months after Victory in Europe on May 8, 1945, less than two months after the defeat of Nazi socialism, the inspirational leader of England, Winston Churchill, was shockingly defeated by the socialist Clement Attlee. Attlee headed the democratic socialist party known as the Labour Party.

The very same people who had fled to the bomb shelters and lost hundreds of thousands of their young men to a Nazi socialist regime turned on a dime and voluntarily elected a socialist. How could that happen? The only possible answer is ignorance, igno-rance of the ideology that founded the Nazi Party, and ignorance that the socialism the British were embracing could lead to author-itarianism.

This willful disconnect between socialism and authoritarian-ism was promoted in the public discourse by naive intellectuals. George Orwell, who most famously roasted Stalin's socialism in his book *Animal Farm,* was nevertheless a self-identified socialist. Neither Hitler nor Stalin was condemned for their socialism, only for their methods. (Not all were blind, of course. Socialist George Bernard Shaw, author of the feminist play *Pygmalion,* did not deny Stalin's crimes—rather he *defended* them.)[1]

Attlee's democratic socialism led to the nationalization of ma-jor industries, including coal, electricity, steel, and the railways. Attlee and his socialist band also created the British socialized health-care service. "But no concentration camps!" protest leftists. Surely the British welfare state must be seen as a win. Right?

The absence of death camps hardly proves that socialism in any form is benign. The degree of violence necessary depends on the degree of state ownership and control. So, yes, the owners of the steel, coal, electrical, and rail companies were threatened with jail if they refused to allow the state to take their companies, but there were not concentration camps. If you want to abolish all private property, the resistance intensifies, and camps, truncheons, and state-sanctioned violence become necessary.

George Reisman is an economist who received his Ph.D. under Ludwig von Mises, the famous Austrian economist. Socialism eventually requires, Reisman argues, "a massive act of theft—the means of production must be seized from its owners and turned over to the state. Such seizure is virtually certain to provoke substantial resistance on the part of the owners, resistance which can be overcome only by use of massive force."[2]

Using the apparatus of state force to take private property does not seem to bother modern self-proclaimed socialists like New York City's Bill de Blasio. In a *New York* magazine interview, he laments that "our legal system is structured to favor private property." De Blasio dreams of a time when society takes heed of its "socialistic impulse" to plan and control property "in accordance with [the people's] needs."[3]

De Blasio is not at all embarrassed to admit his desire for a "city government [that] would determine every single plot of land, how development would proceed. And there would be very stringent requirements around income levels and rents. . . . [along with] a very, very powerful government, including a federal government, involved in directly addressing their day-to-day reality."[4]

At least in New York City, the hope that democracy serves as a check and a balance against government confiscation of property is proving to be wrong.

Advocates for democracy argue that as long as the right to vote continues to exist, people typically will resist the complete abolition of private property. Let's hope this is true, and that de Blasio will be voted out of office before the outright confiscation of private property happens.

If democracy is a check against going "too far" with socialism, that may explain why when "complete" or "real" socialism arrives, it requires so much force to confiscate property that the majority rebels. And why "complete" socialism (with the abolishment of private property) is always accompanied by the destruction of democracy at the hands of a tyrant.[5] So perhaps we should not be at all surprised that, while speaking to a group of union workers in Miami in June of 2019, Mayor de Blasio, pumping his fist righteously in the air, shouted the infamous slogan of murderous Marxist Che Guevara: "Hasta la victoria, siempre!"[6]

While the British and the Scandinavian democracies have flirted with socialism, they've never really had the temerity to use the force necessary to achieve full socialism. As Reisman puts it, "The Communists were and are willing to apply such force, as evidenced in Soviet Russia. Their character is that of armed robbers prepared to commit murder if that is what is necessary to carry out their robbery. The character of the Social Democrats, in contrast, is more like that of pickpockets, who may talk of pulling the big job someday, but who in fact are unwilling to do the killing that would be required, and so give up at the slightest sign of serious resistance."[7]

Britain's cherished democratic values check the full abolition of property and Britain remains protected too by her history of limiting central power. For more than seven hundred years, since the barons gathered at Runnymede and forced limitations on the king, the British have had due process of law. So, instead of Nazism or Bolshevism, England got Scandinavian-style welfarism, a welfare state with high taxes and public debt but no abolition of freely floating prices, the stock market, or most private ownership of business. European democracies, at least so far, have been unwilling to embrace the violence necessary to confiscate and redistribute all property.

The allure of socialism's free goodies, though, continues to find appeal. "Free" health care turned out to be very popular in England. After all, people like "free" stuff. However, "free" health care wasn't exactly free and led to overuse and enlargement of the debt and subsequent tax hikes. The National Health Service became famous for its waiting lines. Health care was essentially rationed by putting the excess demand (sick patients) in a queue.

When Thatcher finally arrived in 1979, the Brits had largely soured on the incompetence and stagnation of government ownership of industry. Most of Attlee's nationalization of industry was reversed except for the National Health Service.

But the question remains: Is violence an inevitable part of socialism? Take Nazism, which did not even represent pure socialism. But though the Nazis did not completely ban private ownership, Mises and Hayek argued that the Nazis essentially negated true ownership via price controls and ultimately production controls. Reisman argues that "the requirements of enforcing a system of price and wage controls" ultimately and inevitably require state violence.[8]

How does enforcement of price controls ratchet up to require totalitarian methods? Well, sellers evade price controls to raise their prices. Buyers jump at the chance to get around the shortages. That's how a black market develops.

Regulatory fines are imposed on any caught using the black market. Fines work as long as food and necessities can still be purchased legally but as shortages spread and prices become prohibitive, fines alone will not stop the black market.

According to Reisman, ultimately "the government has to make it actually dangerous to conduct black-market transactions."[9]

Each black market trade must be accompanied by fear of discovery by the police. Any government wishing to enforce price controls must employ an "army of spies and secret informers." To deter the black market everyone must fear everyone. Any time money changes hands, the government must create an environment where no one is certain whether their customer or supplier isn't an informant or an undercover cop.

Product distribution, including food, breaks down to such a degree that a black market is nearly impossible to deter. Only with the utmost government diligence and spread of fear is there any hope of preventing everyone from trading on the black market.

As wage and price controls lead to shortages and lines, the mass bulk of the public becomes sympathetic to if not a participant in the black market. As Reisman explains, the government "cannot rely on jury trials, because it is unlikely that many juries can be found willing to bring in guilty verdicts in cases in which a man might have to go to jail for several years for the crime of selling a few pounds of meat or a pair of shoes above the ceiling price."[10]

As fines ratchet up, criminal sentences are meted out. As the government resorts to extrajudicial incarcerations, Reisman explains that "the requirements merely of enforcing price-control regulations is the adoption of the essential features of a totalitarian state, namely, the establishment of the category of 'economic crimes,' in which the peaceful pursuit of material self-interest is treated as a criminal offense, and the establishment of a totalitarian police apparatus replete with spies and informers and the power of arbitrary arrest and imprisonment."[11]

So, even without outright state confiscation of property, a form of tyranny coincides with and is indeed necessary to enforce and maintain market-wide wage and price controls. Reisman argues that it is not accidental that state violence ensues: "Clearly, the enforcement of price controls requires a government similar to that of Hitler's Germany or Stalin's Russia, in which practically anyone might turn out to be a police spy and in which a secret police exists and has the power to arrest and imprison people."[12]

Do wage and price controls have to end in tyranny? Only if you want them to be enforced. Without the tyranny of government force, wage and price controls break down as the black market thrives. Even with totalitarian methods of enforcement, it is impossible to completely stifle the black market when the choice comes to buying food illegally or having no food at all.

To be fair, the Nazis were already meting out terror before they got to total enforcement of wage and price controls. However, once you accept that the government can exert organized state violence to control the individual for economic planning, by what logic do you then argue against state planning in reproduction, culture, or any other aspect of human life?

Under a centrally planned state, be it Nazi or communist, "the economic plan" is elevated to national, even patriotic significance. As Reisman writes, "disruption by workers and managers siphoning off materials and supplies to produce for the black market, is something which a socialist state is logically entitled to regard as an act of sabotage of its national economic plan. . . . Consistent with this fact, black-market activity in a socialist country often carries the death penalty."[13]

The more complete the planning, the more complete the control, the more violence becomes acceptable in meeting economic goals. Since central planning doesn't work as well as the marketplace, the citizenry becomes increasingly unhappy with the rationing, the lines, the lack of food, the crowding. The citizenry is told that they must suffer temporarily for the public good. Much of this frustration is directed at the state planners, the government.

As Reisman points out, "it follows that the rulers of a socialist state must live in terror of the people. By the logic of their actions and their teachings, the boiling, seething resentment of the people should well up and swallow them in an orgy of bloody vengeance. The rulers sense this, even if they do not admit it openly; and thus their major concern is always to keep the lid on the citizenry."[14]

Economic chaos and public discontent must be managed and the state must respond by restricting freedom of the press and freedom of speech. Socialism not only owns all the newspapers, broadcast stations, and publishing houses; socialism also feels compelled to try to placate the people's resentment over the economic chaos. So, as Reisman explains, "the socialist rulers' terror of the people" causes them to feel the need "to protect themselves[;] they must order the propaganda ministry and the secret police to work 'round the clock."[15]

Propaganda helps to direct people away from the misery of a centrally controlled economy. Secret police are necessary, as Reisman puts it, "to spirit away and silence anyone who might even remotely suggest the responsibility of socialism or its rulers—to spirit away anyone who begins to show signs of thinking for himself."[16]

These regimes can never admit that socialism is failing. It is always someone else's fault. Reisman writes that socialist rulers become so "desperate [in their] need to find scapegoats for the failures of socialism, that the press of a socialist country is always full of stories about foreign plots and sabotage, and about corruption and mismanagement on the part of subordinate officials, and why, periodically, it is necessary to unmask large-scale domestic plots and to sacrifice major officials and entire factions in giant purges."[17]

Thus, when the Soviets' agriculture plan failed to provide enough food, it was not the government's fault. It was due to saboteurs and even the fault of peasants who resisted collectivization of their farms.

Reisman again: "It is because of their terror, and their desperate need to crush every breath even of potential opposition, that the rulers of socialism do not dare to allow even purely cultural activities that are not under the control of the state. For if people so much as assemble for an art show or poetry reading that is not controlled by the state, the rulers must fear the dissemination of dangerous ideas. Any unauthorized ideas are dangerous ideas, because they can lead people to begin thinking for themselves and thus to begin thinking about the nature of socialism and its rulers."[18]

Complete control of the economy means complete control of all the people participating in that economy. To exert such pervasive control, extraordinary state power is necessary. Since this stifling control also stifles economic growth, resentment becomes widespread and the threat of civil war is ever present.

Sound hyperbolic? Ask the citizens of Venezuela if they can feel civil war in the air. The central theme of socialism is state-organized force. The socialists argue that Stalin, Hitler, Pol Pot, Chavez, Castro, and Kim are all anomalies and not the logical conclusion of socialism. Reisman correctly states, "The inescapable inference to be drawn is that the terror actually experienced in the socialist countries was not simply the work of evil men, such as Stalin, but springs from the nature of the socialist system."[19]

Because state-organized violence is a necessary weapon of socialism, Reisman argues that rather than Stalin being an anomaly he actually may represent the norm in "the process of socialist natural selection. Stalin's unusual willingness and cunning in the use of terror were the specific characteristics most required by a ruler of socialism in order to remain in power." Perhaps complete socialism with complete control selects for the worst, for the most violent and evil.[20]

Some on the left will argue that by that definition of violence, isn't all government predicated upon organized violence? The quick answer is yes. But by acknowledging that government relies on force, we admit what Thomas Paine and the founders of our country knew. Government is a necessary evil *because* it relies on force. Our founders believed that "government is best that governs least" because the bigger government becomes, the more that control, and potentially violence, is necessary to exert government edicts.

We accept a certain minimum amount of government force (or, conversely, loss of individual freedom) to achieve goals that individuals might not voluntarily achieve, like national defense or a legal system. Limited-government libertarians, at least, understand that we accept this "necessary evil" but wish to keep this evil limited by minimizing the tasks we assign to government.

So, yes, force and organized state violence is a function of all government. However, that simply restates Reisman's thesis that when socialists exert control over all aspects of the economy either through wage and price controls or through direct state ownership, government becomes so pervasive as to require also a pervasive utilization of organized state force or violence—also known as totalitarianism.

That said, perhaps we should not express surprise at Stalin or Hitler. If all-encompassing government requires all-encompassing force, perhaps pervasive government's "success" is proportional to the willingness of its leaders to use force.

Chapter 20

HITLER WAS A SOCIALIST

For obvious reasons, no significant party advocates Nazi socialism today. Ever since the general public became aware of the Nazi death camps, no one has wanted the stigma of being anywhere close to Nazism on any political spectrum. So, despite the Nazis literally having "socialist" in their name—the National Socialist German Workers' Party—the left has made a concerted effort to label Nazis as "far-right-wingers."

As George Watson points out: "For half a century, none the less, Hitler has been portrayed, if not as a conservative—the word is many shades too pale—at least as an extreme instance of the political right. It is doubtful if he or his friends would have recognized the description. His own thoughts gave no prominence to left and right, and he is unlikely to have seen much point in any linear theory of politics. Since he had solved for all time the enigma of history, as he imagined, National Socialism was unique."[1]

The description of Hitler being from the "right," however, had largely been cemented by the time of the Spanish Civil War in 1936. By then, as Watson puts it, "most western intellectuals were certain that Stalin was left and Hitler was right. By the outbreak of world war in 1939 the idea that Hitler was any sort of socialist was almost wholly dead."[2]

Socialism is not a direct path to genocide or military imperialism. Still, national socialism was part and parcel to Nazism from the beginning. In 1920, Hitler first presented the Nazi Party a twenty-five-point plan for national socialism. Most of the plan could be found in any Bolshevik platform except for the racial animus against Jews.

Hitler's platform called for "THE GOOD OF THE COMMUNITY BEFORE THE GOOD OF THE INDIVIDUAL." I think both Marx and Bernie would approve of that collectivist motto.

If you weren't informed that the following points were from the Nazis' twenty-five-point plan, you could be excused for believing them to be part of any socialist manifesto, even a "democratic" one. Highlights of Hitler's national socialism included:

- "The state [was to] be charged first with providing the opportunity for a livelihood and way of life for the citizens."
- "Abolition of unearned (work and labour) incomes." (*This plank derives from Marx's belief that the value of a product equaled the labor used to create the product. If the owner or banker who lent the money took any portion of the product's sale price then this "profit" was "unearned."*)
- "Breaking of debt (interest)-slavery." (*Hitler not only accepted Marx's view that the collection of interest was robbing labor but argued against Jews explicitly for collecting interest income.*)
- "Common national criminals, usurers, profiteers and so forth are to be punished with death, without consideration of confession or race."
- "... personal enrichment through a war must be designated as a crime against the people. Therefore, we demand the total confiscation of all war profits."
- "We demand the nationalisation of all (previous) associated industries (trusts)." (*The essence of socialism—state ownership of the means of production*)

- "We demand a division of profits of all heavy industries."
- "We demand . . . immediate communalization of the great warehouses. . . ."
- "We demand a land reform suitable to our needs, provision of a law for the free expropriation of land for the purposes of public utility, abolition of taxes on land and prevention of all speculation in land."
- "The state to be responsible for a fundamental reconstruction of our whole national education program."
- "For the execution of all of this we demand the formation of a strong central power in the Reich. Unlimited authority of the central parliament over the whole Reich and its organizations in general."[3]

Hayek described "the famous 25 points drawn up by Gottfried Feder, one of Hitler's early allies, repeatedly endorsed by Hitler and recognized by the by-laws of the National-Socialist party as the immutable basis of all its actions, . . . [as being] full of ideas resembling those of the early socialists."[4]

And yet, during Hitler's rise and fall, he and his followers fought the communists for political power in Germany. Instead of the battle being seen as a fight between different strands of socialism, purposefully or not, the dispute came to be categorized as right versus left.

Today's left presents the argument that Hitler's attacks on the Communist Party and Bolshevik socialism prove that he was not a socialist. In *National Review*, Jonah Goldberg responds that "when people say Hitler can't be a socialist because he crushed independent labor unions and killed socialists, they need to explain why Stalin gets to be a socialist even though he did likewise."[5]

The left persists in trying to convince us that the Nazis were not socialists because they were not orthodox Marxists. But, as Goldberg writes, while the "German National Socialist economics differed from Russian Bolshevik economics. So what? The question was never, 'Were Nazis Bolsheviks?' Nor was it 'Were Nazis Marxists?' The question was 'Were Nazis socialists?' Demonstrating that the answer is no to the first two doesn't mean the answer to the third question is a no, too."[6]

Reisman laments that today "practically no one thinks of Nazi Germany as a socialist state. It is far more common to believe that it represented a form of capitalism, which is what the Communists and all other Marxists have claimed. The basis of the claim that Nazi Germany was capitalist was the fact that most industries in Nazi Germany appeared to be left in private hands."[7]

But, as we will see, industries were privately owned in name only. State control over industry was so complete that, in reality, owners were essentially stripped of private control of their property.

Some argue that fascism and communism are not variants of socialism, but as Peter Drucker writes, "It's not that communism and fascism are essentially the same. Fascism is the stage reached after communism has proved an illusion, and it has proved as much an illusion in Russia as in pre-Hitler Germany."[8]

If you read the Nazis themselves, they never doubted their socialism and were proud of its distinct brand.

In the *Independent*, George Watson disputes the idea that Hitler was not a socialist. He writes, "It is now clear beyond all reasonable doubt that Hitler and his associates believed they were socialists, and that others, including democratic socialists, thought so too. The title of National Socialism was not hypocritical."[9]

Watson writes: "Hermann Rauschning, . . . a Danzig Nazi who knew Hitler before and after his accession to power in 1933, tells how in private Hitler acknowledged his profound debt to the

Marxian tradition. 'I have learned a great deal from Marxism,' he once remarked, 'as I do not hesitate to admit.'"[10]

George Orwell, the author and socialist, although a critic of Hitler, did still agree that Hitler's rise and dominance proved that socialism works, and that "a planned economy is stronger than a planless one."[11] As Watson describes it, "The planned economy had long stood at the head of socialist demands; and National Socialism, Orwell argued, had taken from socialism 'just such features as will make it efficient for war purposes.'"[12]

Rather than argue that Hitler's Germany was not socialist, Orwell acknowledged at the time: "Internally, Germany has a good deal in common with a socialist state."[13]

Not only did Hitler promote socialism, but he considered socialism to be the unfulfilled mission of Christianity. As Watson explains: "Socialism, Hitler told fellow Nazi Wagener shortly after he seized power, was not a recent invention of the human spirit, and when he read the New Testament he was often reminded of socialism in the words of Jesus. The trouble was that the long ages of Christianity had failed to act on the Master's teachings."[14]

Nevertheless, Hitler, in many ways, accepted and expounded traditional Marxian socialism. Like Marx, Hitler believed "the one and only problem of the age . . . was to liberate labour and replace the rule of capital over labour with the rule of labour over capital."[15]

Hitler, rather than rejecting socialism, considered his brand of national socialism to be an improvement over the Bolsheviks. Hitler believed he improved socialism by adding nationalism and a touch of his conception of Christianity—along with a side of racial hatred.

Hitler's lieutenant Joseph Goebbels also was explicit in describing the Nazi goal of socialism.

In his diary, Goebbels described the Nazi dream for socialism. Goebbels predicted that when Germany defeated the Soviet Union, Bolshevik or Jewish socialism would be replaced by "real socialism." Listening to the Nazis themselves in their own words, it seems they never wavered in their support of socialism. They simply believed they had a better form of socialism to offer.[16]

Likewise, the Nazi Gregory Strasser spoke of his fellow Nazis thus: "We are socialists. We are enemies, mortal enemies, of the present capitalist economic system with its exploitation of the economically weak, with its injustice in wages, with its immoral evaluation of individuals according to wealth and money instead of responsibility and achievement, and we are determined under all circumstances to abolish this system!"[17]

Whether or not the Nazis were socialists is still important. Today's socialists don't want any part of their doctrine tainted with Nazism. Yet the Nazis' history of national socialism and underlying hatred of capitalism are undeniable. None of which is to argue that today's socialists are Nazis or will become Nazis. However, surrendering more and more freedom to the state is something socialism, fascism, and Nazism have in common.

Today's socialists should look harder at what has happened in the past when the rights of the individual are made secondary to the desires of the collective, even in the name of fairness or social welfare. Democratic socialists argue, "Not to worry, the will of the collective will always be represented by the majority!" The question remains: is fully democratic, majoritarian rule immune from human envy, greed, or racial animus? Jim Crow and even lynching were countenanced by majorities in the South for decades. The left might argue that we need better people elected to government, to which Madison replied in Federalist Paper 51, "If men were angels, no government would be necessary."

As long as socialists continue to promote the will of the collective over the rights of the individual, it remains a danger that the determiners of the "collective will" may determine to carry out policies for their own self-interest, their own power, or even their own petty prejudices.

Hitler, like so many megalomaniacs before him, was proud of his unique modifications of Marxism. Hitler believed his great additions to Marxism were to achieve labor's dominance over capitalists without a destructive class or civil war, to make Marxism consistent with nationalism, and to fire up and unite all classes for socialism using racial animus.

Watson summarizes Hitler's confidant Otto Wagener: "Without race, [Wagener] went on, National Socialism 'would really do nothing more than compete with Marxism on its own ground.' Marxism was internationalist. The proletariat, as the famous slogan goes, has no fatherland. Hitler had a fatherland, and it was everything to him. Hitler's discovery was that socialism could be national as well as international. There could be a national socialism."[18]

To Hitler, Wagener confided that "the future of socialism would lie in 'the community of the volk,' not in internationalism . . . and his task was to 'convert the German volk to socialism without simply killing off the old individualists.'"[19] Instead of class struggle killing off the bourgeoisie, the socialist workers' state would come about without destroying the country in the process and without confiscating all property.

Hitler felt that this insight would allow him to succeed where the Bolsheviks had failed in Russia. Complete dispossession of all private property meant, Watson wrote, "Germans fighting Germans, and Hitler believed there was a quicker and more efficient route. There could be socialism without civil war."[20]

So, rather than Hitler rejecting socialism, he found a different route to the same workers' paradise. As Hitler told Wagener, the trick was to "find and travel the road from individualism to socialism without revolution."[21]

As Watson summarizes Hitler's hopes, "Marx and Lenin had seen the right goal, but chosen the wrong route—a long and needlessly painful route—and, in destroying the bourgeois and the kulak, Lenin had turned Russia into a grey mass of undifferentiated humanity, a vast anonymous horde of the dispossessed; they had 'averaged downwards'; whereas the National Socialist state would raise living standards higher than capitalism had ever known."[22]

For the past seventy years, Hitler's horrific murder of millions of Jews and his obsession with race have, as Watson puts it, "prevented National Socialism from being seen as socialist."[23] Failing to see the socialism in Nazism misses that which Hitler saw as his great insight—achieving socialism without civil war and in the name of nationalism driven by racial animus.

Hitler never denied his socialist platform. It can be argued, and easily accepted, that in the end his all-consuming desire for power made any other objectives secondary, but that really is the exact story we find when others, such as Stalin, Mao, and Pol Pot, achieved power. Power for power's sake blinded them, but none of these dictators ever relinquished their goal of socialism.

Chapter 21

THE NAZIS HATED CAPITALISM

As the economic historian Chris Calton writes: "It is now the conventional wisdom that the Nazis were capitalists, not socialists,"[1] despite the name "Socialist" being in the official party name—"the National Socialist German Workers' Party." The long-standing movement to erase socialism from the history of Nazism is not without ulterior purpose. To conclude that the Nazis were capitalist is to cast historical aspersions on capitalism.

As Calton explains, "At a time when many members of the European intelligentsia were still enamored with the Soviet Union, this narrative of the Nazis as capitalists was a welcome lie." No socialist wanted to be associated with Nazism, even though the Nazis proudly proclaimed their socialism. Acknowledging that Nazism was a variety of socialism did not, as Calton writes, "fit cleanly into the Soviet-Marxist worldview, and this false narrative survives today."[2]

A decade before he published *The Road to Serfdom*, Friedrich Hayek had warned the world of national socialism. In 1933, before the depth of depravity of Hitler became known, Hayek wrote in a letter to William Beveridge, the head of the London School of Economics and a Fabian socialist, about the nightmare of national socialism. Even in 1933, Hayek understood that socialists would claim that national socialism was somehow "right-wing." Hayek argued, "Nothing could be more superficial than to consider the forces which dominate the Germany of today as reactionary—in the sense that they want a return to the social and economic order of 1914."[3]

Hayek wrote that the Nazis' "persecution of the Marxists, and of democrats in general, tends to obscure the fundamental fact that National 'Socialism' is a genuine socialist movement, whose leading ideas are the final fruit of the anti-liberal tendencies which have been steadily gaining ground in Germany since the later part of the Bismarckian era, and which led the majority of the German intelligentsia first to 'socialism of the chair' and later to Marxism in its social-democratic or communist form."[4]

As to the argument that Nazism is not socialism because of its affiliation with big business, Hayek replied,

> One of the main reasons why the socialist character of National Socialism has been quite generally unrecognized, is, no doubt, its alliance with the nationalist groups which represent the great industries and the great landowners. But this merely proves that these groups too—as they have since learnt to their bitter disappointment—have, at least partly, been mistaken as to the nature of the movement. But only partly because—and this is the most characteristic feature of modern Germany—many capitalists are themselves strongly influenced by socialistic ideas, and have not sufficient belief in capitalism to defend it with a clear conscience. But, in spite of this, the German entrepreneur class have manifested almost incredible short-sightedness in allying themselves with a movement of whose strong anti-capitalistic tendencies there should never have been any doubt.[5]

As for the Nazi platform, Hayek claimed that it differed from the Bolsheviks "only in that its socialism was much cruder and less rational."[6]

To Hayek, "the dominant feature [of national socialism] is a fierce hatred of anything capitalistic—individualistic profit seeking, large scale enterprise, banks, joint-stock companies, department stores, 'international finance and loan capital,' the system of 'interest slavery' in general."[7]

Hayek recognized that Germans were attracted to national socialism because they "were already completely under the influence of collectivist ideas. . . ." National socialism, rather than being an abrupt break with the Bolsheviks, was rather socialism mixed with nationalism and animated by racial hatred.

Chapter 22

THE NAZIS DIDN'T BELIEVE IN PRIVATE PROPERTY

Despite the common roots of national socialism and Russian socialism, the mainstream media of the day, as well as mainstream thought, refused to acknowledge them. Even after the war, when saner minds might have prevailed, most critics saw only the horrors of the Holocaust and not the link between that horror and the collectivism underlying socialism. Mainstream thought also ignored Stalin's horrors for decades, and when they finally got around to acknowledging the terror of the gulag, they often refused to accept that terror was a consequence of socialism.

Shortly after World War II, in his essay "Planned Chaos," Ludwig von Mises explained the superficial differences between Russian and German socialism.

Mises acknowledged that German socialism "seemingly and nominally, maintains private ownership of the means of production, entrepreneurship, and market exchange."[1] But Reisman points out that Mises "identified . . . that private ownership of the means of production existed in name only under the Nazis and that the actual substance of ownership of the means of production resided in the German government."[2]

Ayn Rand in "The Fascist New Frontier" concurs: "The main

characteristic of socialism (and of communism) is public ownership of the means of production, and, therefore, the abolition of
private property. The right to property is the right of use and disposal. Under fascism, men retain the semblance or pretense of private property, but the government holds total power over its use
and disposal."[3]

Leonard Peikoff reinforces this point in *Ominous Parallels*: "If
'ownership' means the right to determine the use and disposal of
material goods, then Nazism endowed the state with every real
prerogative of ownership. What the individual retained was merely
a formal deed, a contentless deed, which conferred no rights on its
holder. Under communism, there is collective ownership of property de jure. Under Nazism, there is the same collective ownership
de facto."[4]

Under national socialism there was, as Mises put it, "a superficial system of private ownership . . . but the Nazis exerted unlimited, central control of all economic decisions." With profit and
production dictated by the state, industry worked the same as if
the government had confiscated all the means of production, making economic prediction and calculation impossible.[5]

In addition, the Nazis dictated the wages of workers. By 1935,
one's choice of occupation was often dictated by the government.
Employment was guaranteed by the government, but a forced labor camp was not what most workers imagined full employment
would be.

As Adam Young reports, "Every German worker was assigned
a position from which he could not be released by the employer,
nor could he switch jobs, without permission of the government
employment office. Worker absenteeism was met with fines or
imprisonment—all in the name of job security."[6]

The Nazis, like the Soviets, used slogans to reinforce their message. Nazi slogans like "Put the common interest before self" could have just as easily been seen in communist Russia. Substitute the word "fairness" for "the common interest" and you have a talking point for many of today's new democratic socialists in the United States.

Wage and price controls were enacted and interest rates were fixed. As Mises puts it, once prices are fixed, "The authority, not the consumers, directs production. The central board of production management is supreme; all citizens are nothing else but civil servants. This is socialism with the outward appearance of capitalism. Some labels of the capitalistic market economy are retained, but they signify here something entirely different from what they mean in the market economy."[7]

Adam Young describes how extensive the Nazi economic controls became. The Nazis established the Reich Food Estate "to regulate the conditions and production of the farmers. Its vast bureaucracy enforced regulations that touched all areas of the farmer's life and his food production, processing, and marketing." So, while the Nazis, for the most part, did not confiscate the farmland (except those farms owned by Jews), they exerted control over every aspect of how the land was used.[8]

The Nazis paid for this the same way their predecessors had paid for reparations. They simply printed the money and manipulated their foreign exchange rate. Tariffs shut down international trade and wage and price controls wreaked havoc on the economy.[9]

It wasn't just Jewish businesses. As Mises reminds us, the Nazis used the word "Jewish" as a synonym for "capitalist." Even non-Jewish businesses worried that the Gestapo would come for the "white-Jews" next, explaining that the Nazi animus featured both racial and traditional socialist anger toward capitalists.[10]

Economic controls threatened everyone. As one factory owner

complained: "It has gotten to the point where I cannot talk even in my own factory. Accidentally, one of the workers overheard me grumbling about some new bureaucratic regulation and he immediately denounced me to the party and the Labor Front office."[11]

As Ralph Reiland reports, this was official policy: "In this totalitarian paradigm, a businessman, declares a Nazi decree, 'practices his functions primarily as a representative of the State, only secondarily for his own sake.' Complain, warns a Nazi directive, and 'we shall take away the freedom still left you.'"[12]

Young gives us an idea of how extensive the Nazi economic controls were. "The bureaucratization of the economy necessarily followed suit. The minister of economics in 1937, reported that 'Germany's export trade involves 40,000 separate transactions daily; yet for a single transaction as many as forty different forms must be filled out.'"[13]

Our Democratic regulation-loving colleagues should acknowledge the historic parallel of government overregulation and loss of freedom. The current U.S. government is awash in regulations. President Obama set the record for new regulations. In his last year in office he added 95,894 pages of them. In contrast, President Trump added the least amount of regulations in recent history but still managed to add 61,950 pages to the *Federal Register*. To its credit, the Trump administration did roll back some regulations; for example, a regulation mandating the number of cherries that must be used in a frozen cherry pie was repealed. I'm sure there are some democratic socialists complaining right now that our citizenry is no longer protected from the danger of purchasing a pie containing an insufficient number of cherries.

My friend Senator Mike Lee of Utah stacks the *Federal Register* of regulations in his office next to the corresponding legislation passed. The regulations reach to the ceiling and the laws are only a few inches high. The problem is that Congress, for decades, has delegated its authority to write regulations to the president.

While we don't refer to our regulatory state as socialism (yet), the overwhelming regulatory control of business that occurred under the Nazis is a form of government control over the means of production and is, in essence, a form of socialism.

As Young describes it, under Nazi socialism "businessmen and entrepreneurs were smothered by red tape, were told by the state what they could produce and how much and at what price, burdened by taxation, and were forced to make 'special contributions' to the party. Corporations below a capitalization of $40,000 were dissolved and the founding of any below a capitalization of $2,000,000 was forbidden, which wiped out a fifth of all German businesses."[14]

Reisman explains that "what specifically established de facto socialism in Nazi Germany was the introduction of price and wage controls in 1936. These were imposed in response to the inflation of the money supply carried out by the regime from the time of its coming to power in early 1933. The Nazi regime inflated the money supply as the means of financing the vast increase in government spending required by its programs of public works, subsidies, and rearmament. The price and wage controls were imposed in response to the rise in prices that began to result from the inflation."[15]

Wage and price controls led to shortages and ultimately to chaos—not unlike what has happened in Venezuela. The Nazis, like Chavez and Maduro in Venezuela, tried to counteract the shortages with rationing and ultimately with production controls.

Reisman reminds us that "the combination of price controls with this further set of controls constitutes the de facto socialization of the economic system. For it means that the government then exercises all of the substantive powers of ownership."[16]

He continues, "This was the socialism instituted by the Nazis. And Mises calls it socialism on the German or Nazi pattern, in contrast to the more obvious socialism of the Soviets, which he calls socialism on the Russian or Bolshevik pattern."[17]

So, we see that the facts (and the Nazis themselves) argue that Nazism was a branch of socialism. The only reason this debate continues is that today's socialists only want to admit to a lineage of "kinder, more gentle" socialists like the Danish (who are not socialist and utterly reject the description). Today's socialists have seen it in their best interest to arbitrarily assign the Nazis to the "right wing."

This debate still matters as each generation chooses the government and economic system they think will best provide prosperity. So, if you want to be an American socialist, by all means, learn of your forebears, including socialists like the Nazis, who decided to animate their socialism with racial hatred in order to implement it more quickly.[18]

Chapter 23

SOCIALISM
ENCOURAGES EUGENICS

S ome on the left still argue that when a government begins committing genocide they shouldn't continue to be referred to as socialist. George Watson argues otherwise. He writes: "[T]here were still, in Marx's view, races that would have to be exterminated. That is a view he published in January–February 1849 in an article by Engels called 'The Hungarian Struggle' in Marx's journal the *Neue Rheinische Zeitung*, and the point was recalled by socialists down to the rise of Hitler."[1]

Watson continues: "The Marxist theory of history required and demanded genocide for reasons implicit in its claim that feudalism was already giving place to capitalism, which must in its turn be superseded by socialism. Entire races would be left behind after a workers' revolution, feudal remnants in a socialist age; and since they could not advance two steps at a time, they would have to be killed. They were racial trash, as Engels called them, and fit only for the dung-heap of history."[2]

Was that simply a dated, one-off view limited to Engels? Disturbingly, decades before Hitler's deadly "eugenics" camps, many prominent socialists were quite open in their support for government-directed eugenics.[3]

The socialist George Bernard Shaw infamously claimed that

"the only fundamental and possible socialism is the socialization of the selective breeding of Man." Shaw went on to recommend that certain people be eliminated by "lethal chamber," a sinister forewarning of Hitler's camps.

As Jonathan Freedland writes, "Such thinking was not alien to the great Liberal titan and mastermind of the welfare state, William Beveridge, who argued that those with 'general defects' should be denied not only the vote, but 'civil freedom and father-hood.'"[4]

Marie Stopes, a pioneer in birth control, was, as Freedland reports, "a hardline eugenicist, determined that the 'hordes of defectives' be reduced in number, thereby placing less of a burden on 'the fit.' Stopes later disinherited her son because he had married a short-sighted woman, thereby risking a less-than-perfect grandchild."[5]

Likewise, Margaret Sanger, another birth control crusader and socialist, also advocated for eugenics. The same year Hitler ran for the presidency, Sanger gave a speech titled "My Way to Peace."

Sanger argued: "The second step would be to take an inventory of the second group, such as illiterates, paupers, unemployables, criminals, prostitutes, dope-fiends; classify them in special departments under government medical protection and segregate them on farms and open spaces."[6] Sanger's list of "deplorables" would be allowed to leave the camps if they agreed to sterilization. Never one to worry too much about civil liberties, Sanger thought only about 15 million to 20 million Americans would need to be interned in these camps.

Father John J. Conley tells us, "The centerpiece of the [Sanger's eugenics] program is vigorous state use of compulsory sterilization and segregation. The first class of persons targeted for sterilization is made up of people with mental or physical disability. . . .

A much larger class of undesirables would be forced to choose either sterilization or placement in state work camps."[7]

Makes one wonder if Hitler heard her speech. In an era where Confederate statues are seemingly taken down daily, it's amazing that the "liberal" icon and socialist Margaret Sanger is still proudly promoted and lionized as the founder of Planned Parenthood.

The socialist advocates for eugenics were nothing if not blunt. Another prominent socialist, Britain's Harold Laski, predicted the eugenics of the future: "The time is surely coming . . . when society will look upon the production of a weakling as a crime against itself."[8]

The scientist J. B. S. Haldane, known for his socialism, channeled his inner Nietzsche to opine that "Civilisation stands in real danger from over-production of 'undermen.'"[9] Haldane was also unapologetic in his support of Stalin, declaring in 1962 that Stalin was "a very great man who did a very good job."[10]

The eugenicists were not only worried about undesirable genetic traits; they wrongly believed that behavioral traits were inherited. So, if you were poor or lazy, the eugenicists wanted to prevent you from reproducing. As Freedland puts it, "it was not poverty that had to be reduced or even eliminated: it was the poor."[11]

Even the godfather of big-government debt and inflation, John Maynard Keynes, was, as Freedland notes, the director of the Eugenics Society from 1937 to 1944. Keynes advocated for contraception to keep down the numbers of the working class, who were too "drunken and ignorant" to control their production of children.

Today's left would have us forget that the pseudoscience of eugenics was once all the rage among socialists. When reminded of the repugnant views of their fellow travelers, today's socialists might respond that their forebears were simply products of their time, that it's not fair to hold them to our current standards.

But Freedland argues that socialists' support for eugenics was no accident: "The Fabians, Sidney and Beatrice Webb and their ilk were not attracted to eugenics because they briefly forgot their leftwing principles. The harder truth is that they were drawn to eugenics for what were then good, leftwing reasons."[12]

These same socialists believed unreservedly in state planning of the economy. It was not much of a stretch for them to believe in the state planning of families. As Freedland asks, "If the state was going to plan the production of motor cars in the national interest, why should it not do the same for the production of babies?"[13]

To these socialists, individual wants and needs were secondary to society's interests. As Freedland explains, if the "aim was to do what was best for society, society would clearly be better off if there were more of the strong to carry fewer of the weak."[14]

You can excuse these socialists all you want "as men and women of their times," but never forget that they were socialists and that they saw state planning of the family as no different than state planning of the economy or a rancher's planning for his cattle breeding.

As Mises put it: "It is vain for the champions of eugenics to protest that they did not mean what the Nazis executed. Eugenics aims at placing some men, backed by the police power, in complete control of human reproduction. It suggests that the methods applied to domestic animals be applied to men. This is precisely what the Nazis tried to do."[15]

Once the truth of the Holocaust became apparent, Freedland tells us, "eugenics went into steep decline . . . most recoiled from it once they saw where it led—to the gates of Auschwitz. The infatuation with an idea horribly close to Nazism was steadily forgotten."[16]

What should not be forgotten is that the central idea of collectivism, that the individual is less important than the whole, is entirely consistent with allowing the state to eliminate individuals that are a burden to society.

Socialism and eugenics are not a historical anomaly but a historical symbiosis that we risk any time we are tempted to accept an "ism" that elevates the collective over the individual.[17]

Watson writes, "since the liberation of Auschwitz in January 1945 socialists have been eager to forget" their association with state elimination of undesirables. He maintains that "there is plenty of evidence in the writings of H. G. Wells, Jack London, Havelock Ellis, the Webbs and others to the effect that socialist commentators did not flinch from drastic measures. The idea of ethnic cleansing was orthodox socialism for a century and more."[18]

The argument that Hitler's racial animus and ultimate extermination policies somehow disqualify him as a socialist are not justified. As Watson puts it, "Only socialists in that age advocated or practised genocide, at least in Europe, and from the first years of his political career Hitler was proudly aware of the fact."[19]

The socialist intelligentsia, at the time, remained committed to defending the idea that creating a socialist paradise, as Beatrice Webb put it, is like making an omelet: "you can't make an omelette without breaking a few eggs."

Chapter 24

YOUR DEGREE
OF ENTHUSIASM
FOR SOCIALISM MAY
DECIDE WHETHER YOU
LIVE OR DIE

Aleksandr Solzhenitsyn, the famous author and Russian dissident, spent eight years in the Soviet gulag. His books *The Gulag Archipelago* and *One Day in the Life of Ivan Denisovich* brought the horrors of Stalin to the world, although these books were, of course, banned in the Soviet Union.

In *The Gulag Archipelago*, Solzhenitsyn tells the stories of those who were arrested or went missing. The stories are culled from the firsthand reports of 227 prisoners. It is in some ways miraculous that the text was published at all. Solzhenitsyn was still in the Soviet Union. The secretary who had typed the manuscript was arrested and days later killed herself, prompting Solzhenitsyn to quickly get the manuscript to Paris. *The Gulag Archipelago* was finally published in 1973 but was banned for another sixteen years in Russia.

The book contains a particular anecdote about applauding—or

not applauding—Stalin to illustrate the frivolousness and consequences of the arrests. (This anecdote also incidentally connects
with my own personal experience of the consequences of unenthusiastic clapping . . . more on that later.)

Solzhenitsyn paints the scene.

> At the conclusion of the conference, a tribute to Comrade Stalin
> was called for. Of course, everyone stood up (just as everyone had
> leaped to his feet during the conference at every mention of his
> name). . . . For three minutes, four minutes, five minutes, the stormy
> applause, rising to an ovation, continued. But palms were getting
> sore and raised arms were already aching. And the older people
> were panting from exhaustion. It was becoming insufferably silly
> even to those who really adored Stalin.
>
>   However, who would dare to be the first to stop? . . . After all,
> NKVD men were standing in the hall applauding and watching to
> see who would quit first! And in the obscure, small hall, unknown
> to the leader, the applause went on—six, seven, eight minutes!
> They were done for! Their goose was cooked! They couldn't stop
> now till they collapsed with heart attacks! At the rear of the hall,
> which was crowded, they could of course cheat a bit, clap less
> frequently, less vigorously, not so eagerly—but up there with the
> presidium where everyone could see them?
>
>   The director of the local paper factory, an independent and
> strong-minded man, stood with the presidium. Aware of all
> the falsity and all the impossibility of the situation, he still kept
> on applauding! Nine minutes! Ten! In anguish he watched the
> secretary of the District Party Committee, but the latter dared not
> stop. Insanity! To the last man! With make-believe enthusiasm
> on their faces, looking at each other with faint hope, the district
> leaders were just going to go on and on applauding till they fell

where they stood, till they were carried out of the hall on stretchers! And even then those who were left would not falter....

Then, after eleven minutes, the director of the paper factory assumed a businesslike expression and sat down in his seat. And, oh, a miracle took place! Where had the universal, uninhibited, indescribable enthusiasm gone? To a man, everyone else stopped dead and sat down. They had been saved!

The squirrel had been smart enough to jump off his revolving wheel. That, however, was how they discovered who the independent people were. And that was how they went about eliminating them. That same night the factory director was arrested. They easily pasted ten years on him on the pretext of something quite different. But after he had signed Form 206, the final document of the interrogation, his interrogator reminded him:

"Don't ever be the first to stop applauding."[1]

How, pray tell, am I connected to the factory director arrested for unenthusiastic applause? Well, in 2013, Benjamin Netanyahu gave a speech to a joint session of Congress. Just as in presidential State of the Union orations, today's partisan politicians can't contain their enthusiasm and insist on giving a standing ovation to every utterance. It becomes tiresome and ridiculous even if you agree with the sentiment expressed.

The typical State of the Union speech is a twenty-five-minute address turned into a ninety-minute marathon by endless standing ovations. Instead of awe over the great privilege of being present for a joint session of Congress and hearing the president firsthand, you wind up feeling as drained and insincere as if you were attending an overwrought junior high pep rally.

So as Benjamin Netanyahu's speech to Congress was ending, cameras focused in on me standing and applauding—apparently too slowly applauding—the speech. The Internet went crazy with a GIF of me slow-clapping Netanyahu.

Michael Brendan Dougherty described the Internet reaction. "And that's when people lost their minds. You see, Paul wasn't clapping enthusiastically enough. It was a clap gap! How did he fail to catch the clap as it spread through Congress?"[2]

Neocon stutterers like Jennifer Rubin wrote that I was channeling my inner hatred for Israel and all Jews. Not true, of course, but that has never stopped Rubin from writing drivel. In one six-month period, this supposedly "conservative" voice of the *Washington Post* wrote dozens and dozens of articles attacking me. Her attacks, however, simply exposed her as the fake conservative that she is.

Seth Lipsky challenged one of her allegedly "conservative" attacks on me. I had introduced a bill to cut foreign aid to the Palestinian Authority. Rubin dubbed it a "phony pro-Israel bill." The very definition of petty partisanship is when you oppose a bill that you actually agree with simply because you hate the author of the bill.[3]

I have to admit that I did enjoy these snarky keepers of "all-things-politically-correct-regarding-Israel" getting their due with comparisons to the gulag.

Dougherty wrote entertainingly: "Monitoring the relative enthusiasm of applause has an ugly history, mostly in dictatorships" and he recounted Solzhenitsyn's anecdote about not being the first to stop clapping.

Dougherty goes on to remind the authoritarian Rubin, "In the nightmare prison-state of North Korea, Kim Jong Un's own uncle (and the rest of his uncle's family) were executed by the state for 'thrice-cursed acts of treachery.'" Listed among the traitorous deeds: "half-heartedly clapping."

To folks like Rubin, Dougherty wrote: "Foreign policy hawks don't have the power to jail Rand Paul, but they should at least have the good sense to disagree with him like a normal human being." Couldn't have said it better myself.[4]

Matt Purple at Rare.com also came to my defense: "Senator Rand Paul was just convicted of a capital offense against America, Israel, decency, civilization, man, God, and the Occident. Paul attended Israeli Prime Minister Benjamin Netanyahu's address to Congress yesterday, and when the speech wrapped up, he was spotted clapping with what was promptly deemed insufficient enthusiasm."

In reference to Orwell's *1984*, Purple wrote: "Among neoconservatives, this is the equivalent of not getting agitated enough during the Two Minutes Hate."

I don't recount this episode to compare myself in any way to the horrors of the real-life regimes that have and still do kill for the crime of insufficient clapping. I recount this story only to warn of what happens when everyone begins to think so much alike that any dissent, even unenthusiastic clapping, is crime enough to rally the politically correct police for an ostracization.[5]

I've always wondered if Bolsheviks exiled to Siberia by the czar were conscious of the irony, once in power, of sending their opponents to Siberian prisons. One such prisoner was Yevgeny Zamyatin, author of the dystopian novel *We*. *We* was written in 1924. Zamyatin joined the Bolsheviks because the czar had imprisoned him, put him through a sham execution, and banished his books. Ironically, *We* then became the first book banned by the Bolsheviks.

Part IV

Socialism Doesn't Create Equality

Chapter 25

SOCIALISM PROMISES EQUALITY AND LEADS TO TYRANNY

Today's socialists don't want anything to do with Nazi socialism or for that matter Mao's socialism. But the question remains—if Mao's China is not representative of socialism, where are the differences? It is important to remember that the post–World War II revolution that brought Mao to power was fueled by the promises of socialism. Mao promised to redistribute wealth and abolish private property. Mao promised to abolish income inequality and create a more equal society. Anything sound familiar?

Modern socialists' goals are not dissimilar, except for the gulag, the famines, the cultural revolution, oh . . . and the millions of victims, I suppose. But Mao and Stalin and Hitler didn't come to power promising tyranny. They came to power promising equality. It is important to know something of the horrors of Maoism so that we can resist the same calls for government-enforced equality. We can see quite clearly that the more you destroy economic carrots, the more you have to resort to economic sticks. Not everyone wants equality of income, and those citizens must be penalized until they agree.

Richard Ebeling makes clear that "under a regime of comprehensive socialism the ordinary citizen would be confronted with the worst of all imaginable tyrannies." Not by the accident of "thugs" taking over control of socialism but by socialism's very nature, "the individual [is] totally and inescapably dependent on the political authority for his very existence."[1]

Indeed, once you have a centralized government in control of your health care, your child care, your college education, and your employment, you are on the slippery road to the regulation of cultural and scientific work, including what can be published, studied, or researched. After all, if you want the government to pay for it, they control it. In the complete socialist state, Ebeling writes, "Man's mind and material well-being would be enslaved to the control and caprice of the central planners of the socialist state."[2]

Socialism also crushes the spirit of work and entrepreneurship. As Ebeling puts it, socialism weakens "the close connection between work and reward that necessarily exists under a system of private property. What incentive does a man have to clear the field, plant the seed, and tend the ground until harvest time if he knows or fears that the product to which he devotes his mental and physical labor may be stolen from him at any time?"[3]

Today's socialists argue: "No, that is not what we want at all. We want more 'freedom' for the individual. Those who lack wealth under capitalism are enslaved by the rich!" And what of the argument that socialist rulers would be guided by their own self-interest, just as capitalists are, but with the brute force of government at their disposal? Doesn't the government, even now, exert control by withholding or granting funds to individuals and groups who are ever more dependent on them? As the saying goes, "The government big enough to give you everything you want is a government strong enough to take away everything that you have."

Socialists have argued since the time of Plato that political evolution will bring about philosopher-kings who are disinterested in their own material gain. Lenin predicted that class struggle would lead to a "New Soviet Man" guided by altruism and the common good. Instead, history has given us Stalin, Hitler, Mao, Pol Pot, and innumerable other socialist elites who began by pursuing the ideology of equality but ultimately and perhaps inevitably succumbed to a tyrannous accumulation of power—all while preaching egalitarianism, redistribution of wealth, and an age of enlightened "new men" full of hope, change, and altruism. Before anyone signs up with any of today's young socialists, it's worth learning the dark origin and decline of Mao's attempt to create a workers' paradise.[4]

Mao admitted that the socialism he strove for would, at least at first, require war. Mao is famous for saying that "political power grows out of the barrel of a gun." To get that power, Mao decided to weaponize the divide between the rural peasants and the urban capitalist class. Mao saw a path to victory by mobilizing the rural peasants. While Mao believed the Chinese People's Revolution would lead to its own unique socialism, he also saw the Chinese revolution in the context of a worldwide class struggle as Marx had described. Mao, like Marx, believed in the Hegelian notion of the inevitability of socialism. Workers are naturally pitted against owners who, according to Marx, steal "value" from the labor of the workers, which leads to class warfare and ultimately to a synthesis where a workers' paradise comes into being.[5]

Mao, like Marx before him, believed that socialism was a Darwinian destiny. Mao wrote: "Socialism, in the ideological struggle, now enjoys all the conditions to triumph as the fittest."[6]

Interestingly, intervention by European powers played a role in Mao's rise. At the end of World War I, the Treaty of Versailles ceded the Shandong region of China to Japan. This region had been controlled by Germany until her defeat. The socialist movement was able to incorporate Chinese nationalism and pride into its message, setting the stage for the people's revolution of Mao.[7]

Likewise, the chaos of World War II and the unifying opposition to Japanese rule allowed the communists to combine socialism with nationalism to grow its forces. In the ensuing civil war with Chiang Kai-shek, like so many revolutions before and since, the communists "fought against" the injustices and lack of freedom under the rule of Chiang's Kuomintang. But when the communists came to power they, in turn, became the despots they had once despised.

The People's Republic of China was founded in 1949. Factories were nationalized; land was expropriated and divided up among the peasants. Taking everyone's land, as you can imagine, is difficult to do overnight. To stamp out resistance, Mao targeted the bourgeoisie, seeking "to destroy the property-owning class by killing at least one landlord in every village via public execution."[8]

Over an eight-year period, the land was confiscated and the farmers forced to work in gradually larger and larger "cooperatives." These agricultural cooperatives ranged from 100 to 300 families.

The economy was planned from the top down, and the communist government attempted to micromanage several hundred million people.

By 1953, Mao determined that the post–civil war economy and collectivization had progressed enough that he could emulate the Soviets by launching a five-year plan for the Chinese economy. Like Soviet five-year plans, Mao claimed his agrarian socialism was working, but the facts argued otherwise. Nicholas Kristof writes, "China's per-capita income was actually lower, adjusted for inflation, in the 1950s than it had been at the end of the Song

Dynasty in the 1270s." The government conclusion was that the five-year plan from 1953 to 1958 had succeeded, but the truth was the opposite.[9]

In 1958, an optimistic Mao launched "the Great Leap Forward." Collectivization of the farms was completed, and private farming was banned. The goal was to quickly transition Communist China from agrarian socialism to a modern, albeit socialized, industrial nation.

The result was disastrous almost beyond human comprehension. Instead of a Great Leap Forward, what ensued was perhaps the worst man-made famine of all time.

The famine was no accident. When ownership is collectivized, the incentive to work harder, to be more productive evaporates. When the government purchases nearly a third of the crop at prices controlled by the government and regulates the prices of the remaining two-thirds, shortages inevitably occur. Over time the government began to buy more and more of the harvest. The central planners "calculated" a great harvest and so increased export of grain and dictated that land be converted from grain to cash crops. The farmer co-ops were merged into giant people's communes.

Mao did not anticipate the result. Once private property was abolished, so too was the ability to have rental income, to sell land for profit, or to use the land as collateral to borrow money. Peasants were reassigned from farm work to industrial iron and steel work and sent to the cities.

Like all attempts at government-enforced equality, the need for the truncheon arose.

In China, sticks served the purpose of truncheons. Professor Frank Dikötter describes beatings that were meted out by roving bands of communist enforcers. As the Great Leap Forward became the great leap backward, starvation and desperation required more brutality to keep people in line. Victims were buried alive, forced to labor in the subzero cold, with government thugs chopping off ears and noses of any who resisted.[10]

Dikötter describes the descent into darkness:

> On the other hand, the farmers who were herded into giant people's communes had very few incentives to work. The land belonged to the state. The grain they produced was procured at a price that was often below the cost of production. Their livestock, tools, and utensils were no longer theirs. Often even their homes were confiscated. But the local cadres faced ever-greater pressure to fulfill and over-fulfill the plan, having to drive the workforce in one merciless campaign after another. In some places both villagers and cadres became so brutalized that the scope and degree of coercion had to be constantly expanded, resulting in an orgy of violence. People were tied up, beaten, stripped, drowned in ponds, covered in excrement, branded with sizzling tools, mutilated, and buried alive. The most common tool in this arsenal of horror was food, which was used as a weapon: entire groups of people considered to be too old, too weak, or too sick to work were deliberately banned from the canteen and starved to death.[11]

Dikötter traveled to China and examined the local documents concerning the Great Famine. Dikötter's best estimate is that at least 45 million people died throughout China.

Dikötter maintains that "[b]etween 2 and 3 million of these victims were tortured to death or summarily executed, often for the slightest infraction. People accused of not working hard enough were hung and beaten; sometimes they were bound and thrown into ponds. Punishments for even the smallest violations included mutilation and forcing people to eat excrement."[12]

Dikötter found a government report that describes how "a man named Wang Ziyou had one of his ears chopped off, his legs tied up with iron wire and a 10-kilogram stone dropped on his back before he was branded with a sizzling tool. His crime: digging up a potato." He describes another horror story where a father was forced to bury his son alive for the crime of stealing a handful of rice. The famine was so terrible that the government eventually resorted to simply withholding food as punishment.

It's always hard to imagine people resorting to cannibalism, but Dikötter found police records of fifty such cases in one village. One report read, according to Dikötter, "culprit: Yang Zhong-sheng. Name of victim: Yang Ecshun. Relationship with culprit: younger brother. Manner of crime: killed and eaten. Reason: live-lihood issues."

The Chinese still see this famine as largely the result of natural causes, though even the official party line now acknowledges some "planning" mistakes. Millions died at the hands of government equality enforcers.

Mao, never that sentimental, continued to confiscate ever-larger portions of the grain. Dikötter describes it:

At a secret meeting in Shanghai on March 25, 1959, he ordered the party to procure up to one-third of all the available grain— much more than ever before. The minutes of the meeting reveal a chairman insensitive to human loss: "When there is not enough to eat people starve to death. It is better to let half of the people die so that the other half can eat their fill."[13]

The starvation and death became so widespread it was impos-sible to deny. Yu Dehong, a communist functionary in Xinyang during the Great Leap Forward, stated:

[F]ive kilometers from my home, there were dead bodies everywhere, at least 100 corpses lying out in the open with no one burying them. Among the reed ponds along the river embankments I saw another 100 or so corpses. Outside it was said that dogs had eaten so many corpses that their eyes glowed with bloodlust. But this was inconsistent with the facts: people had already eaten all the dogs, so where would there be dogs to eat the corpses?[14]

The Chinese journalist Yang Jisheng describes how China attempted to modernize and follow the Soviet Union's attempt at rapid industrialization, but rather, the Great Leap Forward "brought inconceivable misery, bearing witness to what Friedrich Hayek wrote in *The Road to Serfdom*: 'Is there a greater tragedy imaginable than that, in our endeavor consciously to shape our future in accordance with high ideals, we should in fact unwittingly produce the very opposite of what we have been striving for?'"[15]

Certainly, famine was an unintended consequence, but it was not as if the socialists had not been warned. Hayek had written that any "Great Utopia" that required central planning according to a government blueprint would fail, that any "Great Utopia" that prevented the interaction of free individuals in a free marketplace was doomed to fail.

Dikötter comes to a similar conclusion: "Is there a more devastating example of a utopian plan gone horribly wrong than the Great Leap Forward in 1958? Here was a vision of communist paradise that paved the way to the systematic stripping of every freedom—the freedom of trade, of movement, of association, of speech, of religion—and ultimately the mass killing of tens of millions of ordinary people."[16]

As Yang Jisheng puts it: "In order to bring about this Great Utopia, China's leaders constructed an all-encompassing and omnipotent state, eliminating private ownership, the market and competition. The state controlled the vast majority of social resources and monopolized production and distribution, making every individual completely dependent on it. The government decided the type and density of crops planted in each location, and yields were taken and distributed by the state. The result was massive food shortages, as the state's inability to ration food successfully doomed tens of millions of rural Chinese to a lingering death."[17]

There is no kinder, gentler version of state ownership of the land. Jisheng channels Hayek when he describes China's socialism: "An economy with 'everything being directed from a single center' requires totalitarianism as its political system. And since absolute power corrupts absolutely, the result was not the egalitarianism anticipated by the designers of this system, but an officialdom that oppressed the Chinese people."[18]

Chapter 26

ALL ASPECTS OF CULTURE EVENTUALLY BECOME TARGETS FOR THE PLANNERS

The dangers of socialism don't end with ruining the economy. When the economy fails, it must be blamed on malefactors besides the socialist leaders. Usually the blame falls on dissidents, capitalists, insufficiently productive workers, and foreigners. The economy is sick because the culture is diseased, and the disease must be eradicated. Not every socialist purge turns out as badly as China's, but it's worth exploring how and why China ended up the way it did.

No sooner had the nation begun to recover from the famine of the Great Leap Forward than Mao decided to distract the masses with a new program. The Cultural Revolution was launched in 1966. The Cultural Revolution purged the remaining capitalist and traditional elements from Chinese society and put Maoism at the center of the Party.

Mao, like socialists before and since, maintained that the failure of the Great Leap Forward and the famine was due to outsiders, lingering capitalists, and impure party members. The Cultural

Revolution was to make socialism purer by purging opponents. The Red Guard was formed to enforce the purge.

After the bungled Great Leap Forward, Mao's leadership position in the Chinese Communist Party was threatened. The Cultural Revolution was a way to solidify his position by eliminating his rivals and purifying Chinese socialism. Like Stalin, Mao sought to develop a cult of personality around himself.

A book of Mao's quotations, *The Little Red Book*, was published and distributed far and wide to spread hero worship of Mao. This pocket-sized volume was printed by the hundreds of millions (some say billions). The Red Guard presided over public readings of Mao's wisdom. One such exhortation read: "Be resolute, fear no sacrifice, and surmount every difficulty to win victory!" Flight attendants on Chinese airlines even intoned Mao's words overhead to the passengers. Chinese citizens were expected to have a copy with them at all times.

As part of the Cultural Revolution Mao closed down all the schools, libraries, shrines, and anything else perceived to be traditional. Houses were pillaged, and religious icons and books piled in the streets and burned.

Mao exhorted China's youth to purge the country of any who were sympathetic to capitalism or the "old" ways, to destroy the "four olds"—old ideas, old customs, old habits, and old culture.

The Red Guard would attack people simply for wearing "bourgeois" clothes rather than the gray unisex communist pajamas, which represented complete equality. Mao encouraged the Red Guard to take matters into their own hands. The violence spread unchecked until 1968, when Mao finally intervened. While much of the violence was committed by the paramilitary Red Guard, the government had its hands in the conflict as well. Estimates are that the government killed upwards of 500,000. Military rule was instituted. The violence touched even leading figures in the party. Deng Xiaoping, who would become the most powerful man in China in the 1980s, was purged in 1967. China's current president Xi Jinping's father was beaten and sent into exile. Xi, himself, was a thirteen-year-old boy at the time.[1]

Orders came down from Beijing for all Chinese families to send one child to reeducation camps in the countryside.

Dr. Ming Wang, a friend of mine and a fellow ophthalmologist, was one of those children.

He was born in Communist China in 1960 amid Mao's Great Leap Forward. Ming's family were present to see farmers forced off their farms and into the cities. They experienced the famine firsthand.

Ming was entering high school when the news came that he would not be able to continue his education. According to Dr. Wang's book, *From Darkness to Sight*: "The first aim [of the Cultural Revolution] . . . was to eliminate higher education. Universities across China were shut down. Anyone with knowledge and education was labeled the 'stinking ninth class,' the absolute bottom of the social ranking, beneath even criminals, prostitutes and beggars."

Ming came from a family of doctors. All nine members of his grandfather's family were physicians. Both of his parents were doctors. During the Cultural Revolution, the Red Guard marched on the medical university with clubs to destroy the classrooms and laboratories. Ming's mother heard they were coming and bravely tried to protect her lab. She was beaten so badly that she was not able to rise from bed for one year and lived in pain for the rest of her life. When she finally could walk again, she was exiled to a work camp for two years. Ming was eleven years old at the time.

In 1974, word came that each Chinese family could keep only

one child. Other children would be deported to labor camps. Ming's family chose him, hoping the policy would change before his younger brother reached the age of deportation. Choosing Ming meant he would not be deported—but only if he quit school. So, at the end of junior high, Ming was forced to quit school.

Ming secretly attended the medical university with his father but ultimately was discovered and forbidden from attending lectures.

Ming's story is so moving and extreme that he could be a character in a dystopian novel. In fact, the grotesque concept of preventing the intellectually capable from pursuing higher education and assigning them to menial labor is not that different from the plight of the narrator of Ayn Rand's *Anthem*.[2]

Ultimately, Ming's story brightened as he escaped to America and graduated magna cum laude from Harvard Medical School. He is now a prominent eye surgeon in Nashville.

The Cultural Revolution is said to have ended with Mao's death in 1976, but Tom Phillips writes, "Dikötter believes the nightmarish upheaval also served to destroy any remaining faith the Chinese people had in their Great Teacher. Even before Mao died, people buried Maoism."[3]

One can read of the millions who died during Stalin's terror or Mao's Great Leap Forward and still not grasp the horror of what it was like. Perhaps the best way to try to understand the magnitude of what happened as Mao strove to achieve complete socialism is to listen to the victims tell their stories.

Chen Dake was one of those caught up in the Cultural Revolution. Like Ming Wang, Chen Dake's life was turned upside down by the Cultural Revolution. Both men were part of the mad rush to take the college entrance exam when the Cultural Revolution finally allowed the universities to reopen. It is estimated that in

1977, after a decade of closed universities, approximately 5.7 million students attempted to attend college, in one year.

Chen was accepted to Hunan Normal University to study physics. As a kid, Chen had thought he might want to study literature or history, but in the aftermath of the Cultural Revolution, science seemed the safer course. Chen ended up becoming a famous oceanographer who recently led a team of scientists to the South Pole.

But during the Cultural Revolution, Chen was exiled to the rice paddies of central China to do manual labor. His crime? His parents were intellectuals. While some students did attend university during the Cultural Revolution, others like Chen and Ming were banned because of their ideology.

Mao made room for "acceptable" applicants like peasants—and of course the children of government officials. An example of the politically motivated admissions process recounts a farmer named Zhang Tiesheng who was admitted to college in 1973—even though he answered not one question correctly on the chemistry and physics entrance exam.

Chen remembers the excitement and challenge of competing with the five million college applicants that had built up because of ten years of limited university access.

"I was sent to the countryside after high school and toiled in the rice fields for three years before getting back to the city and entering college," Chen said.

"I barely had time and energy to prepare for the entrance exam, but I guess that's probably true for almost everyone who took that exam. I remember that almost every young person in the countryside where I worked took the exam."[4]

Chen recalls, as Ming does as well, that there was space for only about 5 percent of the five million applicants. To be accepted in 1977 was an extraordinary feat.

The stories of Chen Dake and Ming Wang are testaments to the power of human will in the face of nearly unimaginable hardship and terror. Ming Wang spent much of his childhood singing and dancing to the propaganda songs extolling Mao (the only music allowed) as a way to ensure that he would not be sent to a work camp.

Chen Qigang, who is now a composer living in France, also lived through the Cultural Revolution.

Chen was plucked out of middle school in Beijing and sent to a forced-labor reeducation camp in the countryside. Chen describes what happened to him:

I have always been a very direct speaker. When the Cultural Revolution was starting, I spoke out about what I was seeing. The day after I said something, a big-character poster appeared on campus overnight: "Save the reactionary speechmaker Chen Qigang." I was so young. I didn't understand what was going on. Yesterday we were all classmates. How come today all of my classmates are my enemies? Everyone started to ignore me. I didn't understand. How could people be like this? Even my older sister, who was also at my school, came to find me and asked, "What's wrong with you?" You saw in one night who your real friends were. The next day I only had two friends left. One of them is now my wife.

Chen continues,

At the time, no one really knew who was for or against the revolution. It was completely out of control. The students brought elderly people into the school and beat them. They beat their teachers and principals. There was nothing in the way of law. There was a student who was two or three years older than me. He beat two elderly people to death with his bare hands. No one has talked about this even until this day. We all know who did it but that's the way it is. No one has ever looked into it. These occurrences were too common.

If there had been no Cultural Revolution, then I would not be who I am today. People who haven't been through it can't appreciate how easy everything else is. It wasn't the manual labor. That's a different kind of hardship. This was the worst kind of bitterness. You are constantly told: "You are against the revolution, so therefore you have no right to speak. You don't have freedom. You will have no future in this place. You will not have a good job. Everyone looks down on you."

That burden, that burden on your spirit, is very heavy. It was very different later when I went to France. I could have been criticized. I could have had a different opinion on something artistic. But for me that was nothing. It is nothing. Because it doesn't affect my freedom.[5]

Yang Jisheng, a famous writer and historian, was in high school in 1966. He writes:

People who didn't experience the Cultural Revolution only know that a large number of officials were persecuted, but they don't know that the numbers of ordinary people who suffered were 10 times, a hundred times, more.

They only know that the rebels were the culprits in the Cultural Revolution, and don't know that the rebels were active for only two years. The main culprits were the power holders in different periods. They only know that the Gang of Four and the rebels supported the Cultural Revolution, and don't know that a large number of senior officials also supported the Cultural Revolution for some time.

Unfortunately, now there are some people doing everything

*in their power to cover up the mistakes of history. They treat
one-sidedly extolling the achievements of the past as a "positive
energy" to be exalted, and they treat exposing and reflecting on the
mistakes of history as a "negative energy" to be beaten down.*[6]

Professor Zehao Zhou is haunted by the Chinese Cultural Revolution. Zhou was an eleven-year-old when Mao decided to unleash the Red Guard to purge opposition. Zhou describes the Red Guard as "mostly brainwashed teenage hooligans, [who] stormed into any neighborhood they pleased, assaulted anyone they wanted, and tortured their victims to death with impunity—all in the name of revolution."[7]

Mao encouraged the violence. "Revolution is not a dinner party! Be violent!" Mao declared.

Zhou remembers "the 'Chinese Crystal Night' in the summer 1966 when waves of Red Guards from different factions repeatedly stormed my 'bourgeois neighborhood' in the former French Concession of Shanghai over a period of weeks, terrorizing the innocent, ransacking homes and parading their victims through the streets for the purpose of public humiliation."

Still a child at the time, Zhou could never forget the "screaming, shouting, yelling and cries for help [that] rang out all around me—nearly every household was subjected to such abuse. Chaos was the order of the day."

As the Red Guards closed in on their house, Zhou describes his mother's feverish destruction of any incriminating evidence. "After closing the curtains, she started to burn books, notebooks and the entire collection of family photos. I saw my mother gingerly putting one photo after another into the flames. I had never seen most of them before. The only time I got to see what my parents looked like at their wedding or how my father looked in uniform was in those fleeting moments before each photo started to curl and blacken in the flames."[8]

That first summer of the Cultural Revolution, Mao started the "Destroy the Four Olds Campaign." The Red Guard was goaded to attack anything or anyone who expressed old ideas, old habits, old customs, or old culture.

To this day it is sad to think of five thousand years of Chinese artifacts being burned or destroyed. Zhou explains that "almost 90 percent of Tibet's monasteries and temples were razed to the ground and roughly 74 percent of the historical sites in the birthplace of Confucius . . . were obliterated."

Zhou remembers the Red Guard attacking the local Christian church. They "brought out all of its Bibles into the middle of the street, and set them on fire. That horrific moment—seeing the sky darkened by the floating ashes of burned Bibles—remains seared in my memory even now."

Zhou ponders the ironies: "The result is a curious kind of doublethink. Mao led the country to ruin and is responsible for more deaths than either Hitler or Stalin, but he remains the political idol of millions of ordinary Chinese. The Red Guards were eventually denounced as aberrant radicals, but the ruling faction of the Chinese Communist Party is composed of a significant number of former Red Guards."[9]

To better understand the Cultural Revolution, Karoline Kan interviewed her uncle Lishui, who was and is an unrepentant Red Guard. What is alarming about her description is how "normal" he seemed to her. She describes how "as a young child, when I heard him coming to visit, I would rush out of the house, climb onto his shoulders, and pull his ears."[10]

Kan describes her uncle as "kind and honest" but he "says he doesn't regret a single thing he did—not even today. . . ."

Lishui joined the Red Guard at eighteen, and astonishingly his first raid was on his grandfather's house. When the orders came to eradicate the "Four Olds," Lishui answered the call. What kind of fervor is enough to lead a young adult to raid his grandfather's house?

Kan describes how "terrified of severe punishment, the old man handed over his collection of books and paintings before those young people, including his own grandsons, would find them. The Red Guards piled the books and paintings and burned them. To show his sincerity and to avoid further punishment, my great-grandfather used the fire to boil water in front of the guards."

Kan's great-grandfather had been educated in Confucianism and had been a village leader. Kan reports that "none of that mattered during the Cultural Revolution. My great-grandfather was forced to step on stage and accept criticism, wearing a 'high hat,' which looked like a dunce cap, enumerating his crimes." Lishui, perhaps feeling guilty about harassing his own grandfather, agreed to help his grandfather avoid more punishment by writing down "self-criticisms," a form of forced confessions. According to Lishui:

> My grandfather "was old and his eyes were diseased, so he told me his stories, and I wrote them down. . . . I also guided him to write what the Red Guards would like to hear. I remember a few lines: "I was born in 1899; at eight years old I started studying the Four Books and Five Classics taught by private teachers. I will reflect deeply and profoundly on my past."[11]

Like the Nazi prison guards who blithely followed their orders, it is hard to imagine how Lishui could justify committing terrorism against his own family much less still defend it fifty years later. The power of groupthink or peer pressure, especially when encouraged by the state, is somehow able to motivate "normal" people to commit what most of us would consider highly "abnormal," abhorrent acts.

Today's socialists who choose to write off such horror as an anomaly need to explain why history shows the same story time and time again—when governments take on sufficient power to enforce state ownership of property, the leaders ultimately become ruthless and barbaric.

Millions of people were killed under Mao. It is easy to become inured to violence when you hear such large, almost unbelievable numbers. So it is useful to meet a few of Mao's victims.

Fang Zhongmou had been a member of the Communist Party. In fact, she had served in the People's Liberation Army. Her enthusiasm for Mao's regime waned, however, when her husband was charged with being a "capitalist roader," a nonspecific accusation equivalent to being a sympathizer of capitalism. The government detained her husband on multiple occasions and made him submit to "struggle sessions."

In the privacy of her home, Fang Zhongmou lashed out at Mao. Her family informed the authorities. Fang retaliated by burning a portrait of Mao. Her husband and son turned her over to soldiers. She was subsequently executed.[12]

It's hard to imagine families turning in their family members, but this was not uncommon when everyone lived in fear of everyone else, including their own family.

Bian Zhongyun was an early victim of the Cultural Revolution. She was a vice principal at the well-known Beijing Normal University Girls High School. Mao encouraged the Communist Party youth to denounce traitors, and so they did. Bian fit the profile as an intellectual with a college degree and a well-to-do family background.

The students and the Red Guard became a mob. They harassed, beat, and tortured her. She was warned not to return to school. When she did, the student mob beat her with table legs with protruding nails. Bian died of her wounds.[13]

I remember the Chinese Ping-Pong players of the early 1970s, when the exchange of players between the United States and China became known as "Ping-Pong diplomacy." But a decade or so before Ping-Pong diplomacy, three Chinese players were hounded to their deaths by the Chinese government.

Rong Guotuan, Fu Qifang, and Jiang Yongning, though they were originally from Hong Kong, competed for China in the 1950s and 1960s. Rong became the first Chinese player to win the World Table Tennis Championship in 1959. Because they had been born outside of mainland China, the hysteria of the Cultural Revolution made them suspect. They were subjected to "struggle sessions" and beatings and then accused of spying. Ultimately, all three would commit suicide, with Rong leaving a note denying that he was a spy.[14]

The terror was so pervasive that there likely was no Chinese citizen alive in the late 1970s who did not know of someone who had been killed, tortured, or sent to a forced labor camp. Even as Deng Xiaoping began to relax Mao's terror, Chinese citizens still lived an uncertain existence.

Chapter 27

IF NO ONE HAS TO WORK,
NO ONE WILL

A few years ago, NPR did a fabulous story on China's rise from the ashes of Mao's Marxism to allow a modicum of freedom. The story takes place in the small village of Xiaogang in 1978. Several farmers have come together in a dirt-floor shack to sign a secret compact. To these farmers, this contract was dangerous. They still feared the terror of Mao and believed that if this contract were discovered, they could be executed.

The farms had been owned by the collective since private property was abolished in the 1950s. To defy common ownership of any farmland was very risky.

Yen Jingchang, one of the farmers at this secret meeting, said that "[b]ack then, even one straw belonged to the group. No one owned anything."

One of the men present remembers a farmer asking at a local communist meeting, "What about the teeth in my head? Do I own those?" The party official responded: "No. Your teeth belong to the collective."

Jingchang said in those days, "In theory, the government would take what the collective grew, and would also distribute food to each family. There was no incentive to work hard—to go out to the fields early, to put in extra effort."

According to Jingchang, it didn't matter how much effort you expended: "Work hard, don't work hard—everyone gets the same. So, people don't want to work."

Since the collective farms never produced enough food, there was chronic hunger and a sense of desperation. A small group of farmers decided to act.

According to NPR, "in the winter of 1978, after another terrible harvest, they came up with an idea: Rather than farm as a collective, each family would get to farm its own plot of land. If a family grew a lot of food, that family could keep some of the harvest."

It had been nearly thirty years since anyone had "owned" his or her labor or the fruits of their harvest. This "new" old idea went against thirty years of communist dictates, which is why the farmers met in secret to discuss a new compact.

One by one they filed furtively into the agreed-upon farmer's home. As NPR described it, this home was "like all of the houses in the village, it had dirt floors, mud walls and a straw roof. No plumbing, no electricity."

Despite the danger, the farmers agreed to try privatizing the land—they formalized the agreement and wrote it down as a contract. One of them, Yen Hongchang, wrote out the agreement.

In the contract, the farmers agreed to apportion the land between families. The families would not get to keep the entire harvest. There still would be taxes and a portion for the collective, but for the first time in a generation, the vast amount of the harvest would go to the family that grew the crop. The more you grew, the more you and your family would profit.

The farmers were anxious about the government's response. There were rumors that the harshness of Mao was abating, but the farmers still felt the need to include a provision in the contract that if any of them were executed the remaining farmers would take care of their children.

The contract was kept secret. NPR reported, "Yen Hongchang hid it inside a piece of bamboo in the roof of his house."

What they couldn't hide was the dramatically increased harvest. Farmer Hongchang estimated that the harvest was bigger than the last five years together. A miracle occurred, albeit a miracle known at least since the time of Adam Smith: incentives do matter.

As NPR reported: "Before the contract, the farmers would drag themselves out into the field only when the village whistle blew, marking the start of the work day. After the contract, the families went out before dawn."

Yen Jingchang explained: "We all secretly competed. Everyone wanted to produce more than the next person."

Self-interest and reward allowed the same farmers on the same land to grow five times the amount of food grown when everyone—and therefore no one—owned the land.

NPR reported "that [the] huge harvest gave them away. Local officials figured out that the farmers had divided up the land, and word of what had happened in Xiaogang made its way up the Communist Party chain of command."

The farmers worried that they would be executed, but they were lucky to have taken this risk just as Deng Xiaoping was coming to power. Deng and his lieutenants were deciding to allow a little Adam Smith to creep in and give a boost to the moribund socialism that had, by that time, killed millions of Chinese.[1]

On the one hand, it is a great relief to see the horrific socialism of Mao thaw enough to allow at least some version of private property and profit to exist. Yet it is an immeasurable calamity that tens of millions of Chinese had to die before the Chinese discovered the horrors that come when a government tries to enforce complete socialism. Let's hope today's American socialists will realize that violence is not an aberration but a necessary tool if you want a society made "equal" by redistribution of wealth and property.

Chapter 28

THE CURE FOR FAILED SOCIALISM IS ALWAYS MORE SOCIALISM

Pol Pot is now infamous as a mass murderer: the architect and executioner of the killing fields of Cambodia. But first and foremost, Pol Pot was a socialist. Before he created the persona Pol Pot, he was just Saloth Sar, the son of a well-to-do small farmer. The day Saloth Sar won a government scholarship to study in France, the fate of millions of Cambodians was sealed. In France, Saloth Sar became enamored with Marxism, visited socialist Yugoslavia, and joined the French Communist Party.[1]

When he returned to Cambodia, he began writing under the pseudonym Pol Pot, advocating for revolution and organizing a communist resistance. By 1960, Pol Pot had become a leader in the Khmer People's Revolutionary Party and renamed it the Workers' Party of Kampuchea, which later became the Communist Party of Kampuchea.

Pol Pot's Marxist education in France might have all been for naught if the Vietnam War had not come to Cambodia's border. Pol Pot saw an opportunity and moved his operations to the northeast border with Vietnam to ally his revolution with the North Vietnamese communists.

The big breakthrough for recruitment came in 1969 when the

Vietnam War arrived at the Cambodian border. There's nothing like U.S. bombs dropping on your countrymen to encourage enlistment. The bombing continued for four years, with tens of thousands of Cambodians killed.

In addition to the U.S. bombing of Cambodia, America backed a coup in 1970 by Lon Nol. Pol Pot allied with the deposed leader Prince Norodom Sihanouk and thousands of recruits flocked to Pol Pot and his communists.[2]

There is a foreign policy lesson here that the foreign policy swamp-dwellers in Washington, D.C., still fail to understand. The blowback from constant intervention in everybody's civil war often leads to unintended consequences. Virtually every time the United States chooses sides in another country's civil war, there is a backlash that encourages the growth and resistance of the other side. Not to mention that more often than not, the United States chooses to support "the lesser of two evils."

Popular resistance to the U.S.-backed coup allowed the Khmer Rouge to grow strong enough that they laid siege to Phnom Penh and took over the capitol in 1975. Pol Pot gave himself the title "Brother Number One." Within hours of the takeover of the capitol, the population was ordered into the countryside. It is estimated that over two million people were expelled from Phnom Penh alone. It's likely that history has never seen, and hopefully will never see again, such a massive forced exodus.

The Khmer Rouge, like the French revolutionaries, even established their own calendar. The day they conquered Phnom Penh began "Year Zero."[3]

Pol Pot then ambitiously went about creating "complete socialism" or complete abolition of private property. The Khmer Rouge instituted their socialism by banning access to world markets and abolishing money, all private property, all market exchange, and prices. They then expelled all urban dwellers to the countryside.

Pol Pot's goal was to avoid the food shortages that plagued communist Russia.

Vincent Cook describes Pol Pot's attempt at pure socialism as "being the one Communist movement in history to actually attempt the full and consistent implementation of the ideals of Karl Marx."[4]

The Khmer Rouge tried to put in place what Marx and Engels advocated for in *The Communist Manifesto* of 1848: "The theory of the Communists [that] may be summed up in the single sentence: Abolition of private property."[5]

As Morgan O. Reynolds, a retired professor of economics at Texas A&M University, puts it, the Khmer Rouge not only strove for Communism in all its so-called glory, they seemed hell-bent on bringing Plato's *Republic* to life in Cambodia. From Plato's *Republic*:

> ... what has been said about the State and the government is not a dream, and although difficult not impossible ... when true philosophers are born in the reigning family in a state, one or more of them, despising the honors of this present world which they deem mean and worthless ... will begin by sending out into the country all the inhabitants of the city who are more than ten years old, and will take possession of their children, who will be unaffected by the habits of their parents; these they will train in their own habits and laws, which will be such as we have described: and in this way the State and constitution of which we were speaking will soonest and most easily attain happiness, and the nation which has such a constitution will gain most.[6]

What made Pol Pot so dangerous is that when the economy collapsed, he drove ever harder toward socialism. When mass starvation broke out, he persevered unrelentingly in pursuit of total socialism. Where many communist regimes before him had tacitly accepted a little capitalism here and there, Pol Pot was uncompromising. He achieved, more than his predecessors, the true goal of abolishing all private property and he didn't seem to mind if it took more than a few broken skulls.[7]

Of course, it didn't work. Even after he killed more than a million "resisters," starvation killed another million or more. Estimates are that the Khmer Rouge may have killed between 13 and 30 percent of the Cambodian population during Pol Pot's regime.[8]

Not surprisingly, complete confiscation of property takes an extraordinary amount of force. No resistance to the collectivization of property was tolerated. Not only were property owners who resisted killed, but intellectuals, opposition leaders, and anyone of wealth was systematically eliminated.[9]

The massacres were not all of landowners resisting collectivization. As James Pierson reminds us, "Pol Pot and his comrades sought to follow the socialist example set by Mao—that is, to purge the socialist movement of impure elements, which resulted in the massacre of religious and national minorities, intellectuals, and those living in cities."[10]

The killings were so numerous that bullets had to be conserved. The Khmer Rouge resorted to clubbing their victims to death.

Like Pol Pot, the other Khmer Rouge leaders were from well-off families. The leadership of the Khmer Rouge were educated in law and economics and like Pol Pot received at least some of their education in Paris during the 1950s. Marxist-communist ideals were not just slogans; the leadership authored essays espousing their socialism. As Reynolds points out, though, "Like Lenin and his fellow armchair intellectuals, none of the Cambodian philosopher-kings ever did manual labor for a living or managed any enterprise."[11]

Choeung Ek served as one of the killing fields; 8,895 bodies were dumped in mass graves there.[12]

Choeung Ek is about an hour's drive from Phnom Penh. Today there is a memorial there. Travel writer Elaine McArdle describes what lies "behind the gates of the once tranquil orchard" as a "mass grave for almost 20,000 men, women and children who fell victim to the Khmer Rouge regime and many of whom were tortured before their deaths."

McArdle describes "the incredible sadness that surrounds the site. Visitors wander around in silence . . . tears streaming down their faces. Fragments of bones surface during heavy rain and rags of clothing still protrude from the ground."

In the center of Choeung Ek is a giant tree they call "the Killing Tree." It is said that the Khmer Rouge bashed the heads of children against the tree to save ammunition. The children were "preventative killings" to prevent them from growing up to avenge their parents' executions.

The memorial culminates at the Buddhist Stupa, where McArdle tells us, "thousands of skulls [are] arranged in order of age and sex . . . many of which display signs of trauma. It's impossible not to stare into the empty sockets and wonder what tortures they suffered and what horrors they witnessed before their death."[13]

It's tempting to ask what if? Georgie Anne Geyer was a foreign correspondent for the *Chicago Daily News* in the late 1960s covering Vietnam and Southeast Asia. She happened to interview Prince Norodom Sihanouk just before the Khmer Rouge took over.

She asked Sihanouk: "What are you going to do about the Cambodian students going to France?"

As Geyer remembers:

*The quintessentially voluble Sihanouk looked very serious for a
moment. Then he spoke slowly. "They are learning a strange kind of
French Marxism, which they are mixing with our ancient Khmer
mysticism," he said. A pause. "I have now forbidden our young
people from going to France to study."*

*Still another pause. Then he looked me straight in the face, with
a sad look that is etched in my memory, and added, "But it may be
too late."*[14]

In 1997, when Pol Pot was finally turned over to international
authorities, Geyer admitted that it had been too late. As Geyer
put it: "The toxic Soviet European Marxist genie had been let out
of the bottle to poison what had been a peaceful and prosperous
Southeast Asian land. All the beautiful traditions of Cambodia's
national life soon gave way to the horrors committed by those students who went to France."[15]

As they say, ideas have consequences and bad ideas can have
disastrous consequences. Combine bad ideas, socialism, and U.S.
intervention in Vietnam and Cambodia and you have a recipe for
disaster. War especially rewards survival of the most brutal. When
"the most brutal" also have received the messianic message of
Marxism, you have a recipe for genocide.

As Geyer reports: "Under Pol Pot's coldly fanatical, French
Marxist–trained eye, his guerrillas mercilessly drove masses of
Cambodians out of the cities. In that once-prosperous countryside I had known, upward of 1 million Cambodians were savagely
put to death on ideologically correct collective farms. Officials,
intellectuals, even people who merely wore glasses, were killed,
usually by blows of hoes to the back of their head."[16]

So massive were the killings that they required bureaucratic
centers to process the executions. Experts believe Tuol Sleng in

Phnom Penh "processed" twenty thousand prisoners, many of whom were tortured and killed—but, as Geyer points out, "only after they were driven to the 'confessions' that Pol Pot so loved and pored over."[17]

War selected for Pol Pot's barbaric savagery, but it was the ideology he imbibed as a young communist in France that fueled the "complete socialism" of the killing fields. Scholars estimate between one and two million people were killed. A Yale University study had identified twenty thousand mass grave sites that according to their estimates indicate about 1.3 million executions.[18]

How could so much killing occur without the people coming together to resist? Solzhenitsyn explained in *The Gulag Archipelago* that for violence to become genocide it requires ideology:

> *Macbeth's self-justifications were feeble—and his conscience devoured him. Yes, even Iago was a little lamb, too. The imagination and spiritual strength of Shakespeare's evildoers stopped short at a dozen corpses. Because they had no ideology. Ideology—that is what gives evildoing its long-sought justification and gives the evildoer the necessary steadfastness and determination. That is the social theory which helps to make his acts seem good instead of bad in his own and others' eyes.... That was how the agents of the Inquisition fortified their wills: by invoking Christianity; the conquerors of foreign lands, by extolling the grandeur of their Motherland; the colonizers, by civilization; the Nazis, by race; and the Jacobins (early and late), by equality, brotherhood, and the happiness of future generations.... Without evildoers there would have been no Archipelago.[19]*

It's hard not to wonder about what is lost when a generation is essentially exterminated. What alternate future could Cambodia have had if not for the "complete socialism" of Pol Pot? Geyer looks back nostalgically at Cambodia before Pol Pot when she writes: "There is a surfeit of guilt to go around for the destruction of that lovely little country. If the French colonialists had left Vietnam earlier and not held on to their overseas empire, the whole area could have had moderate leaders. If the United States had not gotten into Vietnam, and then not invaded Cambodia, Pol Pot would never have found the colonial excuse and the support for his movement. If, if, if . . ."[20]

One would have thought that at least the international community would have contemporaneously condemned the atrocities of the Khmer Rouge. Instead, the United Nations General Assembly voted to allow the Khmer Rouge to retain its seat in the UN until 1993. But then again, the "Human Rights" Committee of the UN has historically been a rogues' gallery of human rights violators.[21]

In the end, it wasn't Cambodians who defeated Pol Pot but an invasion from his onetime ally, the Vietnamese. After the fall of the Khmer Rouge government in 1979, Pol Pot escaped to Thailand to live in exile for another eighteen years. He continued to insert himself into what was left of Khmer Rouge politics, including ordering the execution of his self-appointed replacement. Even the Khmer Rouge finally tired of him and handed him over to the international court, but not until 1997. He died, presumably from suicide, in custody.

As with Stalin or Hitler, the left wants to write off Pol Pot as a historical oddity unconnected to his underlying ideology of socialism.

Reynolds understands that the killing fields should not "be dismissed as crazy, fanatical, or insane and then quickly forgotten."

Reynolds believes "close inspection reveals nothing illogical or irrational about the Khmer Rouge and Cambodia, given their goals." In fact, according to Reynolds,

> [Their goals] were to completely replace the market economy with socialism. To be sure, it was much more determined and extreme than most socialist efforts, but this only makes the Cambodian experiment all the more essential to understand as an example of the pre-eminent issue of our age—socialism versus capitalism, collectivism versus individualism, death versus life. Originally, the word "socialism" was coined to express opposition to individualism. The brutal attempts of the Khmer Rouge and other communists to suppress all traces of individuality are not irrational but quite predictable and intelligible.[22]

Witnessing the killing fields of Cambodia, Vincent Cook writes, "It is not enough to say of Pol Pot, as Prince Sihanouk did: 'Let him be dead. Now our nation will be very peaceful.' We must also acknowledge that a Pol Pot–type passion for equality remains a threat to the peace and well-being of every nation even if the former dictator himself is dead. Rather than retreating into amnesia about the crimes of the Khmer Rouge, we should never forget that the killing fields of Cambodia will stand forever as a grotesque monument to egalitarianism, and take heed that those who preach the egalitarian gospel of envy are, whether they know it or not, apostles of Pol Pot."[23]

Morgan O. Reynolds, writing at FEE, warns that in the killing fields, "the bones of millions of Cambodians suggest why living human beings will never reach socialism." And, I might add, should never attempt such foolishness.[24]

Chapter 29

POETRY CAN
BE DANGEROUS
UNDER SOCIALISM

Joseph Stalin supposedly said a single death is a tragedy; a million deaths is a statistic.

How dangerous was it to lampoon Stalin? Well, the poet Osip Mandelstam found out the hard way when he recited but didn't even write down the following lines about Stalin:

> His unwieldy fingers are greasy like worms.
> His words are as staunch as the weights made of lead.
> Like roaches his whiskers lengthen in laugh.
> And teasingly shine, his polished boot-flaps.

Stalin was not amused.

Mandelstam, one can only imagine, was busting a gut trying not to laugh as he recited his little satirical ditty to his friends and literary colleagues, Boris Pasternak and Anna Akhmatova.

They didn't appear to enjoy his good humor as Mandelstam closed with:

> He forges decrees in a line like horseshoes,
> One for the groin, one the forehead, temple, eye.

He rolls the executions on his tongue like berries.
He wishes he could hug them like big friends from home.[1]

As the story goes, fear consumed both Pasternak and Akhmatova. Pasternak reportedly replied to Mandelstam as he finished his satirical epigram to Stalin: "What you just read . . . is not poetry, it is suicide. You didn't read it to me, I didn't hear it, and I beg you not to read this to anyone."[2]

Either the walls had "ears" or Mandelstam couldn't resist reciting his little ditty to others. Whatever the details may have been, Mandelstam was arrested shortly thereafter in the spring of 1934.

In an extraordinary call, Stalin called Pasternak to get his opinion of the "crime."

When Pasternak received the call from Stalin, he didn't exactly prove himself a profile in courage. Stalin said of Mandelstam: "He's a genius, he's a genius, isn't he?"

Pasternak avoided the question, saying, "But that's not the point."

"Then what is?" Stalin asked.

Pasternak suggested they meet to talk.

"About what?"

"Life and death," he said.

Stalin hung up without replying.[3]

Nikolai Bukharin, a prominent member of Bolshevik leadership from the beginning, did, however, intercede on behalf of Mandelstam.[4]

When Bukharin visited the spy chief Genrikh Yagoda to try to help Mandelstam, Yagoda thought the poem so entertaining he committed it to heart and recited it to Bukharin. Mandelstam's widow recorded that while Yagoda may have found humor in the poem, he would "not have hesitated to destroy the whole of literature, past, present and future, if he had thought it to his advantage. For people of this extraordinary type, human blood is like water."[5] Bukharin's visit did, however, help to shorten Mandelstam's sentence.

Yagoda himself would ultimately suffer the same fate he had meted out to thousands when he was arrested and executed in 1938. I wonder if Yagoda remembered Mandelstam's lampoon of Stalin as he awaited his executioners. Similar to the guillotine of the French Revolution, Stalin's party purges eventually got around to killing the killers.[6]

It's easy from the comfort of America, decades later and an ocean away, to question why Pasternak wasn't more courageous. But before judging him too harshly, realize that millions of people died at Stalin's whim. Not only was every individual at risk but often families were sent to camps for "crimes" of a single family member.

Indeed, even Mandelstam himself, from his camp, tried to ingratiate himself with Stalin by writing odes to glorify his rule. For that matter, so did Pasternak and Akhmatova.

Akhmatova in the 1950s penned a poem "In Praise of Peace" (and Stalin), including the line: "Legend speaks of a wise man who saved each of us from a terrible death." After Mandelstam's return from exile in 1937, he also published an "Ode" to Stalin that he vainly would read in public in an attempt to win back the favor of the dictator. While it is tempting to ridicule these poets today, one should imagine life in a country where everything from the economy to the arts to even sports was controlled by one man, Stalin.[7]

Soviet purges often meant not only killing the person, but erasing them completely from the collective memory. It wasn't as neat and clean as Orwell devised it with unauthorized histories, photographs, books flushed down the memory hole. It was messier and bloodier.

Milan Kundera, in *The Book of Laughter and Forgetting*, captures just such a moment in the communist occupation of Czechoslovakia:

> *In February 1948, the Communist leader Klement Gottwald stepped out on the balcony of a Baroque palace in Prague to harangue hundreds of thousands of citizens massed in Old Town Square. That was the great turning point in the history of Bohemia. A fateful moment.*
>
> *Gottwald was flanked by his comrades, with Vladimír Clementis standing close by him. It was snowing and cold, and Gottwald was bareheaded. Bursting with solicitude, Clementis took off his fur hat and set it on Gottwald's head.*
>
> *The propaganda section made hundreds of thousands of copies of the photograph taken on the balcony where Gottwald, in a fur hat and surrounded by his comrades, spoke to the people. On that balcony the history of communist Bohemia began. Every child knew that photograph, from seeing it on posters and in schoolbooks and museums.*
>
> *Four years later, Clementis was charged with treason and hanged. The propaganda section immediately made him vanish from history and, of course, from all photographs. Ever since, Gottwald has been alone on that balcony. Where Clementis stood, there is only the bare palace wall. Nothing remains of Clementis but the fur hat on Gottwald's head.*[8]

Barely a year later Orwell would depict just such an authoritarian cleansing of history in *1984*, where "the past was erased, the erasure was forgotten, the lie became the truth."[9]

One result of Gorbachev's glasnost was that the Russian people were allowed to begin to remember the victims. In 2018, a memorial to some of Stalin's victims was dedicated at Kommunarka. The memorial wall lists 6,609 victims of Stalin's Great Terror. According to Carl Schreck and Nikita Tatarsky, "Kommunarka was one of three areas in Moscow used by the NKVD for mass executions and burials during the Great Terror, in which some 700,000 people perished."[10]

The memorial, though, is not without controversy. Almost all of the names listed were true victims of Stalin. However, at least eighty-eight were killers from the ranks of Stalin's secret police who ultimately were, in turn, also purged and executed.

Activist Andrei Shalayev objected that Stalin's killers were honored alongside the "true" martyrs of Stalin. Carl Schreck and Nikita Tatarsky reported that Shalayev, in his own small protest, affixed a sign to two nearby trees that "in fine print, [lists] the names of what he calls 88 of the most 'odious' perpetrators of Stalin's death machine who are also listed on the memorial."

Shalayev has a point. It's hard to imagine a list of Holocaust victims that also included Nazis that Hitler later had killed.

At Kommunarka memorial, a sad irony is that an accomplished linguist named Yevgeny Polivanov, who fell victim to one of Stalin's purges, is listed just yards away from his notorious interrogator, Valentin Filatovich Grigoryev, who, in turn, was executed three years later.

As Schreck and Tatarsky tell us, "On October 1, 1937, as Soviet dictator Josef Stalin's brutal purge raged, a brilliant, one-handed Russian linguist [named Polivanov] penned a complaint from Moscow's notorious Butyrka prison about his treatment by the NKVD secret police."[11]

Yevgeny Polivanov, who was said to know eighteen languages, picked his words carefully as he pleaded with the court: "I request a halt to the severe interrogation methods (physical violence), as these methods compel me to lie and only serve to confuse the investigation. Furthermore, I am close to losing my mind." His signature on each page of his forced confession shows his deterioration as the weeks of interrogation wore on. Finally, after four months he was executed.

One can imagine Polivanov's family's anger upon seeing his killer's name at the memorial at Kommunarka.

When Stalin died in 1953, the Soviet government "rehabilitated" his victims or their surviving relatives. "Rehabilitate" seems a bit of a sterile and impractical way to sort through the victims. It is hard to imagine how "rehabilitating" someone killed by Stalin means anything. But in the legalistic world of Soviet socialism, it meant granting access to schools, position, travel, even food for the victim's descendants as a form of reparation. According to Schreck and Tatarsky, "the Soviet government [ultimately] rehabilitated . . . nearly 270,000 people who perished in his purges or faced other forms of repression."[12]

Altogether Stalin is estimated to have imprisoned 25 million people. From poets to scientists to peasants, more than 10 percent of Russians encountered the gulag in one form or another.

Orlando Figes, in *The Whisperers*, explores the complex psychological reactions of victims and their families to the Stalin purges. Figes concludes that "one lasting consequence of Stalin's reign" was "a silent and conformist population."

Americans, myself included, have always wanted populations to rise up and resist dictatorship. As a kid, I could never get my mind around the idea that one dictator could control millions of people.

Part of the answer is omnipresent police and terror. According to NPR, Figes brings that terror to life:

When Nina Kaminska was a teenager in Stalin's Moscow, she came home late after a party and discovered that she had forgotten

her key. She rang her family's apartment doorbell and waited . . .
and waited.

Her father finally answered the door in a full suit and tie. He
had always expected his doorbell to ring in the middle of the night,
and he had dressed to be taken away by the secret police. When he
saw that it was only his daughter, he slapped her face.[13]

The constant fear led to whispers. There were two kinds of
whisperers. One whisperer informed on their neighbor. Like the
Vichy French or Herod's Sanhedrin, these whisperers turned in
their neighbors and friends. The other whisperer spoke quietly so
as not to be heard or turned in to the secret police. The Russians
developed two distinct words to describe each kind of whisperer.

One man controlled millions by, as NPR describes it, "relying
on 'mutual surveillance,' urging families to report on each other in
communal living spaces and report 'disloyalty.' Many people did
what they could to survive, but they dealt with shame and guilt
long after Stalin's reign."[14]

To get an idea of the fear that drove people to inform upon their
neighbors, Figes tells the stories of landed peasants, or kulaks, that
were rounded up by Stalin, nearly two million by some estimates.
The kulaks were peasants but considered "rich." They were often
landowners and resisted the confiscation of their land.

The story of Antonina Golovina, who was exiled when she was
eight, captures the lifelong stigma of being the daughter of a kulak. When the secret police came to their home, Antonina and her
brothers and her mother were "given just an hour to pack a few
clothes." Their destination? A remote region of Siberia. Her father
was a kulak, and he was sentenced to three years in a Gulag labor
camp. Their multigenerational house was destroyed.

Antonina and her family somehow survived the frozen tundra

of Siberia. But many of their camp inmates did not. The ground was too frozen to bury the dead, so they were piled up until spring, when they were disposed of in the river. Antonina tells of how winter snow destroyed a couple of the barracks, and the prisoners were forced "to live in holes dug in the frozen ground."

Ultimately Antonina's family and their father were released and reunited. But, under the Stalinist regime, they were still seen as suspect. Instead of growing up to become Ayn Rand's heroine Kira, who refuses to join the Communist Party and dies trying to escape Russia, Antonina, like thousands of others, saw no way out. She joined the Communist Youth League. She hid her "kulak" roots. As Figes describes it: she "even forged her papers so that she could go to medical school. She never spoke about her family to any of her friends or colleagues at the Institute of Physiology in Leningrad, where she worked for forty years." Antonina joined the Communist Party and blended in.

Antonina only became brave enough to talk of her past when Gorbachev allowed the thawing of glasnost. Glasnost's opening allowed thousands of still-living victims and their families to speak out without fear of repercussions.[15]

Some victims rebelled more than others. Yevgenia Ginzburg was a Communist Party member who in 1937 got caught up in one of the insane purges that saw enemies within the party. Ginzburg was a professor who taught the history of the Communist Party. When a prominent Bolshevik leader and personal friend of Stalin's was assassinated, Ginzburg was arrested. Unlike many others arrested in the Great Purge, she fought back but was ultimately convicted. Her husband was given fifteen years and their personal property was confiscated. Despite her protests, her trial was said to have taken seven minutes.

She feared her verdict would include a death sentence, but the court sentenced her to a prison camp. Her autobiographical response to the court is both triumphant and unapologetic:

> To live! Without property, but what was that to me? Let them confiscate it—they were brigands anyway, confiscating was their business. They wouldn't get much good out of mine, a few books and clothes—why, we didn't even have a radio.
>
> My husband was a loyal Communist of the old stamp, not the kind who had to have a Buick or a Mercedes . . . Ten years! . . . Do you [the judges], with your codfish faces, really think you can go on robbing and murdering for another ten years, that there aren't people in the Party who will stop you sooner or later? I knew there were—and in order to see that day, I must live. In prison, if needs be, but I must at all costs live! . . . I looked at the guards, whose hands were still clasped behind my back.
>
> Every nerve in my body was quivering with the joy of being alive. What nice faces the guards had! Peasant boys from Ryazan or Kursk, most likely. They couldn't help being warders—no doubt they were conscripts. And they had joined hands to save me from falling. But they needn't have—I wasn't going to fall. I shook back the hair curled so carefully before facing the court, so as not to disgrace the memory of Charlotte Corday. Then I gave the guards a friendly smile. They looked at me in astonishment.[16]

The reference to Corday is to the woman seen by many as a heroine for assassinating Jean-Paul Marat during the French Revolution.

Chapter 30

IT'S NOT SOCIALISM
WITHOUT PURGES

Socialists love to talk about being inclusive, and about bringing everyone into the process. They say they value the free and fair exchange of ideas. However, they also acknowledge that socialism requires a supermajority to function. How do you get everyone to agree on a path forward? The easiest way is to deplatform those who don't agree.

I met Jon Utley when I was elected to the U.S. Senate. In a city where the conservative intellectual movement often seems to be on the wane, Jon remains a strong proponent for free markets, a less interventionist foreign policy, and limited government. In other words, he is an old-school constitutional conservative.

As publisher of *The American Conservative*, Jon's voice is an important one as populism and nationalism attempt to supplant conservatism. Jon came to conservatism, like many other intellectuals of the twentieth century, after his family first flirted with communism.

Jon's mother, Freda Utley, was born in England. As England languished in the 1920s, she embraced the new communism of Russia. She married a Russian Jewish economist, Arcadi Berdichevsky, and moved to Russia, where Jon was born.[1]

But all did not go as planned and even government officials were not immune from Stalin's wrath.

At 2 a.m. on April 14, 1936, the KGB came calling. As Jon describes it, "In those days, they would arrest someone and then look for something they'd done." Jon's father was arrested in one of Stalin's purges of his own communist ranks.

Georgie Anne Geyer describes Jon's mother's turmoil: "Freda, unable to help him, soon used her and Jon's British passports to return to England, where she mobilized important leftist friends, people like George Bernard Shaw, Bertrand Russell, and Harold Lasky, to try to find out where Arcadi was and even sent a letter directly to Stalin. What camp in the Gulag, that web of labor camps that eventually killed untold millions? What part of that white barrenness of the Arctic? Even the knowledge that he had died— and how and where and when—would be some sort of solace! But the Soviets were never into solace."[2]

Jon's father was presumed dead, but the details were not revealed until Jon traveled back to Russia in 2004 to see for himself. His father had died in Vorkuta, a Soviet concentration camp in the far north of Russia. Camp records revealed that he had been executed in 1938 for being a leader in a hunger strike and "provoking massive discontent among the prisoners."

When Jon visited the camp where his father was killed he was struck by the fact that "twenty million people are estimated to have died in these camps, but they are almost forgotten. There are hardly any museums or exhibits of communist camps. Many emptied ones were burned down at the time of Nikita Khrushchev, but mostly they were scavenged by poor peasants for anything usable, and then the remains, built of wood and cheap brick, just rotted into the forest or tundra. They were poorly built by unskilled prison labor, and many were temporary and moved when timber or easily mined minerals were depleted from nearby."

Vorkuta was so far to the north that prisoners often arrived via the Arctic Sea. How cold was it? Utley explains that "during the winter, daylight is less than three hours long and temperatures go to 40 degrees below zero." One can scarcely imagine what it must have been like to endure such circumstances.

Solzhenitsyn describes the deadly winters from the point of view of the prisoner: "When you're cold, don't expect sympathy from someone who's warm."[3]

Jon and his mother were able to flee to England and ultimately to the United States because she still held an English passport. Fortunately, according to Jon, "Knowing the prohibition against taking Russian-born children out of the country, they had put only my mother's name on my birth certificate."

With her husband's presumed death and her immersion into American culture, Freda Utley wrote *The Dream We Lost* in 1940, one of the first accounts of the terror and misery of communism.

Jon asks the same question so many ask: "why didn't they resist more?" The answer, according to Jon, is that millions were condemned and executed for resistance, but the movement lacked momentum because the prison camps were very isolated and their horrific conditions kept secret.[4]

Jon describes how he felt as he stood in the brick quarry where his father was executed: "I guess I felt a certain peace as to where he was; it ended a question. Actually, it's a sort of peaceful thing to know what happened because my mother never knew what happened to him. I always wondered what he would have been thinking of, of what was in his mind when he was killed, or whether he would ever have dreamed that his son would find the place where he died."[5]

How massive were the Soviet pogroms? In 1932 and 1933, an estimated 7 to 11 million people were killed by Stalin. Most of these were kulaks like Antonina Golovina's family who resisted the Soviet land grab. Collectivization of the farms caused food production to plummet, and the ensuing famine saw millions more die.

The combined number for those killed under Lenin and Stalin likely exceeds sixty million, a mind-boggling number.[6]

Part V

Where Are
These Angels?
The Philosophy
of Socialism

"I think you're taking a lot of things for granted. Just
tell me where in the world you find these angels who
are going to organize society for us?"

—MILTON FRIEDMAN

Chapter 31

SOCIALISM EXPECTS SELFLESS RULERS AND CITIZENS

From the very beginning, one criticism of socialism has been its utopian nature. Even Marx criticized the voluntary socialist communes in America as utopian.

The word "Utopia," though, is much older than socialism; it comes to us from Thomas More's book by that name, written in 1516. The word is translated from the Greek as "no place." Interestingly, the word also phonetically sounds like "eu" topia, which would mean true or good place. More may have intended to make a double entendre when he created the word. Critics are still debating which meaning he intended as the primary definition.

Nor do critics agree on whether More's work was meant to be satire or instruction. Controversy still exists as to whether More presents a road map to a "perfect" place or a satirical look at an undesirable one.

The same can be said of Plato's *Republic*. Is his idealized Republic, Kallipolis—run by guardians or philosopher-kings—to be taken literally? If so, as in More's Utopia, it is hard to explain the defense of slavery, government-regulated reproduction, and total central planning in Plato's Republic.

Perhaps the most destructive aspect of utopian philosophy is its claim to be inevitable, that as history unfolds a utopian version of paradise is the endpoint.

In *The Republic*, Plato presents a utopian inevitability of history, the idea that history is linear and going somewhere. Plato puts forward that government will evolve from timocracy (a ruling class of warriors, like ancient Sparta) to oligarchy (rule by the wealthy few) to democracy to tyranny.

In Kallipolis, the philosopher-kings rule as disinterested persons, not for their own selfish interests but for the good of the whole. But the dilemma is that such selfless philosopher-kings defy human nature, leading to false and impractical expectations.

Plato's *Republic*, in a way, foretells the fatal flaw of the twentieth-century totalitarian disasters. If we give up our freedom to a strong central government, Plato promises that we will receive philosopher-kings as selfless rulers. But in reality, we wind up with Hitler, Stalin, and Mao.

Over time, the word "utopia" or "utopian" has become not an ideal but a pejorative. No one wants their ideas to be called utopian because it means they are impractical, unworkable, naive.

Did Plato, or More for that matter, really see their utopias as models for perfection to be aspired to, or did they intend for them to be interpreted satirically as warnings? It is particularly hard to imagine that More wanted us to interpret his Utopia literally since it allowed slavery and condoned divorce (More was later executed for opposing, among other things, King Henry VIII's divorce).

Because humankind is not selfless (and even if it were, no two people would ever agree on what the utopian ideal would be), the standards for a utopia are naive. The leaders would have to be superhuman to overcome natural self-interest and find agreement on what exactly the ideal striven for by all would be.

Richard Kilminster summarizes the argument in Chad Walsh's *From Utopia to Nightmare*: "the traditional articles of faith underpinning all utopian thinking are that man is good and perfectible and can live in harmony ruled by rulers who will not be corrupted by power."[1]

Herein lies the real danger of utopia. Karl Popper explains: "[T]he Utopian attempt to realize an ideal state, using a blueprint of society as a whole, is one which demands a strong centralized rule of the few, and which therefore is likely to lead to a dictatorship. . . ."[2]

Writing toward the end of World War II in 1944, the philosopher Ludwig von Mises makes a similar point in his *Omnipotent Government*: "At the bottom of all totalitarian doctrines lies the belief that the rulers are wiser and loftier than their subjects and that they therefore know better what benefits those ruled than they know themselves." Essentially, those who would presume to plan society are, at their core, elitists.[3]

Popper's writing came of age during World War II, when the world was becoming aware of the authoritarian nature of Nazi and Stalinist socialism. Intriguingly, the bogeymen of today's politics—Charles Koch on the right and George Soros on the left—both profess admiration for Karl Popper.

Koch admired Popper's conclusion that to be scientific, a theory must be falsifiable. As Popper put it: "A theory which is not refutable by any conceivable event is non-scientific." Popper maintained that the "genuine test of a theory is an attempt to falsify it or to refute it. Testability is falsifiability." To Popper, Marxism was a pseudoscience because Marx's argument of the inevitability of class warfare and ultimately of communism was untestable and really on par with a religious belief.[4]

Soros, though seen now as the "Daddy Warbucks" of the left, for many years used his Open Society Foundations to oppose totalitarianism. Soros agreed with Popper that historical determinism leads to closed societies ruled by authoritarians.

Popper's observations about determinism, therefore, garnered praise from all across the ideological spectrum. Popper, while not necessarily a defender of laissez-faire capitalism, was a fellow traveler of the Austrian free-market advocates and was a colleague and friend of Hayek at the London School of Economics.

One of Popper's great contributions is showing the link between central planning and state violence. Popper explained that once it is accepted that government will centrally plan society, "any difference of opinion between utopian engineers must therefore lead, in the absence of rational methods, to the use of power instead of reason, i.e. to violence."[5]

Popper felt that Plato advocated in *The Republic* for a version of Sparta where the needs of the collective trumped the rights of the individual. In Sparta, the state selected out and eliminated weaklings by tossing infants off a cliff or into a pit of water. Males were separated from parents and introduced into military training at a young age. Slavery was accepted and censorship was common. Popper believed that it was not coincidental that the Nazis idolized the Spartans.[6]

Utopian visions are naive because they require a perfect society with perfect leaders. Utopias are dangerous because humankind is not perfect. Indeed, utopias require leaders willing to wield absolute power to conquer man's true nature, to take and redistribute his property. Consequently, utopias select not for perfectly selfless leaders but for the opposite—people who are capable, willing, and unrestrained in their use of force to achieve utopian ends.

Popper recognized that utopians who proposed that they knew which direction history needed to go and wanted to push history in that direction would inevitably have to use force and violence to achieve their goals.

Think about the concept of history having a direction for a moment. Think about your own life. When you do, see if you agree with me that history is directional or linear only in retrospect. Looking back, we tend to see purpose and pattern resulting from our own desire to put order and meaning to the events of the past.

Tolstoy put it this way: "Every man lives for himself, making use of his free-will for attainment of his own objects, and feels in his whole being that he can do or not do any action. But as soon as he does anything, that act, committed at a certain moment in time, becomes irrevocable and is the property of history, in which it has a significance, predestined and not subject to free choice."[7]

Tolstoy, like others in the nineteenth century, thought the answer to history's progress was the discovery of the cyclical nature of history with a healthy dose of divine intervention. Free will was subjugated to a vast, inevitable fate called "Progress."

In *The Whig Interpretation of History*, Herbert Butterfield articulates why those who see history as a progression or linear development are naive or utopian in their outlook. He wrote that the "historian can draw lines through certain events, . . . and if he is not careful he begins to forget that this line is merely a mental trick of his; he comes to imagine that it represents something like a line of causation. The total result of this method is to impose a certain form upon the whole historical story, and to produce a scheme of general history which is bound to converge beautifully upon the present—all demonstrating throughout the ages the workings of an obvious principle of progress."[8]

Why is it a big deal to believe or not believe in the linearity of history or in historical determinism?

Because utopias are often built on the notion that they are the apotheosis of history's unfolding, that they are inevitable. Marx certainly believed that the class struggle was inevitable but would produce a paradise or utopia where the state would wither away. Believing that history has an inexorable course takes a great leap of faith. The ramifications of perceiving history to have some linear purpose are a big deal, probably much bigger than most of us realize. To believe that history has a direction and that any one individual or government should assist history along that path is not only utopian but ultimately dangerous. Just ask the victims of the gulag or Auschwitz. The eventual ends always justify the temporary means, however horrible.

Both the Soviets and the Nazis believed that they were creating their version of paradise on earth. For the Soviets it was to be a workers' paradise. For the Nazis a monoracial utopia.

It is said that those who fail to grasp history are in danger of repeating history. Understanding utopian ideas ensures that nobody forgets the millions of lives lost to utopian nonsense.

Karl Popper understood that the utopianism of historical determinism and tyranny are not benign but rather are directly related to the millions of people who were killed by Stalin, by Hitler, by Mao. These genocides all came about as a result of utopian ideas and a utopian concept of history.

Popper dedicated his 1957 book, *The Poverty of Historicism,* thus:

> *To the memory of the countless men, women, and children of*
> *all creeds or nations or races who fell victim to the fascist and*
> *communist belief in the Inexorable Laws of Historical Destiny.*

A friend of mine, William J. Murray, writes in the dedication of his book *Utopian Road to Hell*:

To the tens of millions who lost their lives to the misguided twentieth-century efforts to create Utopia here on earth, whether that be the Nazi "Thousand-Year Reich" or the failed Soviet experiment with communalism, and to hundreds of millions more who suffered through starvation and enslavement.

The science of Marxism required the acceptance of the utopian notion that selfless guardians will rule in the interests of the nation and that selfless citizens will accept this rule without question. It did not take long to discover that the prerequisites for this utopia defied the nature of man.

The Soviets acknowledged that Marxism would require a breed of men and women with new traits and expectations. So they sought to create a new type of person, the "New Soviet Man."

Leon Trotsky described the "man of the future" like so:

Man will make it his purpose to master his own feelings, to raise his instincts to the heights of consciousness, to make them transparent, to extend the wires of his will into hidden recesses, and thereby to raise himself to a new plane, to create a higher social biologic type, or, if you please, a superman.... Man will become immeasurably stronger, wiser and subtler; his body will become more harmonized, his movements more rhythmic, his voice more musical. The forms of life will become dynamically dramatic. The average human type will rise to the heights of an Aristotle, a Goethe, or a Marx. And above this ridge new peaks will rise.[9]

As Murray N. Rothbard describes it: "the Marxian cadre, the possessors of the special knowledge of the laws of history . . . will proceed to transform mankind into the new socialist man by the use of force."[10]

Nikolay Chernyshevsky and other radicals of the mid-nineteenth century acknowledged that man's nature, his inherent selfishness, might be an impediment to their utopia. So they created a "new man" who would see "service to mankind" as in his selfish interest. Chernyshevsky wrote in *What Is to Be Done?* of a "new" man who would find "rational selfish" pleasure in serving the interests of society.[11]

Fyodor Dostoyevsky wrote *Notes from Underground* as a direct response to Chernyshevsky's *What Is to Be Done?* Dostoyevsky, like Chernyshevsky, had been greatly influenced by the radicals or nihilists of the day. Both he and Chernyshevsky had been sentenced to the firing squad only to be given a last-minute reprieve.

Such an experience would no doubt have a lasting effect on anyone. Add four years of hard labor in Siberian exile and you have the recipe for a life-changing experience. Dostoyevsky the nihilist sympathizer became Dostoyevsky the critic. Dostoyevsky came home from prison aware that a slavish submission to reason did not leave a place for the individual.

Chapter 32

PROGRESS COMES FROM REBELS AND DREAMERS

In the 1850s, Dostoyevsky visited the Crystal Palace in England. For him, the Crystal Palace became a symbol of the godless, man-made utopia. It was built in 1851 as part of the Great Exhibition. It was nearly a million square feet under a cast-iron and plate-glass ceiling.[1]

In "Winter Notes on Summer Impressions," Dostoyevsky writes of the crowds gathered to gawk at the Crystal Palace: "that a terrible force . . . has united all the people . . . into a single herd. You become aware of a gigantic idea; you feel that here something has already been achieved." Dostoyevsky fears that what has been achieved is the "ultimate" and if recognized as such, leaves nothing left to strive for.[2]

In *Notes from Underground*, Dostoyevsky rejects the modern, man-made Crystal Palace as a symbol of the nihilist or socialist desire to plan man's future with rational mathematical certainty. The Underground Man worries that when the Crystal Palace comes it will be "frightfully dull (for what will one have to do when everything will be calculated and tabulated), but on the other hand everything will be extraordinarily rational."[3]

The Crystal Palace, like the anthill, once completed leaves nothing left to be attained. The Underground Man argues that central to man's nature is a desire to create, a predestination to strive. In fact, "the process" of creating may be even more important than what is created.

But how will man continue to strive if he is simply an automaton destined to fulfill a mathematical equation of self-interest? Perhaps the "only goal on earth to which mankind is striving lies in this incessant process of attaining . . . in life itself, and not in the thing to be attained."[4]

The rationalists argued that free will does not exist and that man acts in a calculated fashion to accomplish what is in his or her self-interest.

Dostoyevsky's Underground Man argues that anyone who believes men will act in unison in their best interest ignores an aspect of man's nature that is inescapable:

"One's own free unfettered choice, one's own caprice, however wild it may be, one's own fancy worked up at times to frenzy—is that very 'most advantageous advantage' which we have overlooked, which comes under no classification and against which all systems and theories are continually being shattered to atoms."[5]

Sarah J. Young, the author of two scholarly books on Dostoyevsky, points out that the Underground Man has two answers to the Crystal Palace utopia: "you can behave gratuitously, i.e. perform a pointless irrational act: you can stick out your tongue," or you can act in a destructive way—"throw stones at it."

The fact that atheism was intermixed with nihilism and socialism also pushed Dostoyevsky in the opposite direction. While the Underground Man rails against a world rigidly structured by reason, he also endlessly considers the need for faith. Some critics even classify Dostoyevsky as a "Christian novelist."

The three brothers Karamazov represent the spectrum from doubt to fervent belief, but Dostoyevsky so masterfully develops each brother's point of view that some critics still debate whether he sides more with Ivan and the Inquisitor than with Christ.

One criticism of Ayn Rand, and Chernyshevsky as well, for that matter, is the one-dimensionality of their characters. The characters are archetypes rather than realistic, conflicted individuals. Dostoyevsky's characters, however, are rich in depth and not always definable or categorical.

Young attributes "these very significant ambiguities" to what makes "Dostoevsky such a complex and interesting writer."

The radicals and socialists of the time were also known as nihilists. Young writes: "Contrary to the Nihilists' view of human nature as rational," Dostoyevsky believed "that human beings are full of contradictions and dualities" that are irrational.

Dostoyevsky saw Chernyshevsky's Crystal Palace as a false utopia. Today few people have heard of Chernyshevsky's *What Is to Be Done?* although it is said to have been Lenin's favorite book.

Notes from Underground may have begun as Dostoyevsky's response to Chernyshevsky's rationalistic and altruistic world, but it was also, as scholar Adrian Wanner describes, an expression of Dostoyevsky's distaste for "scientific positivism."

Positivism argues that history can be examined objectively, just like physics and math. Opponents such as Popper argued that it is impossible to quantify much of what history studies. History cannot develop experiments or mathematical models, and there are no general laws of history.

While the Underground Man hated the idea of a Crystal Palace world, Russian novelist Yevgeny Zamyatin envisioned a future community where everyone already lives in one. His novel, *We*, does not explicitly refer to the Crystal Palace, but Zamyatin's citizens live in vast glass buildings that may be his reimagining of it.

When Zamyatin wrote *We*, the Bolshevik regime was still in its infancy. Despite having been a supporter of the Bolsheviks, Zamyatin presciently understood what would happen when the rights of the individual were made subservient to the needs of the collective. *We* is the grandfather of all twentieth-century dystopian novels but has its roots in the dispute between Dostoyevsky and the mid-nineteenth-century socialist writers.

In *We*, the people live in buildings made entirely of glass. Zamyatin's narrator, D-503, describes the scene with almost religious fervor: "On days like this the whole world is cast of the same impregnable, eternal glass as the Green Wall, as all our buildings. On days like this you see the bluest depth of things, their hitherto unknown, astonishing equations. . . ."[6]

Zamyatin, Dostoyevsky, and Chernyshevsky are linked together in the debate both for and against utopia. All three share the distinction of having been arrested by the czar. Zamyatin was first arrested during the Russian revolution of 1905 for his association with Bolsheviks. He was sent into exile in Siberia but escaped and was then arrested again in 1911. Despite being a reformer and a Bolshevik sympathizer, he became disturbed by the violence and intolerance of communists as well, particularly their censorship of the arts.

Zamyatin wrote *We* in 1920, and by 1921 it became the first book banned by the Soviet censorship board. *We* was smuggled out of the Soviet Union and first published in the United States in 1924. It would finally be published in the Soviet Union only in 1988.

In his 1921 essay "I Am Afraid," Zamyatin wrote: "[T]rue literature can only exist when it is created, not by diligent and reliable officials, but by madmen, hermits, heretics, dreamers, rebels and skeptics." Sounds sort of like an homage to the Underground Man.[7]

Zamyatin requested exile and with the help of Gorky left the Soviet Union in 1931.

Some critics maintain that Zamyatin is the creator of the modern genre of dystopian novels. Margaret Atwood wrote of Zamyatin:

> There were a lot of utopias in the nineteenth century, wonderful societies that we might possibly construct. Those went pretty much out of fashion after WWI. And almost immediately one of the utopias that people were trying to construct, namely the Soviet Union, threw out a writer called Zamyatin who wrote a seminal book called We, which contains the seeds of Orwell and Huxley [as well as Ayn Rand's Anthem]. Writers started doing dystopias after we saw the effects of trying to build utopias that required, unfortunately, the elimination of a lot of people before you could get to the perfect point, which never arrived.[8]

The links from Chernyshevsky to Dostoyevsky's *Notes from Underground* to Zamyatin's *We* are many. Chernyshevsky's "desirable" Crystal Palace becomes Dostoyevsky's object of derision becomes Zamyatin's glass cubes, where all are exposed to the eyes of the state.

The harangues of the Underground Man are still valid and pertinent today. As today's socialists promote the scientific rationalism of the green agenda and socialized medicine, the rebellion of the individual against the collective is still apropos.

Dostoyevsky's Underground Man rebels against the rationalism of the state: "2 times 2 equals 4 . . . Is no longer life, but the beginning of death." In *We*, D-503, at least in the beginning, accepts the rationalism of the state:

> The multiplication table is wiser and more absolute than the ancient God. It never—repeat, never—makes a mistake. . . . And

there's nothing happier than figures that live according to the elegant and eternal laws of the multiplication table. No wavering, no wandering.—Truth is one, and the true path is one. And that truth is two times two and that true path is four.[9]

The certainty of 2 + 2 = 4 becomes a metaphor for the all-knowing, all-powerful, rational state. At first glance in *1984*, Orwell seems to flip the metaphor as Winston cries out that 2 + 2 still does equal four. To Winston, his ability to still know that 2 + 2 = 4 is his last refuge of freedom.

In *1984*, as Winston is being tortured by the state, he believes that "[f]reedom is the freedom to say that two plus two make four."

Has Orwell flipped the metaphor or is he making a finer point? Perhaps the point is that in *1984*, the government has become so powerful as to be irrational. So, Winston identifies 2 + 2 = 4 as his rebellion. And the state tortures him to agree to the irrational 2 + 2 = 5.

Adrian Wanner describes the contrast: "In Dostoevsky and Zamyatin's dystopian dictatorships of reason [where 2 + 2 = 4], madness [where 2 + 2 = 5] becomes a strategy of resistance."

Wanner explains Orwell's different approach to the metaphor of 2 + 2. "Orwell's use of the formula '2+2=5' inverts the relationship of reason and madness laid out by . . . [Dostoyevsky and Zamyatin]."[10]

Orwell's inversion of the dogma of 2 + 2 = 4 implies, perhaps, that the society based on reason that the socialists strove for somehow has been supplanted. That Winston still strives for a world in which there is objective truth and reason, where two plus two still equals four, seems to imply that the pursuit of reason as a guide is not necessarily the problem. The problem arises when the dictatorship of the proletariat allows reason to become seduced and supplanted by power.

Wanner quotes Orwell himself "as insisting that this novel was not intended as an attack on socialism . . . but as a 'show-up of the perversions to which a centralized economy is liable and which have already been partly realized in Communism and Fascism.'"

To Orwell, striving for a reason-driven society (the socialist ideal) is not necessarily the problem. The terror of totalitarianism occurs when the lure of power requires absolute submission even to the irrational. Where Dostoyevsky saw the freedom to act, even in an irrational way, as an act of rebellion against power, Orwell recognized, likely from the tyranny of Stalin and Hitler, that when power is centralized in the name of creating a society of reason, power ceases to impose reason but creates an irrational logic of its own. As such, $2 + 2$ must equal 5.

The tyranny of Orwell is tyranny that has evolved beyond pursuit of reason and now requires submission for submission's sake. Accepting the irrational $2 + 2 = 5$ becomes the submission of reason to power.

The mathematical certainty of $2 + 2 = 4$, the very same that the Underground Man railed against, is adopted wholesale and recited as creed by the guardians of *We*.

Zamyatin's D-503, as a scientist and supporter of the One State, is initially as religiously devoted to the multiplication tables as the next guy. Love, however, lets doubt creep in and causes him to question everything that he has previously accepted at face value.

In *We*, society seems to have accepted reason's mandate to act according to their self-interest. Like Chernyshevsky's "new men," they act according to "psychological egoism" (the deterministic doctrine that people necessarily pursue the goals they believe to be in their best interest).

Normative egoism, by contrast, is the ethical doctrine that people ought to pursue their best interests. Ergo, people can understand and deduce what their best interests are—thus, acting in one's best interest is not simply a psychological instinct. Normative egoism is a doctrine with moral implications, where people choose to act in their self-interest, and the choice is voluntary. Normative or ethical rational egoism is closer to the objectivism put forward by Ayn Rand.

The psychological egoism of Chernyshevsky leaves no place for free will. The Underground Man responds to those who argue you can have free will and rational egoism:

> You will scream at me . . . that no one is touching my free will, that all they are concerned with is that my will should of itself, of its own free will, coincide with my own normal interests, with the laws of nature and arithmetic.
>
> Good heavens, gentlemen, what sort of free will is left when we come to tabulation and arithmetic, when it will all be a case of twice two make four.[11]

What so inflames Dostoyevsky's Underground Man about the Crystal Palace is that it answers all questions. It leaves no place for doubt. It leaves no place for man's irrational love of "destruction and chaos," which the Underground Man contends is equivalent to "real suffering." Dostoyevsky writes, "Suffering is the sole origin of consciousness," and "Consciousness, for instance, is infinitely superior to twice two makes four."

Ultimately, it isn't suffering or well-being that the Underground Man chooses to base his actions on but rather "caprice." He fears the Crystal Palace because he is "afraid of [the] edifice, that it is of crystal and can never be destroyed and that one cannot put one's tongue out at it, even on the sly."

What today's socialists utterly fail to understand is the central planning required to create a society based on reason precludes a fundamental aspect of freedom: the freedom to act irrationally, the freedom to act out, the freedom to simply stick one tongue's out at the state.

When the Crystal Palace is finally completed, when the workers' paradise is here, what then will men strive for? When history ends and the state melts away, what then? The great insight of Dostoyevsky is that even if it were possible to achieve such a nirvana it should still be opposed, because a fundamental aspect of who we are is our desire to attain. "Man is a creative animal," says the Underground Man, "destined to strive consciously towards a goal." And we need the impetus to strive—a utopian goal achieved eliminates that impetus. Finding any utopia, arriving at any Eden, is not to be desired because the end of history would in actuality be the end of a fundamental part of man's nature.[12]

Chapter 33

FREEDOM IS NOT THE INEVITABLE OUTCOME OF HISTORY AND MUST BE PROTECTED

I s it possibly that simple? That a hundred million people killed by Hitler, Stalin, Mao, and Pol Pot were all the result of utopian ideas?

The horror of utopian determinism, once recognized, is no longer accepted by thinking people, right?

Unfortunately, there are still modern historians, such as Francis Fukuyama, who believe in the utopian concept that history is developing in a linear fashion, that there can be an end of history.

Fukuyama, like Hegel, believes that as history unfolds there will come a time when all internal contradictions in ideas resolve themselves and an "end to history" ensues. Hegel saw the American and French revolutions as indicative of the end of history.

Marx also believed history was moving directionally toward an "end of history" that culminated in a workers' paradise. Hegel saw the dialectical process of ideas being countered by opposing ideas and their subsequent resolution or synthesis as the driver of history. Popper viewed both Hegel's and Marx's historical determinism as dangerous because once the planners were convinced of the inevitability of the workers' paradise, they also became convinced of their own unlimited authority to coerce the "inevitable" end of history.[1]

Fukuyama's announcement in the late 1980s, as the Berlin Wall fell and the Cold War came to a close, that the world was now approaching an "end of history" moment alarmed followers of Popper. Even though Fukuyama argued that the "end of history" he was announcing would be followed by an era of liberal democracy, some worried that Fukuyama's embrace of historical determinism would encourage modern-day zealots to assume, since liberal democracy was inevitable, that perhaps a little war here and there to nudge us toward it was in order. This concept was doubly worrying since there already existed in Washington a well-connected cabal promoting this neoconservative foreign policy.

Elizabeth Glaser puts Fukuyama in a contemporary context: "When he wrote 'The End of History?', Fukuyama was a neocon. He was taught by Leo Strauss's protege Allan Bloom, author of *The Closing of the American Mind*; he was a researcher for the Rand Corporation, the think tank for the American military-industrial complex; and he followed his mentor Paul Wolfowitz into the Reagan administration."[2]

Although Karl Popper's arguments predate Fukuyama, they still are spot-on. Fukuyama is a contemporary Hegelian. So, when Fukuyama announced the "end of history" and the triumph of liberal capitalist democracy, many observers worried that the deterministic doctrines that encouraged first Hegel and then Marx were being resurrected.

Fukuyama argued that the world now understood that democracy provided greater prosperity than centrally planned economies. Big government–planned economies, even communist states, would now wither away and be replaced by capitalism. Sounds great, if you ignore that Fukuyama's theory is based on the same "end of history" suppositions of Marx that morphed into the totalitarian dystopias of the twentieth century.

Timothy Stanley and Alexander Lee wrote in the *Atlantic Monthly*, "Fukuyama's logic was a bit too reminiscent of the pseudo-Hegelian historical determinism that Marxists and Fascists deployed to disastrous effect earlier in the 20th century. . . ." The events of the last thirty years have not confirmed Fukuyama's thesis.[3]

Not only is history not over, but much of the world is still headed away from liberal democracy.

Stanley and Lee remind us that "a new Cold War has broken out [and] China's 'Marxist capitalism' suggests you can have wealth without freedom."

China may have "wealth without freedom" but they don't have "wealth without capitalism." China's wealth might be described as proportional to the degree of her rejection of socialism. But Stanley and Lee are correct that for whatever capitalism it has embraced, China has not by any analysis accepted liberal democracy.[4]

Just as Marx incorrectly believed that history was inevitably going to resolve itself in a workers' paradise, so too was Fukuyama wrong. Fukuyama's argument that history is inevitably evolving toward liberal democracy, not tyranny, has been defied by the facts. Throughout the Middle East, dictatorships continue. Russia and China cannot be said to be inevitably headed toward liberal democracy.

Though critical of Fukuyama's thesis, Roger Kimball argues that some criticisms of Fukuyama "were based on a simplistic misreading of his thesis. For in proclaiming that the end of history had arrived in the form of triumphant liberal democracy, Francis

Fukuyama did not mean that the world would henceforth be free from tumult, political contention, or intractable social problems. Moreover, he was careful to note 'the victory of liberalism has occurred primarily in the realm of ideas or consciousness and is as yet incomplete in the real or material world.'"[5]

The only problem with that defense is that it's hard to imagine an "end to the history" of ideas that is independent of actual history. Fukuyama himself points to real, historical episodes such as the French and American revolutions as indications that the "end of history" was nigh.

So, if "the longing for recognition" is satisfied and the end of history is paramount, how do we know it unless we look to real-life history or current events? If man has come to the end of his ideological journey and chosen liberal democracy, wouldn't it be fair to look around and see if current events reflect that? If Fukuyama meant only the "end of the history of ideology," how would one know it had come to pass without looking at real history to determine if, indeed, people's ideological conclusions had spilled over into real action?

Fukuyama wrote boldly, "What we are witnessing is not just the end of the Cold War, or a passing of a particular period of postwar history, but the end of history as such: that is, the end point of mankind's ideological evolution and the universalization of Western liberal democracy as the final form of human government." He was committing the same deterministic errors that Marx did. Kimball responds that "these were the sorts of statements—along with Francis Fukuyama's professed conviction that 'the ideal will govern the material world in the long run'—that rang the alarm."

Making the case that liberal democracy is the best form of government would not have been so controversial. Popper himself agreed that democracy was not perfect but the least evil form of government and therefore preferable. What alarmed people was the mathematical certainty with which Fukuyama proclaimed the new era and his claim that liberal democracy was historically inevitable.[6]

Like Marx and Hegel, Fukuyama argues that "history [should be] understood as a single, coherent, evolutionary process, . . . taking into account the experience of all peoples in all times."[7] Seems a rather sweeping claim, at once both naive and utopian. Fukuyama's attempt to marry history and evolution are reminiscent of Marx trying to equate the dialectic with the "science" of evolution.

Fukuyama goes on to argue that history's "evolutionary process [is] neither random nor unintelligible." This is quite the assertion: history is not random or unintelligible. What about unknowable? If the future is unknowable, then history is orderly and unfolding according to an intelligible plan only in retrospect and really only in the biased eyes of the beholder.

Fukuyama writes: "Both Hegel and Marx believed that the evolution of human societies was not open-ended, but would end when mankind had achieved a form of society that satisfied its deepest and most fundamental longings. Both thinkers thus posited an 'end of history': for Hegel this was the liberal state, while for Marx it was a communist society."

Even Fukuyama admits that recent history argues against his end-of-history thesis: "[it is] . . . a very old question: Whether, at the end of the twentieth century, it makes sense for us once again to speak of a coherent and directional history of mankind that will eventually lead the greater part of humanity to liberal democracy."[8]

Fukuyama admits to an abundance of critics: "The most profound thinkers of the twentieth century have directly attacked the idea that history is a coherent or intelligible process; indeed, they have denied the possibility that any aspect of human life is philosophically intelligible."

He describes the historians who refute the linearity of history as possessing a "profound pessimism [that] is not accidental, but born of the truly terrible political events of the first half of the twentieth century."

Nevertheless, Fukuyama asserts that "liberal democracy remains the only coherent political aspiration that spans different regions and cultures around the globe."

Few would argue against liberal democracy as an aspirational goal. If Fukuyama only expressed hope for history's direction, the commendable might outweigh the concern. Fukuyama accepts the mathematical certainty and scientism that Dostoyevsky's Underground Man and Popper, among others, warn us of. History "has proceeded according to certain definite rules laid down not by man, but by nature and nature's laws." To Fukuyama, $2 + 2 = 4$ applies to the historical actions of men. How very Marxian of him.

If history were inevitable, would such a conclusion dampen the fire that Jefferson thought necessary in each generation? If people accept historical determinism, the danger exists that charlatans, like Hitler and Stalin, appear on the national stage promising the people that history's march toward progress and national success goes through them. Contrary to a notion that history's end is desirable would be that history's end should scare the hell out of any of us who would resist "homogenization."

Fukuyama tries to convince us that history is headed toward a liberal, democratic utopia. But regimes of the twentieth century inform us that the "end of history" can go either way. While there is an argument that many countries have headed away from the autocracy of the Iron Curtain, there still remain plenty of countries clinging to the model of a single-party, strongman rule.

Dostoyevsky would argue that part of the recognition of self-worth is that "most advantageous advantage" of free will, even the freedom to act simply out of caprice. For Hegel and Fukuyama, though, recognition comes about by war. Fukuyama and Hegel seem blasé about war. Fukuyama writes unemotionally that "war is fundamentally driven by the desire for recognition. . . ."[9] Hegel saw war as necessary: "War protects the people from corruption which an everlasting peace would bring upon it."[10]

Kimball quotes the German thinker Hans Blumenberg: "If there were an imminent final goal of history, then those who believe they know it and claim to promote its attainment would be legitimized in using all the others who do not know it . . . as a mere means." Once the "final solution" is believed to be an option, it becomes certain that some totalitarian, a Hitler or a Stalin, will use that "ideology of historical inevitability" to justify whatever means are necessary.

Kimball reminds us that "the twentieth century has acquainted us in terrifyingly exquisite detail with what happens when people are treated as 'moments' in an impersonal dialectic."[11]

The danger of historical determinism is that it provides philosophical cover for any megalomaniac who seeks to prove that his or her program is historically inevitable.

Both the left and right often succumb to the "end of history" ideal. Stanley and Lee point out that "leaders across the political spectrum have been quick to adopt this form of historical determinism."

"Hillary Clinton . . . has . . . a similar outlook in the realm of foreign policy," Stanley and Lee write. "She has subtly distanced herself from Barack Obama's cautious realism abroad and instead used discrete references to the past to justify aggressively exporting liberal values across the globe as often as possible. Given that history has 'proved' how great liberalism was in previous battles against tyranny, the argument goes, liberalism will inevitably win out if we pick enough fights and put enough muscle behind it."[12]

Neoliberals like Clinton are virtually indistinguishable from neoconservatives like Bill Kristol in their support for military intervention in Libya, Syria, Afghanistan, Yemen, Somalia, Mali, Niger, etc. The only difference is the liberal neocons are more honest about their goal of nation building.

If history were, indeed, unfolding toward liberty, we would still need to understand what is meant by liberty. Left and right sometimes do agree that freedom is the goal, only they differ on their definition of freedom. Positive "liberty" is what today's socialists yearn for. Positive liberty can also be described as the "freedom" to get something concrete, such as health care, a car, a house, or food.

Can man really discover self-worth in the command economy of Venezuela or the autocracy of Cuba? Of course not. The question remains, though, whether there are still enough Americans who put their faith in the individual, and in liberty, to ensure that our nation resists the siren call of "free stuff" that socialism offers. Time will tell.

From my perspective, the cautionary moral of a utopia is: don't succumb to any end-of-history utopias from the right or the left. Don't accept any preordained linearity to history. Because simply that acquiescence, that attenuation of free will, may be enough to allow the recurrent strongman in history to justify his or her edicts as science or evolution or simply as the inevitable.

Part VI

Never Let a Crisis
Go to Waste:
Socialism
and Alarmism

"You never want a serious crisis to go to waste. And
what I mean by that [is] it's an opportunity to do
things that you think you could not do before."

RAHM EMANUEL

Chapter 34

SOCIALISM LEADS
TO CRONYISM

Today's socialists sometimes claim they're not against all capitalism, just crony capitalism. They point to the bank bailout (aka the Troubled Asset Relief Program, or TARP) of 2008 as a prime example.

After the market discovered that subprime mortgages were bundled together with traditional safe mortgages and called AAA securities, the government solution was to bail out the biggest banks for their bad decisions. The result? Furor erupted on both the right and the left.

From the right came the Tea Party movement. I know because I was there. I spoke at the very first Tea Party rally at Faneuil Hall in Boston in December 2007. This was one year before the election of President Obama. Those on the left and in the media often portray the genesis of the Tea Party movement as a protest against Obama. This is false. The citizens at the first Tea Party rallies came together because they were worried about the accumulation of government debt, the housing collapse, and the concern that we'd transfer trillions from responsible citizens to irresponsible ones.

From the left came the Occupy Wall Street movement, upset that the nation's wealthy were using a government bailout to protect themselves from bad decisions.

Both left and right were correct: the bailout was the very definition of crony capitalism. For a decade, the big banks had been
allowed to reap enormous profits, but now that their bad decisions
were coming home to roost, the taxpayer was being forced to cover
their losses. What other industry could bring down the economy
through malfeasance and get nearly a half trillion in loans to make
sure the key players survived?

Some of today's socialists claim that the capitalism they oppose
is precisely this kind of crony capitalism. Bernie Sanders, to his
credit, voted against the $350 billion bank bailout, although he
did vote for a $15 billion bailout of the automotive industry. It's
difficult to understand how bailing out banks is crony capitalism
but bailing out the billion-dollar car industry is not. Consistency,
though, has never been a big concern for the left.

Progressives are right to decry crony capitalism. However, they
should recognize that socialism is just another form of cronyism.
Byron Schlomach, director of the 1889 Institute, a free-market
think tank in Oklahoma, writes, "crony capitalism is more akin to
socialism than it is to free enterprise. . . ." He is absolutely correct
in this observation.

Schlomach explains:

> Privilege and prosperity of elites side-by-side with unemployment
> and economic stagnation perfectly describes socialist economies
> like Cuba and Venezuela. There, government officials and
> their favored cronies do well while the masses languish. Then-
> expatriated Soviet historian Michael Voslensky's 1984 book
> "Nomenklatura" described the privileged class of party elites in
> the Soviet Union, who enjoyed lives of relative ease and luxury. He
> pointed out that every sort of class exploitation Marx and Lenin
> accused the capitalist system of committing occurred in the Soviet
> Union, in spades, and was committed by communist leaders.[1]

When Alexandria Ocasio-Cortez complains about special tax breaks for Amazon, she needs to understand that she is complaining about markets not being free enough. As Schlomach explains: when "government rewards some businesses and not others with tax breaks or outright subsidies, it is a socialistic practice. Whether or not they actually succeed, government officials are attempting to control the flow of resources in our economy with state and local economic development deals. By definition, this is socialistic, because socialism involves, after all, government control of resources."

Today's socialists compound their error by failing to realize that socialism also grants privileges to a new class of elites: government planners. As Schlomach explains: to "those who see socialism as a counter to the elitism they see in capitalist economies, think again. History teaches that, due to socialism's centralized nature, there is no place more replete with cronyism than one practicing socialism."[2] In other words, there is no bigger elite than a government elite.

Another rallying cry of the new socialists is that "the rich" aren't paying enough in taxes. In the shining face of increased prosperity, reduced poverty, and record-low unemployment in America, Bernie and the gang are reduced to using "income inequality" as their evidence of capitalist failure. After all, it is unfair that we can't all live like Beyoncé and Jay-Z.

Our socialist friends conveniently ignore the fact that our top 1 percent of income earners already pays nearly 40 percent of our income tax revenue and the top 10 percent pays nearly 70 percent of the total.[3] And yet Bernie and other liberal millionaires and billionaires like Warren Buffett, Howard Schultz, and Bill Gates frequently whine and opine that they should be paying more to the U.S. government. They wring their hands in frustration at the injustice of their inability to pay more money.

Fortunately, Adam Brandon, president of FreedomWorks, gave these wealthy victims a simple solution to this vexing problem with a link to the donation page PayYourFairShareFirst.com. He wrote in the *Washington Examiner*, "Why wait for Congress to demand more money? The federal government has a donation page available right now for these economic altruists to lead by example." FreedomWorks even tweeted the website link to Gates, Buffett, Bernie, and the gang to ensure that they were fully aware that there was nothing standing in their way of paying more to Uncle Sam. Not one of them responded to the opportunity.

As Brandon wrote,

> *Is it possible they are not being sincere? After all, Bill Gates led Microsoft while it moved profits offshore to dodge billions of dollars in taxes. Howard Schultz cofounded a venture capital group that invested in a financial firm that helped wealthy people dodge hundreds of millions in taxes. For decades, Warren Buffett avoided paying billions of dollars in taxes by taking advantage of what is now called the "Buffett Loophole." . . . Remind me again, which political party is the party of big business? Sorry, Sen. Elizabeth Warren, but the "robber barons" of the 21st century are voting Democrat, not Republican. When big business colludes with Big Government, it happens at the expense of the rest of us. . . . Yet, Democrats want to force millions of families into a complicated tax code that wastes time and hard-earned money. Why? Because they feel guilty for being rich. The solution to their guilt is a therapist, not a tax hike. Regular families can't afford teams of lawyers and lobbyists dedicated to avoiding taxes. We work hard and play by the rules. If Democrats want to punish themselves with extra taxes, they can make a voluntary donation to the federal government and leave us out of it.*[4]

Chapter 35

IF SOCIALISTS CAN'T
FIND A CRISIS,
THEY WILL CREATE ONE

ost socialist governments rise up claiming to be the solution to a widespread economic disaster, such as peasants starving while corrupt leaders wage pointless wars. However, today's socialists have to overcome the longest economic expansion in American history.

When Alexandria Ocasio-Cortez arrived in Washington, she set off a race on the left to see who could endorse the most extreme proposals. If you first heard about the "Green New Deal" by word of mouth, you might be forgiven if your initial impression was one of disbelief.

The cost alone is mind-boggling. Former Congressional Budget Office (CBO) director Douglas Holtz-Eakin estimates that the low-carbon electricity grid alone will cost $5.4 trillion. The "New Zero Emissions Transportation System" will cost about $2 trillion. Ocasio-Cortez's program for a "guaranteed job for everyone"—somewhere between $6.8 trillion and $44.6 trillion. Wow!

"Medicare for All"—over $30 trillion. Guaranteed Green Housing, $1.6 to $4.2 trillion, and "Food Security," $1.5 billion. Anybody else alarmed that the projects are so grandiose that the cost can only be approximated to within a few trillion dollars?

But is the Green New Deal socialism? Let's consider how AOC and Bernie and their merry troupe of socialists will accomplish their dream. How and who will close down the fossil fuel factories? What government SWAT team will shut down the automobile manufacturers and the gas stations? Who will force the people from their current homes into "green living quarters"?

And what about all those carbon-producing cows? AOC is ready with an answer. In the outline she and Senator Edward Markey released, they explained that they "set a goal to get to net-zero, rather than zero emissions, in 10 years because we aren't sure that we'll be able to fully get rid of farting cows and airplanes that fast."[1]

Don't laugh. California is well on its way to regulating cows out of existence. According to the *Los Angeles Times,* the San Joaquin Valley Air Pollution Control District claims that "gases from ruminating dairy cows, not exhaust from cars, are the region's biggest single source of a chief smog-forming pollutant."[2]

It would be funny if these climate change alarmists weren't serious. It's not only cows these crazies want to eliminate, but humans as well. CO_2 exhalers—aka all animals, including humans—are a big part of the problem, according to environmentalist Diane Francis. Writing at the Canadian *National Post,* she claims that "the world's other species, vegetation, resources, oceans, arable land, water supplies and atmosphere are being destroyed and pushed out of existence as a result of humanity's soaring reproduction rate."

Francis's answer? She believes that a "planetary law, such as China's one-child policy, is the only way to reverse the disastrous global birthrate currently, which is one million births every four days."[3]

Think about that. In addition to eliminating the belching cows, some environmental extremists actually propose emulating China's mass abortion and mandatory reproductive limitations.

Beyond the mind-boggling costs and outright lunacy of restricting the populations of humans and cows, the Green New Deal also promises a primary goal of socialism—communal ownership.

AOC's legislative resolution calls for "providing and leveraging, in a way that ensures that the public receives appropriate ownership stakes . . . [in] businesses working on the Green New Deal mobilization," as well as "community ownership" in "local and regional economies."

The original overview released for the Green New Deal also offered a guaranteed job and income even for those "unable or unwilling" to work. The concept of a universal basic income (UBI) is not new. Even such libertarian stalwarts as Hayek and Milton Friedman succumbed to the allure of distributing welfare in a less destructive way.[4]

We already have a variant of universal basic income in the form of the Earned Income Tax Credit and the Child Tax Credit. Together the government spends about $100 billion each year on refundable tax credits that are really "tax credits" in name only—as the payments are not limited to taxes that an individual has paid. In other words, these tax credits are simply a transfer payment from other workers. As Robert Bellafiore writes at TaxFoundation.org, "Today, tax credits provide a negative income tax rate to the bottom two quintiles, causing their income to increase."[5]

Even though Milton Friedman promoted the concept, he likely would blanch at what the program has become. The Cato Institute has reported that there is a 25 percent fraud rate in the Child Tax Credit program, costing around $6 billion annually.[6] There have been repeated allegations that the Child Tax Credit program does not require proof of legal residence in the United States and that illegal aliens use the program to receive what are essentially welfare payments. In addition, because the government does not require

Social Security numbers for the children claimed, it is very easy to claim nonexistent children in order to defraud the American taxpayer.

José Niño writes at Mises.org that proponents of these tax credits fail to understand Frederic Bastiat's "concept of the 'seen and the unseen'":

> When a transfer policy like the UBI is implemented, what is seen is the transfer of money from one sector of the economy to humbler sectors. However, what is not seen is the money that productive sectors of the economy lose out on. Under normal circumstances, this same money would otherwise be allocated towards business expansion and other ventures that increase worker output and worker incomes.[7]

Indeed, the bigger this transfer program becomes, the more money is drained away from productive enterprises that create sustainable jobs supported by consumer interest in their services or products.

Conservatives who support refundable tax credits often support them as an alternative to the high bureaucratic costs of our current welfare state. But inevitably, these tax credits have accumulated on top of and in addition to all of the other welfare programs.

A guaranteed job or income may sound appealing but it is simply another variant of the fallacy of "something for nothing" and should be rejected.

Today's socialists present the Green New Deal as absolutely necessary for the world's survival. It's not as if we aren't already spending exorbitant sums to ward off this "devastating military attack," as Bernie describes climate change. *Forbes* magazine estimated that in Obama's first term we spent $150 billion on subsidies for green energy projects and to combat climate change—plus another $8–$10 billion in wind and solar tax credits. Not to mention a few more billion dollars spent by states that require their utility companies to purchase costly "green" energy.[8]

Around the world the money spent on climate change is truly staggering. In 2013 the Climate Policy Initiative reported that "global investment in climate change" reached $359 billion that year. And yet, the CPI declared that the sum "falls far short of what's needed." How much is needed, you ask? They suggest a modest $5 *trillion*.[9]

So what are we getting for all this money? According to Stephen Moore, Senior Fellow at The Heritage Foundation, "the real scandal of the near trillion dollars that governments have stolen from taxpayers to fund climate change hysteria and research [is that,] by the industry's own admission, there has been almost no progress worldwide in combating climate change."

Trillions of taxpayer dollars transferred to government-favored "green" industries and the climate alarmists continue to beat the drum for more money.

The "green socialists" are never satisfied. As Moore explains, the "green socialists" believe "the only 'solution' is for the world to stop using fossil fuels, which is like saying that we should stop growing food."[10]

Consider this quote from former United Nations climate official Ottmar Edenhofer who co-chaired the UN Intergovernmental Panel on Climate Change working group on Mitigation of Climate Change from 2008–2015:

"One has to free oneself from the illusion that international climate policy is environmental policy. This has almost nothing to do with the environmental policy anymore, with problems such as deforestation or the ozone hole.

"We redistribute de facto the world's wealth by climate policy," said Edenhofer.

He described the world climate summit in Cancun, Mexico, as "actually an economy summit during which the distribution of the world's resources will be negotiated." At least he is being honest about his objective.[11]

Edenhofer's goals are certainly not the exception. In 2015, Christiana Figueres, executive secretary of the UN's Framework Convention on Climate Change, made the following statement:

> *This is probably the most difficult task we have ever given ourselves,*
> *which is to intentionally transform the economic development*
> *model for the first time in human history. This is the first time*
> *in the history of mankind that we are setting ourselves the task*
> *of intentionally, within a defined period of time, to change the*
> *economic development model that has been reigning for at least*
> *150 years, since the Industrial Revolution.*[12]

Figueres's lofty language reveals a breathtaking ignorance of the "historic transformations" brought about by Stalin and Mao.

In their own words, climate alarmists are using the "crisis" of climate change to scare people into relinquishing the freedom and prosperity of capitalism in exchange for a global socialist welfare state.

Basically they want to let poor, undeveloped countries emit unlimited carbon dioxide. After all, as even Edenhofer acknowledged, "in order to get rich one has to burn coal, oil or gas." And they want to put heavy carbon restrictions on developed countries like the United States. While that will slow our economy and limit our freedom, Edenhofer thinks we deserve it because we "have basically expropriated the atmosphere of the world community."[13]

None of which is to say that we shouldn't make every effort to curb pollution. In fact, the United States actually is successfully reducing pollution. The dirtiest decade in America's history was likely at the height of the Industrial Revolution. Most emission levels are down, dramatically so for mercury and sulfur dioxide. Even the Environmental Protection Agency (EPA) admits that over the past two decades, American emissions have fallen 7.5 percent. According to the BP Statistical Review of World Energy, the United States actually reduced CO_2 more than any other nation in 2017.[14]

The problem is that China and India have not slowed their emissions. As Steve Moore writes at the *Washington Times*, "For every ton of reduced pollution the United States emits, China and India produce almost 10 more tons. This means it doesn't really matter how much America reduces its greenhouse gases because China and India cancel out any and all progress we make."

Climate change advocates agree that the problem is a worldwide one, thus their advocacy for the Paris Accord that President Trump did not join, to great condemnation from the left. Yet, as Moore points out, "Not a single EU [European Union] nation is within 80 percent of its respective target for emission reduction, according to Climate Action Network Europe (CANE). In its official EU report, CANE said, 'All EU countries are failing to increase their climate action in line with the Paris Agreement goal.'" It's telling that we do not hear much about the shortcomings of our European friends, who are often portrayed in the media as being more progressive on climate change.[15]

Chapter 36

SOCIALISM AND CLIMATE CHANGE ALARMISM GO TOGETHER

Even the most ardent climate change alarmists acknowledge that this debate is about more than pollution or temperature changes. To many climate activists, it's really about replacing capitalism with socialism.

Self-identified socialist and *Grist* columnist Eric Holthaus makes no bones about the true goal of climate change politics. He tweeted, "If you are wondering what you can do about climate change: The world's top scientists just gave rigorous backing to systematically dismantle capitalism as a key requirement to maintaining civilization and a habitable planet."[1]

In other words, nothing to debate here. The scientific consensus is that the planet can only be saved by eliminating capitalism.

Socialist Matthew Huber, in his essay "Five Principles of a Socialist Climate Politics," writes that "the climate struggle is less about knowledge and more about a material struggle for power."[2]

He argues that "[c]limate change is a class problem." To Huber, "this seems obvious enough. Rich people are responsible for causing climate change and the poorest bear the costs of droughts, rising seas, and floods."

For socialists like Huber, "your carbon footprint is not really the problem." He contends that the problem is not just pollution, but that capitalism allows "profit from the production of the commodities you consume." His answer: "nationalizing the fossil fuel industry." (So much for their claim that they really don't want Venezuelan-style socialism . . .)

The Green New Deal is presented by today's socialists as absolutely necessary for the world's survival. To them, the science is settled and there is no room for debate. Anyone with the temerity to question is labeled a heretic, a "climate change denier."

The notion that an issue is settled and that dissent will not be tolerated is the epitome of "groupthink." Irving Janis, who invented the term "groupthink," warned that "the more amiability and esprit de corps there is among the members of a policy-making in-group, the greater the danger that independent critical thinking will be replaced by groupthink. . . ."

To label the enthusiasm of climate change activists as "esprit de corps" is likely an understatement.

In a disturbing example, NBC's *Meet the Press* host Chuck Todd announced, "We're not going to give time to climate deniers. The science is settled, even if political opinion is not."[3] These "climate deniers" include science Nobel laureates as well as a recipient of NASA's Medal for Exceptional Scientific Achievement. But *Meet the Press* doesn't want to confuse us with the scientific findings of those Luddites—after all, it's a bigger ratings boost to feature AOC announcing that the world will end in twelve years! When our major media outlets close their minds and refuse to offer both sides of complex subjects, we should all be concerned.

In response to the *Meet the Press* pronouncement, Michael Guillen, Ph.D., who holds degrees from both UCLA and Cornell in physics, mathematics, and astronomy and was an award-winning physics instructor at Harvard for eight years, wrote that "if you are absolutely, 100 percent convinced" that "humans are having a decisive, apocalyptic impact on the climate," then "you have a right to say your mind is settled, or your politics are settled. But never say the science of this or any equally complex subject is 'settled.'"

He continued with a history lesson for *Meet the Press*'s producers. "[A]s everyone now knows, Einstein—like Copernicus, Galileo, and scores of other vindicated 'deniers' over the centuries—ultimately disproved the vaunted scientific consensus. . . . But, above all, heed Einstein's wise words about how science really works. 'No amount of experimentation can ever prove me right,' he observed, 'a single experiment can prove me wrong.'"[4]

For instance, cofounder and fifteen-year leader of Greenpeace Patrick Moore, Ph.D., and zoologist Susan Crockford, Ph.D., write that "the 2007 prediction that two-thirds of the world's polar bears would disappear when summer sea ice declined dramatically has obviously failed. It is ironic that activists have long insisted that polar bears are endangered by loss of ice created by human-caused climate change. In fact, both polar bear and walrus populations have increased dramatically in recent decades due largely to restrictions on hunting."[5]

Researchers also are finding evidence that the loss of glaciers may not be as dramatic as predicted. According to a March 2019 article in *National Geographic*, "NASA's Oceans Melting Greenland (OMG) project has revealed Greenland's Jakobshavn Glacier, the island's biggest, is actually growing, at least at its edge." The article quotes NASA oceanographer Josh Willis: "The thinking was once glaciers start retreating, nothing's stopping them. We've found out that's not true."[6]

This is a noteworthy acknowledgment in the era of "settled science." No word yet from AOC on whether this has altered her claim that "[t]he world is gonna end in 12 years if we don't address climate change."[7]

Dr. Moore, however, reminds us that "predictions that 'we only have 10 years left' began in 1989 and have continued unabated ever since . . ." and yet as each apocalyptic deadline approaches and passes it becomes necessary to establish new timelines for world-ending events. "To the contrary," Moore and Crockford write, "NASA has recently demonstrated conclusively from satellite records that our CO_2 emissions are greening the Earth. This has resulted in higher yields in agriculture and forestry, and more efficient use of water by vegetation generally. In fact, there is nothing occurring in weather or climate today that is anywhere near out of the ordinary with the past 10,000 years of this Holocene Interglacial Period."

The same alarmist proclamations followed by unapologetic corrections attaches to predictions on global temperatures.

Recently the United Nations Intergovernmental Panel on Climate Change released a study predicting worldwide extinction of thousands of species if the average global temperature rises 2 degrees Celsius by 2040. The *New York Times,* never shy about spreading alarm, predicted "a world of worsening food shortages and wildfires, and a mass die-off of coral reefs as soon as 2040—a period well within the lifetime of much of the global population."[8]

Meanwhile, Chris Mooney and Brady Dennis at the *Washington Post* reported that climate scientists recently had to admit that their predictions on rising global temperatures "contained inadvertent errors that made their conclusions seem more certain than they actually are."

British mathematician Nicholas Lewis discovered that the climate scientists were "biasing up significantly, nearly 30 percent, the central estimate."[9]

As Mooney and Dennis point out: "Lewis has argued in past studies and commentaries that climate scientists are predicting too much warming because of their reliance on computer simulations, and that current data from the planet itself suggests global warming will be less severe than feared."[10]

Seems like even the vaunted "scientific consensus" occasionally accepts its comeuppance. Why is it a big deal if a prediction is off a degree or two? The secret is to follow the money. William Nordhaus of Yale estimates that the cost of keeping global temperature rise to 2.5 degrees Celsius over the next eighty years would be $134 trillion. So, if climate predictors are off by one degree, and we accept their predictions, we are talking about trillions and trillions of dollars in cost.[11]

Even the official UN mouthpiece for climate change, the Intergovernmental Panel on Climate Change, acknowledges that predicting global temperatures a hundred years from now is not an exact science. In a 2001 report, the IPCC concluded, "The long-term prediction of future climate states is not possible."[12]

The climate alarmists have managed to turn a general consensus that something is happening, and humans are causing at least part of it, into a false 100 percent consensus that catastrophic things are happening, and humans can stop it.

When climate alarmists wail and gnash their teeth over rising ocean levels, I like to remind them that the oceans rose some four hundred feet in the last twenty thousand years, well before man began burning fossil fuels. I remind them that once upon a time people walked across the Bering Strait, now covered by four hundred feet of ocean.[13] Perhaps nature itself has something to do with climate change?

If you really want to challenge the climate change alarmists, ask them to name the three main causes of geologic climate change or if they've heard of the Milankovic cycles.

In the 1920s, the Serbian geophysicist and astronomer Milutin Milankovic proposed three reasons to explain the extreme climate change cycles in the earth's history.

1. The earth's tilt varies over long periods of time and when the earth is more tilted the climate is colder.
2. The earth's tilt wobbles (axial precession), so the direction of the tilt varies and when the direction of the tilt is more completely away from the sun in winter, the climate is colder.
3. The earth's orbit is eccentric and varies over long periods of time. Currently, the earth is closer to the sun in winter. Over long cycles of time the earth ends up being farthest away from the sun during winter.

To this day, no science has disproved Milankovic's insights. My question to the alarmists is, how much of climate change is related to nature and how much to man? The alarmists gaze back confused at the question. I egg them on—"no, really, what percentage? Is climate change 90 percent nature or 90 percent man or perhaps we don't know?"

The global warming crowd admits no such ambiguity. John P. Reisman writes at OSS Foundation, "It is safe to say that virtually 100% of this warming event is human induced, caused, or instigated by human industrial processes and output of industrial Green House Gases."[14]

Yet Reisman admits elsewhere on the foundation website that global warming is both a natural cycle and affected by human influence. "What does the science say? Both are true. In the natural cycle, the world can warm, and cool, without any human interference."

So, Reisman and his fellow travelers admit that the climate has a natural cycle but they are certain that the current warming trend is 100 percent from man for two main reasons:

According to Reisman: "In the natural cycle, the Milankovitch cycles lead the change and most everything else follows. The difference is that in the natural cycle CO_2 lags behind the warming because it is mainly due to the Milankovitch cycles. Now CO_2 is leading the warming. Current warming is clearly not natural cycle."

(This may be true, unless the overall trend in temperature over the next thousand years turns out to be colder temperatures—then rises in CO_2 will have been seen to lag behind warming.)

Their second reason for believing that climate change is 100 percent human caused is that historically ice ages last about 80,000–90,000 years and intervening warm periods last about 10,000–20,000 years. Currently, we are thought to be past the peak of the Milankovic warming cycle and headed back toward another ice age. Climate change advocates believe that the last forty years of warming indicate a reversal of the cooling trend that should be occurring.

But it also may be true that the recent forty-year history of temperatures rising are simply a temporary reversal of the cooling trend. Historical data show that climate change is easily seen to trend up and down when viewed on a timeline of thousands of years but when viewed on a timeline of single years, temperatures often reverse direction for hundreds of years.

Unfortunately, a rational discussion of how much of climate change stems from natural causes and how much from man is increasingly disallowed.

I worry that such closed-mindedness threatens the level of skepticism and curiosity that true scientific inquiry requires. It seems that the intellectually honest answer—"we don't know exactly how much of the cause is nature and how much is man-made"—is becoming impossible given the religiosity of the debate.

It is important to note that very few skeptics of climate change dogma, myself included, deny that man-made emissions play a role in climate change. Skeptics simply want to continue to examine the question before spending trillions of dollars on predictions that continue to evolve with each new study.

So, the next time a young socialist comes up to scold you for driving an SUV or riding on a plane or eating a hamburger, ask them if they've heard of the Milankovic cycles.

Considering the desire of so many in the climate change industry to silence debate, as well as their antipathy toward capitalism, one has to wonder if there is another motive behind their efforts . . . Perhaps global redistribution of wealth or a worldwide socialist welfare state?

Chapter 37

SOCIALIST GREEN
NEW DEAL ALLOWS
FOR NO DISSENT

The Soviets were not very subtle with their propaganda. When the state owns all media outlets, dissent becomes a crime. Isaak Babel, the Russian writer whom the Soviets executed in 1940, once made this remark concerning the pervasiveness of Soviet surveillance and control of speech: "Today a man only talks freely to his wife—at night, with the blankets pulled over his head." My wife, Kelley, and I sometimes feel the same way, never knowing when our iPhones are eavesdropping.[1]

Robert Conquest, in *Reflections on a Ravaged Century*, describes the Soviet propaganda regime: "The censorship body, GLAVIT, is believed to have employed seventy thousand full time staff, concerned not merely to eliminate incorrect facts and promote correct falsehood but also to ensure that the correct ideological spin was put on every published item."[2]

Today we don't have central government control of thought and speech, but between the spin of the cable news networks and the political correctness of the social media networks we are approaching a state where people are becoming afraid to voice their true opinions except under cover of blankets.

In November 2018, Twitter permanently banned Canadian

feminist Meghan Murphy for asserting that "men are not women." According to Twitter, such statements "violate their rules against hateful conduct."

"What is insane to me," Murphy wrote in response to her Twitter ban:

> ... is that while Twitter knowingly permits graphic pornography and death threats on the platform (I have reported countless violent threats, the vast majority of which have gone unaddressed), they won't allow me to state very basic facts, such as "men aren't women."
>
> This is hardly an abhorrent thing to say, nor should it be considered "hateful" to ask questions about the notion that people can change sex, or ask for explanations about transgender ideology. These are now, like it or not, public debates—debates that are impacting people's lives, as legislation and policy are being imposed based on gender identity ideology. . . . [3]

God forbid anyone on Twitter have the audacity to refer to the name Bruce Jenner, which is verboten and considered "deadnaming," using a transgender person's legal or birth name. Murphy was guilty of this crime also.

In contrast, consider Democrat Pennsylvania state representative Brian Sims, who aggressively yelled at and filmed three girls, ages thirteen and fifteen, who were quietly praying on the sidewalk outside a Planned Parenthood. This forty-year-old man, a hulking former football player and elected official, tweeted video of the girls while saying, "I'll give $100 to anyone who can identify these three." He verbally attacked the girls for both their faith and their racial ethnicity in the video, while encouraging his followers to dox them. How was this not considered a threat to the safety of these young girls?

Doxing individuals with whom you disagree on social media is threatening behavior, pure and simple. It is potentially a dangerous call to action for unstable and violent people. Sims's attempt to dox was especially outrageous considering that it was against children. Twitter did nothing. The mainstream media was completely silent, despite hundreds of tweets at CNN to report on this elected official's disturbing behavior.

The next month the bearded brute was back, proudly tweeting video of himself stalking and intimidating an elderly lady praying the rosary outside of the same building. For over eight minutes Representative Sims bullied and castigated the diminutive woman, repeatedly insulting her as "an old white lady" while she tried to get away from him, shoulders hunched and head lowered against his assault. The video is truly painful to watch. Again, deafening silence from Twitter on whether Sims violated rules against hateful conduct.

Twitter prefers to only censor speech it disagrees with while ignoring egregious, threatening speech and stalking behavior that supports its political point of view. While most of us recoil at any censorship of free speech, Nicole Russell, writing at the *Federalist*, points out the problem: "Of course, Twitter is a private company and can do whatever it likes. But they have billed themselves as an open platform, one that welcomes debate, ideas, and sharing. In an April article about how Twitter turned toxic, *Fast Company* reported that Alex Macgillivray, Twitter's first general counsel, used to say, 'Let the tweets flow.'"[4]

What ever happened to the "live and let live, speak and let speak" attitude of the wide-open public forum of the Internet?

Russell informs us that "[e]ven Amnesty International voiced real disgust with Twitter's lack of policing actually awful tweets: 'Twitter's inconsistency and inaction on its own rules not only creates a level of mistrust and lack of confidence in the company's reporting process, it also sends the message that Twitter does not take violence and abuse against women seriously—a failure which is likely to deter women from reporting in the future.'" To which I would again point to its lack of response to the threatening, ageist, racist, misogynist, and anti-Christian tweets by Brian Sims, despite thousands of complaints demanding action.

Even Twitter's CEO, Jack Dorsey, admits that social media has a "left-leaning" tendency and he acknowledges that conservatives at Twitter "don't feel safe to express their opinion." The question remains: What, if anything, should government do to protect speech on private platforms?[5]

Some Republicans, like Ben Sasse of Nebraska, confuse Internet bans of conservatives by private companies as equivalent to university bans of conservative speakers. Jack Shaffer at *Politico* points out the improper analogy:

> In an unfortunate analogy . . . Sen. Ben Sasse (R-Neb.) compared [Twitter banishing conservatives] to the "de-platforming" in vogue on many liberal campuses these days. There is a huge difference between protesters driving an invited speaker off-campus, which is what happens in de-platforming, and a publisher deciding what content he chooses to print. In the former example, an invited speaker is silenced through coercion. In the latter, a proprietor makes his editorial decision about what he will print. The Washington Post *can't be accused of de-platforming me just because it won't publish my letter.*[6]

Ergo, campus de-platforming is far more concerning than the decisions of private platforms about whom they will host. Conservatives, though, want something done. Isn't there something we can do?

My answer has typically been that government should assiduously remove any governmental barriers to entry for the next

"Twitter" and make certain that there are no governmental protections of monopoly in the social media arena.

Some conservative Internet voices have asked that we reconsider granting legal immunity to social media giants like Facebook and Twitter. The legal immunity prevents users from suing Facebook or Twitter for allowing users to post something that might be libelous. This protection makes sense in that social media could not exist if Facebook or Twitter had to defend a lawsuit every time a poster told someone to "STFU."

However, the legal immunity should not protect Facebook or Twitter from lawsuits concerning their breach of the user agreement. This aspect of legal immunity is currently being examined and may be the cudgel necessary to prevent the situation that Russell believes exists now: "Instead of the 'Thought Police' and 'Big Brother,' now we have Jack Dorsey and Twitter."

Even under current law, it may be possible to file a class action suit against Facebook if they breach their user agreement by sharing information the user never agreed to. If the user agreement were indeed breached, imagine a billion-person class action . . . [7]

It's not just Twitter; Facebook has also jumped on the bandwagon of censoring conservative speech. Michael Nunez at Gizmodo writes:

Facebook workers routinely suppressed news stories of interest to conservative readers from the social network's influential "trending" news section, according to a former journalist who worked on the project. This individual says that workers prevented stories about the right-wing CPAC gathering, Mitt Romney, Rand Paul, and other conservative topics from appearing in the highly-influential section, even though they were organically trending among the site's users.[8]

Facebook is not only blocking conservatives, it is also advancing stories that fit its management's liberal bias.

> *Several former Facebook "news curators," as they were known internally, also told Gizmodo that they were instructed to artificially "inject" selected stories into the trending news module, even if they weren't popular enough to warrant inclusion—or in some cases weren't trending at all. The former curators, all of whom worked as contractors, also said they were directed not to include news about Facebook itself in the trending module.[9]*

But before we empower big government to police private venues of speech, conservatives should examine the issue carefully.

I remember when I was sixteen—a long time ago (1979)—I wrote to the matriarch of the conservative movement—Phyllis Schlafly—opposing the fairness doctrine. Schlafly and other conservatives were mad that the three main television networks were heavily liberal in bias (they were). Conservatives wanted the government to enforce a "fairness doctrine" to guarantee equal time for a conservative point of view.

I remember typing the letter on a typewriter (if you're under age forty-five, Google it). I think I quoted Mises. I never heard back from her, but I still think it's important that conservatives not get so carried away that we throw out the First Amendment rights of companies in the fury over private censorship.

Meanwhile, au courant socialists like Representative Ocasio-Cortez and Representative Chellie Pingree don't seem overly concerned about protecting the First Amendment rights of private companies with whom they disagree. Flexing their power and position as new members of Congress, the two sent a letter to Facebook, Microsoft, and Google criticizing their sponsorship of LibertyCon, a conference hosted by Students for Liberty. The event featured speakers and panels discussing libertarian ideas on a range of topics from the pros and cons of regulating the Internet to universal basic income.

So what was the terrible offense that motivated these Democrat representatives to dash off letters of complaint? LibertyCon featured a presentation by a retired statistics professor from American University who had the audacity to argue that perhaps "there should be a more dispassionate review of the data surrounding climate science, and more room for debate about causes and effects." This idea is, of course, tantamount to "climate change denial," according to Ocasio-Cortez and her ilk, and therefore must be roundly condemned—no, *silenced* at all costs.

In an article for the *Federalist*, Jason Pye and Daniel Savickas wrote, "It's quite upsetting that two members of Congress would take time to send a letter making sure private companies get back in line after they sponsored a conference at which one presentation among dozens did not align with these politicians' opinions on the climate. The conference also featured a debate on the merits of a carbon tax, and included a speaker who made the libertarian case in favor of such a tax."

Calling the Ocasio-Cortez–Pingree letter a "veiled form of intimidation," Pye and Savickas rightly make the point that members of Congress have absolutely no business condemning private companies for sponsoring events that encourage young people to think for themselves about politics, current events, and the role of government. They wrote:

The 19th-century British philosopher John Stuart Mill stated that if an idea "is not fully frequently and fearlessly discussed, it will be held as a dead dogma, not a living truth." If members of Congress take issue with certain opinions, they should be willing to fearlessly discuss them in a public forum, as the attendees of LibertyCon did. They should be confident in their convictions and trust the merits of their arguments. Our leaders who swore an oath to defend the Constitution should not only defend free speech, but be the foremost advocates for open discussion wherever possible.[10]

It is disturbing that, not two months into her official government position, Democratic socialist Ocasio-Cortez was already muscularly engaging in the foremost behavior of historical socialist dictators: the intimidation of private citizens who express viewpoints that government officials do not agree with in order to silence speech.

Liberals like to portray themselves as champions of freedom. However, from economic liberty to freedom of speech, the first individuals to stifle freedoms are usually those same liberals. Just take a look at what is happening on college campuses where conservative speakers and groups are being deplatformed, protested, and intimidated in an effort to silence their viewpoints.

I personally dealt with this when I was a professor for a semester at George Washington University. When my deputy chief of staff, Sergio Gor (who had attended George Washington), helped arrange my class with the administration, many on the faculty vociferously complained that I wasn't qualified to teach an entry-level undergraduate class. The Political Science department didn't want me, and neither did the English department. Finally we settled on my dystopian novel course being an elective without a department. I found it intriguing, however, that the student body was much more receptive, as my course was completely filled and had a lengthy waiting list within a couple of hours.

Our friends Kimberly Guilfoyle and Donald Trump Jr. often

appear on college campuses and have dealt with protests and hateful vitriol. Going a step further, liberals now want to stifle speech online. On his social media, Don has highlighted many examples of followers being muted or blocked by major social media companies in order to suppress conservative speech. Followers have sent screenshots to Don showing that their accounts had automatically unfollowed him without their consent or knowledge.

Instagram even blocked Don Jr. from posting about the Jussie Smollett hoax—which they later claimed was "an error." It takes someone like Kimberly or Don, with over five million followers between them, to raise awareness before accounts get restored.

The visceral hatred on social media contributes to this madness. And when suppressing dissent through the usual channels doesn't work, some resort to more extreme methods. We have seen this poison erupt in both threats of violence and actual violence. I was at the baseball field practicing for the charity congressional baseball game when the shooting occurred in June 2017. I was ten feet from a young staff member as a madman shot him on the right field warning track, just seconds after Steve Scalise was shot in the hip at second base. For a few seconds, I couldn't tell which direction the shots were coming from. I had been standing in the right field batting cage adjacent to the field but separated by a twenty-foot fence.

When the first shot rang out, I thought it might just be an isolated shotgun blast. At home in Kentucky, it's not uncommon for us to hear people hunting or shooting for target practice in the bottomland surrounding our neighborhood.

There were about twenty congressmen and senators present and a half-dozen staffers helping. Seconds after the first shot was fired, I heard the sounds of rapid fire as more than a hundred shots rang out. I escaped the batting cage and found cover behind a large willow oak next to it.

As I crouched among the large roots of the tree, two staffers were running from left field close to the shooter toward me as fast as they could. The shooter fired at them the entire way as they ran along the warning track to right field. One of them was hit as he dove into the dirt just on the other side of the twenty-foot fence dividing us.

The other young man scaled the fence in less than five seconds amid gunfire. The staff member who had been shot in the calf made his way toward the first base dugout.

Finally, after what seemed like eternity but was likely only about three or four minutes, the heroic Capitol Hill police and Alexandria police began to return fire. The three of us behind the willow oak made a dash for it over a fence, across a soccer field, and into the street, where by chance a Capitol Hill staffer on his way to work stopped in the middle of the road and picked us up.

I consider myself to be in good shape, but I was struggling to breathe to the point that they all asked if I was okay. As our nerves thawed and our hearts quit beating out of our chests, I realized that I was still wearing my batting helmet. One of the staffers said that he heard the shooter yelling, "This is for health care." Later we would find out that the shooter had a history of anger and violence, including bashing his neighbor in the face with the butt of a rifle. We also learned that he was a rabid Bernie Sanders fan.

I don't point that out in any way, shape, or form to blame Bernie or folks on the left for inciting the shooting that nearly cost Steve Scalise his life. (His entire blood supply was replaced in the first twenty-four hours after the shooting and it is a miracle he is alive. He does, however, live with very significant permanent injuries.)

I refer to this terrible episode not because it is the fault of the left or the right but because both sides need to acknowledge that in a country of 330 million citizens there are unstable, violent people among us and we must all consider our rhetoric when debating what we believe is best for the country.

I was the victim of politically motivated violence not once but twice in 2017. I was viciously and cowardly attacked from behind while working in my yard wearing noise-canceling headphones to protect my hearing from the mower. The assailant was a vocal Internet hater of President Trump who also was known about town as a critic of my opposition to socialized medicine. Despite the fact that my attacker admitted to the police and the courts to having zero communication of any kind with me or any member of my family for more than a decade (other than a casual wave from the car when we rarely spotted him), his legal team's spin that we were in an "ongoing lawn care dispute" was repeatedly stated in the media as fact.

I suffered six broken ribs, three of them displaced fractures. In a displaced fracture, the ends of ribs grind upon each other until they began to fuse. I won't go through the gory details of two pneumonias, a pulmonary contusion, and fluid and blood leaking around my lung. Add to that my cell number and home address being doxed during the Kavanaugh hearings, and a California man threatening to kill me and my family with an ax, and I had a bad year.

I don't blame anyone on the left for the violence of the man who attacked me. I actually blame the media for stoking and exaggerating the country's differences and making them personal, even more so since the election of President Trump.

Today the media feels justified in accusing the president's supporters of hatred, violence, and bigotry, to the point of blind acceptance and false reporting of hoax hate crimes such as the staged "lynching" of actor Jussie Smollett, a fake attack that left the "victim" with no injuries and yet was described as "brutal," "harrowing," and "chilling" for weeks in the media. Before the truth was revealed, Ocasio-Cortez actually criticized some in the media for referring to the hoax as only a "possible" hate crime. Representative Rashida Tlaib, the poster child for hostile incivility when she shouted that we should "impeach the motherf***er" in reference to President Trump, wrote, "the right wing is killing and hurting our people." Senators Kamala Harris and Cory Booker both called the attack "an attempted modern day lynching" while simultaneously pushing for their new antilynching legislation.

GQ quickly published an article condemning the Smollett "crime" that argued that "the racist, homophobic attack on Smollett is Far Right America's endgame." For comparison, consider that after I was attacked and suffered six broken ribs and a pleural effusion of my lung that led to two serious cases of pneumonia, GQ gleefully headlined its story on my assault with this: "Rand Paul Sounds Like the Worst Person to Have as a Neighbor." Their bias is breathtaking.

In an article for *National Review* titled "Hate-Crime Hoaxes Reflect America's Sickness," Andy Ngo wrote:

Jussie Smollett's hoax is symptomatic of America's illness. Because of the mainstreaming of academia's victimhood culture we are now in a place where we place more value on being a victim than on being heroic, charitable, or even kind. Victims or victim groups high on intersectionality points are supposed to be coveted, treated with child gloves, and believed unreservedly. Their "lived experience" gives them infinite wisdom. Those who urge caution are treated as bigots.[11]

It wasn't just the Jussie Smollett hoax. There was the vandalization of an Indiana church painted with homophobic slurs and pro-Trump language—which turned out to be the work of the church's gay organist, who hoped to "mobilize a movement." Or what about extensive coverage of the Muslim woman who falsely claimed that a group of Trump supporters attempted to tear off her hijab in an attack at a New York subway station? Or the Michigan woman who falsely claimed a white man "threatened to set her on fire if she did not remove her hijab"? All of these stories were breathlessly reported in the media as evidence of Trump supporters' violence and viciousness. All were false. We are in an age of new propaganda, where the media's power rivals that of the state.[12]

Chapter 38

FAKE NEWS AND PROPAGANDA ON THE RISE IN AMERICA

There is probably no more egregious example of the Internet's mob vigilantism and the media's stoking of those flames than the grossly inaccurate, in many cases deliberately false, reporting of the scene at the Lincoln Memorial between the teenagers from Covington Catholic High School in Kentucky, the Black Israelite hate group, and the Native American activist Nathan Phillips. By seizing on only a small clip of nearly one hundred minutes of video and ignoring all context, the media, led by the *New York Times* and the *Washington Post*, reported that the boys were "mobbing and taunting" the Native Americans. The *New York Times* headline blared "Boys in MAGA Hats Mob Native Elder at Indigenous Peoples March." Twitter lit up with celebrities and pundits rushing to condemn the boys, trying to outdo one another with their righteousness, their indignation, and their outrage.

It grew uglier and uglier. Mere words would not suffice; calls for violence ensued. Prominent actors, writers, and pundits of all stripes were screaming for the boys and their parents to be doxed, to be physically attacked, to be sexually molested. CNN legal analyst Bakari Sellers fantasized about the sixteen-year-old's "punchable face," as did the former CNN personality Reza Aslan. CNN pundit Ana Navarro called them "asswipes" and *Saturday Night Live* writer Sarah Beattie offered oral sex to anyone who "manages to punch the MAGA kid in the face." These calls for violence were coming from highly privileged, highly paid, ostensibly well-educated adults in America's media today. None were fired or even criticized by CNN or *SNL* for their embarrassingly lowbrow calls for violent attacks on teenagers.

In the cesspool of social media our famous and respected journalists and actors called for violence against a sixteen-year-old kid for his "privilege," and his "white smirking face." I wonder who has more "privilege" in America today—these wealthy and influential actors and media personalities or a high school kid from a small town in Kentucky where the average family income is $42,000 a year?

Soon more details came to light as people started posting the full video. My friend Congressman Thomas Massie refused to be cowed by the torch-and-pitchfork mob and immediately stood up for his constituents in a series of tweets and retweets of Robby Soave's excellent article in *Reason* magazine. Anyone who watched the full video could see and hear the racist, homophobic, and filthy bile that had been spewed at both the boys and the Native Americans by the Black Israelites, a recognized hate group.

The Black Israelites can be seen antagonizing the Native Americans during their ceremony, using a bullhorn to amplify their racist insults, calling them "drunkards in the casinos," "savages," and "Uncle Tomahawks." They ridiculed their religious and cultural beliefs as "idol worship of buffalos and eagles." When a Native American woman attempted to stop their abuse, the Black Israelites yelled back, "Where's your husband? Let me speak to him."

The boys, who were waiting for their bus, were seen standing and watching the men from a distance, saying nothing. And then the Black Israelites, a group of grown men, started spewing their hatred at the boys, calling them "faggots, incest survivors, and dirty ass crackers." They called a black Covington student the n-word and shouted that his classmates were going to eat his organs.

The boys never responded in kind. When the Black Israelites yelled, "President Trump is a homosexual . . . It says on the back of the dollar bill that 'In God We Trust,' and you give faggots rights," the boys started booing and a couple of them yelled back, "That's racist, bro"; "That's rude"; "We don't judge you." Indeed, the kids were remarkably composed in what was undoubtedly a confusing and embarrassing situation, especially for teenagers, as passersby heard them being attacked on a loudspeaker by this group of aggressive men. It's not as if the kids had an option to leave the area, since the Lincoln Memorial was the meeting point for their bus.[1]

The boys asked for permission to sing their school spirit cheers to drown out the hateful language being hurled at them while they waited for the bus. Anyone who has ever attended a sports game against a Catholic boys school knows that these kids have a series of loud, boisterous, funny cheers, usually led by one or two shirtless boys. These pep rally cheers are part of the spirit and culture of these schools, something my family and I enjoyed watching from our apartment balcony overlooking the Gonzaga College High School football field in Washington.

The boys were already dancing, whooping, and hollering when Native American activist Nathan Phillips did not take the most convenient route to the top of the memorial, which he claimed was his objective, but suddenly veered left and walked right into the center of the boys' group, beating his drum. Some of the boys were bewildered by his sudden appearance, and can be heard saying,

"What is happening?" in the video. Other boys understandably assumed that Phillips was showing his support to them in their attempt to drown out the invective from the Black Israelites—after all, they had both been verbally attacked by the same vile group of men for the last hour.

The point is, the kids were clearly dancing and whooping well before Phillips walked into their midst. They continued dancing and cheering to the beat of his drum as he entered their space and stopped to beat his drum within a few inches of the face of sixteen-year-old Nick Sandmann. It is worth noting that, in the video, Sandmann is standing on a higher step while Phillips beats the drum in his face, which is the only reason that they appear to be eye to eye. This boy, or "beast" as Phillips described him to the media, is a head shorter than Phillips.

The fact is, the Covington boys did not approach Nathan Phillips and his fellow Native Americans at all, much less "mob, taunt, and surround" them as they were conducting a sacred ceremony. This lie was repeated over and over, even after many of Nathan Phillips's statements were found to be utterly untrue or misleading, including his claims to be a "recon ranger" and a "Vietnam times veteran." He falsely claimed to be a Vietnam veteran in a video posted to the Native Youth Alliance Facebook page in January of 2018.

Once the larger story and video proof became undeniable, one would have expected more of a mea culpa from the media, but the "clarifications" were tepid at best. After falsely smearing minors with "Boys in MAGA Hats Mob Native American Elder at Indigenous Peoples March," the *New York Times* put forth the lame and cowardly "Fuller Picture Emerges of Viral Video of Native American Man and Catholic Students."

As Caitlin Flanagan wrote in the *Atlantic*, "CNN, apparently by now aware that the event had taken place within a complicating larger picture, tried to use the new information to support its own biased interpretation, sorrowfully reporting that early in the afternoon the boys had clashed with 'four African American young men preaching about the Bible and oppression.'" CNN, the *New York Times*, the *Washington Post*, and their countless parrots were all loath to correct a reported story, however false, that so neatly tied their hatred for President Trump, "toxic masculinity," and "white privilege" into a convenient box.[2]

Shockingly, even days after the nearly one hundred minutes of YouTube footage exonerated the students, CNN's Chris Cuomo was still sanctimoniously shaming and lecturing the boys and their parents on national television, while refusing to fully report on the racist, sexist, and homophobic taunts by the Black Israelites, the true instigators. He briefly described the Black Israelites' words as "unduly provocative." Cuomo's tepid description of their hateful, repugnant language was combined with his continued reverence for Nathan Phillips, despite the proven falsehoods in his statements, such as his description of the boys as "beasts" and the Black Israelite agitators as "their prey."[3]

It is not surprising, then, that data from a Pew Research Center poll of over 5,000 people shows that over two-thirds of Americans consider the media to be biased and 58 percent believe that the news media "do not understand people like them." Sixty-eight percent of Americans believe that journalists and reporters have bias toward one side in political and social issues. These numbers are even starker for Republicans, where the polls show 86 percent believing in reporter bias versus 52 percent of Democrats.[4]

To their credit, some of the actors and journalists apologized for their rush to judgment and tweeted honest regret for their digital vitriol against the boys. Rich Lowry, Jamie Lee Curtis, and

Kara Swisher come to mind. But others took the coward's way out and deleted their nasty tweets with no apology. Bill Kristol was predictably one of the latter. Tucker Carlson pointed out that we shouldn't have been at all surprised by Kristol's wormlike deletion sans apology. "After all, he still hasn't apologized for the Iraq War," Tucker reminded us. Newly elected Minnesota representative Ilhan Abdullahi Omar falsely wrote that the boys "were taunting five black men before they surrounded Phillips and led racist chants." She, too, quietly deleted the tweet without apology or correction to her lies, an ignoble beginning to her tenure in the U.S. House of Representatives.

As their story fell apart, the media pundits scrambled for anything else they could use to continue casting the kids as the villains. In the end, it came down to the smirk.

"Well, why was this kid smirking? How dare he smirk?" they demanded. His outraged accusers left no room for the possibility that his expression might be that of a sixteen-year-old kid who was nervous, embarrassed, or confused about how to react to a strange man who had suddenly walked up to him and started beating a drum in his face. Could the boy have been waiting for the man to say something, as he claimed? Could he have been wondering if it would be rude to walk away? Absolutely not, scolded our thought monitors in the media. His smile was the smirking face of white privilege, they lectured, and for that alone he is condemned.

Consider CNN's Bakari Sellers's defense of his repugnant tweet suggesting that Nick Sandmann should be punched in the face: "My tweet was metaphorically responding to the smugness of those students. It's metaphoric to talk about one's smugness, or smirking." Perhaps Bakari should learn to use metaphors that reflect thoughtfulness and insight, not brutishness and hate. Apparently that level of writing ability is not a requirement to work for CNN, given Ana Navarro's embarrassing potty-mouth insults.[5]

But back to the smirking. Tina Jordan of the *New York Times* retweeted this Facebook post from Marlon James, calling it "the single best commentary I've read on the Covington Catholic boys":

> *Here's the thing about Covington Catholic School Boy. He didn't shout, he didn't rage, he didn't threaten and he did not even lift a finger. Because he's not even twenty years old, and already knows he never has to. He just stood there with his smirk, the line sealing his white privilege. A smirk saying that nothing you speak matters, your existence doesn't matter, your protest doesn't matter, your dignity doesn't matter, not even the fact that you were here first matters. You're a joke because I find you funny, you're a target because I got my bullseye on you, and you are nothing because I won't even remember you by the time I get home. This is racism boiled down to the core, bigotry in excelsis.[6]*

So, as the pundits could no longer credibly accuse the boys of mobbing, taunting, or using racist language, they increasingly justified their outrage by concentrating solely on the boy's young face, its whiteness and its expression. Suddenly all that was necessary to deserve hateful national condemnation was to wear a hat supporting the president of the United States while smiling. As the obsession with Nick Sandmann's facial expression grew, many writers and Twitter users began posting photos of him with this quote from George Orwell's ever-prescient *1984*:

> *It was terribly dangerous to let your thoughts wander when you were in any public place or within range of a telescreen.... In any case, to wear an improper expression on your face (incredulity when a victory was announced, for instance) was itself a punishable offense. There was even a word for it in Newspeak: facecrime, it was called.[7]*

Chapter 39

WELCOME TO
THE PANOPTICON:
FACECRIME, PRECRIME,
AND THE
SURVEILLANCE STATE

I n China, "FaceCrime" is not conjecture but today's reality. Billion-dollar facial recognition companies such as Sense-Time and Megvii are transforming China's ability to have omnipresent surveillance of its citizens as they go about their daily lives. Chinese citizens are given social credit scores and rewards for participation in community activities such as volunteer work or blood donations. Those with low scores can be similarly punished and denied access to jobs, loans, the ability to book flights or train travel—virtually any freedom the Chinese government seeks to deny them.

What could give you a low score? Buying too many video games, posting what the government deems to be "fake news" online, smoking in a nonsmoking area . . . basically whatever the government decides. Perpetrators of "crimes" as minor as jaywalking are publicly shamed on massive digital billboards. Citizens are even judged for their facial expressions as they ride trains. Better not smirk when passing a billboard with a photo of Dear Leader!

The repercussions are not benign. As Harry Cockburn describes in the *Independent*: "Millions of Chinese nationals have been blocked from booking flights or trains as Beijing seeks to implement its controversial 'social credit' system, which allows the government to closely monitor and judge each of its 1.3 billion citizens based on their behavior and activity."

Cockburn writes, "Punishments are not clearly detailed in the government plan, but beyond making travel difficult, they are also believed to include slowing internet speeds, reducing access to good schools for individuals or their children, banning people from certain jobs, preventing booking at certain hotels and losing the right to own pets."[1]

James O'Malley reports that one's social credit score is quite elaborate and arbitrary: "the province of Qingzhen uses more than 1,000 different metrics that can impact a citizen's score. If you hire a child worker for your business, you lose five points, and if you sell coal that doesn't meet regulatory guidelines, you lose 10 points." The system would seem highly dependent on who exactly judges each infraction.

In one Chinese province, a recording that announces to callers that you are "untrustworthy" punishes people with bad debt. Likewise, you can be blacklisted if you don't sort your recycling according to the rules. God forbid that your dog barks at night. A bad social credit score can lead to the government confiscating your pet.[2]

As Anders Corr wrote in an article for La Croix International,

Xinjiang is a test bed for how far a state can control a population in the age of high technology. It is a panopticon, in which no

Chinese citizen is quite sure whether a particular communication,
transit, or purchase has been tracked, or whether it would really
matter to an official who did track it. But individuals do know that
data is tracked at least sometimes by a human behind the screen,
and sometimes that tracking results in detention, torture or worse.
So the risk-averse individual molds his behavior in anticipation to
what he thinks the CCP might like were it watching.

Corr went on to warn us that there are those in the west who
would seek to emulate China in an effort to better police its citizenry, noting that the Brookings Institution "collaborated with
Huawei on a 2017 paper that promoted 'safe cities,' a marketing
term for smart cities controlled by a police brain fed by a nervous
system of networked intelligence feeds."[3]

You might be surprised to find that Big Brother's facial recognition has even found its way into the restroom. In 2017, the Temple
of Heaven in Beijing began to require facial recognition to acquire
toilet paper. If you haven't attempted to get any toilet paper in the
past nine minutes, you are eligible for 80 centimeters of toilet paper. Lo Bei, a representative of the facial recognition device, ap-
pears not to be overly concerned with the freedom to wipe: "For
most people, 80cm of paper should be enough." God forbid anybody gets some bad Kung Pao chicken before visiting the Temple
of Heaven.

You might laugh, but imagine what life will be like once facial
recognition invades every sphere of life. Frankly, I would have
guessed that cameras in the bathroom would have been one of the
last, not the first, areas of privacy invaded.[4]

How is this social credit system working in China? Liu Hu, a
journalist in China, was arrested, fined, blacklisted, and to top it
off named as a "Dishonest Person" by the Supreme People's Court.

His punishment? He was banned from flying and traveling by train and also forbidden from buying property.

Can you get off the list? Maybe. It's kind of like the "no fly" list. No one tells you if you are on it until you try to fly, and it's like pulling teeth to get off the list. Remember when the late Ted Kennedy found out he was on the "no fly" list? Like most violations of civil liberties, the Chinese government presumes guilt first and it's your responsibility to try to prove your innocence. Of course, you must suffer the punishment while trying to prove your innocence.[5]

Facial recognition company Megvii boasts that it will "build the eyes and the brain" for the Chinese government and allow the police to obtain powers "beyond what is humanly possible." The goal is not only to be able to facially recognize China's billion and a half citizens but to be able to predict crime before it occurs. The system will be fully implemented by 2020, with the objective of making it "difficult to move" for those declared to be "untrustworthy."

Sounds like science fiction? Well, it was . . . until it became reality.[6]

Philip K. Dick foresaw the coming of "PreCrime" in his 1956 short story "The Minority Report." Steven Spielberg adapted it for the big screen in 2002 as American politicians were clamoring to sacrifice freedom for the hope of security in the wake of the 9/11 attacks.

Minority Report is set in the year 2054. The government has conscripted three clairvoyants, called "pre-cogs," that can predict crime before it happens. A PreCrime unit gets leads from the "pre-cogs" and arrests people before they commit crimes. Crime becomes a relic of the past.

For the public to acquiesce to the criminal arrest of people before they actually commit a crime requires the acceptance that, at some level, we do not possess free will but are slaves to a preordained or determined future. *Minority Report* raises the question: Is there only one future ahead of us that cannot be altered by our will?

Some have argued that *Minority Report* is not unlike our real-life attempts to preempt terrorist acts. More and more in America, we are convicting people not of actual crime but of "conspiring" to commit a crime that never occurs.

The Mueller investigation of "Russian collusion" in fact has led to dozens of indictments for the "crimes" of falsely testifying about activities that themselves were not really crimes.

In an article for *Slate*, David Edelstein recognizes the parallels between Dick's science fiction and the zeal of today's prosecutors. He writes, "In some ways the certainty that PreCrime feels with regard to their convicting the right person may exceed our current certainty when our government convicts individuals of 'conspiracy' to commit a crime that we are not always certain they will commit or a crime that the government has conspired to encourage them to commit."

Edelstein's response to the movie's central question, though, is worrisome:

"Would you surrender a slew of civil liberties for a world without crime? Assuming that the right people were always jailed for the right reasons, I'd think about it long and hard."

Edelstein's acquiescence to the idea that all would be good "if the right people were jailed" begs the question: If no crime is ever committed, could we ever be certain that a crime would have been committed? In what world could it be just to imprison a person for something they never did, but might have contemplated?[7]

Writers of each successive generation ask if we are there yet. Is *1984* here? Are we now arresting people based on the prediction that they will commit a crime?

Orwell tries to answer this question:

"I do not believe that the kind of society I describe necessarily will arrive, but I believe (allowing of course for the fact that the book is a satire) that something resembling it could arrive. I believe also that totalitarian ideas have taken root in the minds of intellectuals everywhere, and I have tried to draw these ideas out to their logical consequences."[8]

Do we already live in the 2054 world of *Minority Report*? Stephen Carson argues, in a way, yes: "More and more the State makes crimes of actions that don't cause any harm, but might. Drunk driving, an improper paperwork trail for a large transfer of money, violation of any of a multitude of gun purchasing regulations. The point is no longer merely to punish the wrongdoer, but to prevent the crime from happening in the first place."

Minority Report, as Carson writes, demonstrates "the injustice of a 'justice' system that punishes not for actual crimes, but for ones that are yet to be committed . . . the ultimate 'tradeoff' of liberty for security."[9]

A perfect example of this is the metastases of surveillance and traffic cameras in America's urban centers. While big-government liberals love them (especially the Democrat mayors in our major cities), these snooping eyes disproportionately wreak havoc on the lives of the poor and minorities today.

It's the poor person whose life spirals out of control when a ridiculously expensive speeding ticket from a traffic surveillance camera arrives in the mail, goes unpaid, doubles and triples, and then results in their car being booted or impounded. Now that person cannot get to work. And the spiral continues. Worse yet, in many cities you are jailed for nonpayment of fines.

My wife, Kelley, and I know firsthand how draconian some of these traffic fines are. She parked outside of our D.C. apartment one night, and set the alarm early so she could move it. Not early enough. It was being towed away as she burst out to the street the next morning. She went online to pay the $400 in tickets and towing fees, only to discover that apparently we had gotten a speeding ticket from a traffic surveillance camera months before. (Yes, I was driving.) The ticket had been mailed to our former apartment and not forwarded . . . so it had doubled and tripled for nonpayment. Now we owed $700. She was furious and decided to go down to the DMV and fight.

She described her experience that day in a speech she gave as part of her advocacy work for criminal justice reform. In it, she wrote:

> *The Washington, DC, DMV is an interesting place, not that I'm recommending it—but I did learn a lot during my six hours there. As I waited in the large room filled with people waiting for our numbers to be called, I became conscious of the fact that I could pay my fines and fees—and most of the other people there probably couldn't, not without serious difficulty anyway.*
>
> *My number was called, and I went in with four others to a small room with an adjudicator. We were brusquely ordered not to talk and to silence our phones. I sat there and listened to a woman in her seventies, who had her car towed like I had, explain that she had been helping a friend get home after her release from the hospital for heart surgery. She was only parked for a few minutes as she helped her friend to her apartment.*
>
> *The lady tried to show release papers from the hospital to make her case. She also said that she was on a fixed income and would have great difficulty paying the costly fines. The adjudicator refused to look at the papers. "Unless you have a notarized letter from the owner of the apartment complex then your ticket and towing fees still stand," she said flatly. As she walked past me, the look on that poor lady's face broke my heart.*

The next person was an immigrant from Nigeria. He had a costly ticket for making an illegal left-hand turn—recorded by DC's ubiquitous traffic surveillance cameras. He spoke with a heavy accent and the adjudicator was having trouble understanding him. The man kept saying the word "con" while pointing at the grainy image on the screen captured by the surveillance camera.

Finally, the person next to me bravely spoke up. "Ma'am," he said, "maybe you could enlarge the image. He is trying to show you something." She did, and suddenly we could all see what the young man was trying to show her: the entire left-turn lane was filled with traffic cones. He had no choice but to turn from the lane he was in. The adjudicator told the man his ticket was waived. We all broke into spontaneous smiles and subtle but giddy high-fives in support of our fellow beleaguered motorist. "Finally somebody is getting justice in this place," I muttered to the guy next to me. "Victory against the man!" he said as he grinned back.

But seeing the relief on the young man's face as he walked out made me angry at the unfairness of excessive tickets for minor violations. $200 might as well be $2,000 for someone who is barely getting by. Imagine it being doubled or tripled.

I submitted my apartment lease and copies of utility bills to prove that I didn't know about the speeding ticket and got my fines reduced from $700 to $500, but at that point, it barely mattered. All I felt was a searing awareness of what $500 meant to me versus the other people in that room. He might lose his car over $500. She might not be able to pay her rent. And so the spiral begins.

In many cities, you go to jail for nonpayment of traffic tickets. Surveillance cameras and excessive fines for minor violations are truly big government at its worst, because they hurt vulnerable people the most.

NPR writes, "To understand some of the distrust of police that fueled the protests in Ferguson, [Missouri,] consider this: In 2013, the municipal court in Ferguson, a city of only 21,000 people, issued 32,975 arrest warrants for nonviolent offenses, most of which were driving violations."

And it goes beyond the "crime" of traffic violations. Despite resistance from libertarians on the left and the right, some worry that PreCrime is already here. In Chicago, the police have installed a crime-predicting computer algorithm that they used recently to deploy a large gang raid. This PreCrime software compiles a Strategic Subject List (SSL) that reviews personal data to come up with a "danger rating."

Karen Sheley of the ACLU responds: "There's a police database that's populated with secret information, and people can't challenge the accuracy of it."[10]

Simon McCormack, also of the New York Civil Liberties Union, writes: "We are taking one step closer to the dystopian world of *Minority Report* without any discussion of the serious privacy concerns that are implicated, [when we install] controversial advanced cameras, license plate readers, and facial recognition technology in New York's airports and other transportation hubs . . . [and] sensors and cameras at 'structurally sensitive' points on bridges and tunnels."

According to McCormack, technological advances are allowing for "a transformative surveillance system—one that has the potential to put thousands and thousands of people's images and data in a massive database that could be easily misused by the government in ways we haven't even imagined yet."

The danger in having the government collect so much data is, according to McCormack, made worse in that it's "not yet clear how the information will be stored and who will have access to it."

McCormack also worries that facial recognition technology often misidentifies minorities. "A 2012 study, highlighted in the *Atlantic*, for example, found that a facial recognition algorithm failed to identify the right person nearly twice as often when the photo was of a black person."[11]

Slowly but surely, we are seeing more examples of "PreCrime" prosecutions in America. Take, for example, license plate readers. The horrendous case of Robert Harte bears repeating. Robert and his wife often shopped at a gardening store in their neighborhood. Unbeknownst to the Hartes, the police were monitoring cars in the parking lot as part of a marijuana investigation. The police were recording the license plates of all the customers.

The Hartes did not hear about this investigation by a polite knock on the door but rather when a SWAT team burst into their home with semiautomatic weapons drawn to interrogate Harte, his wife, their seven-year-old daughter, and their thirteen-year-old son. As McCormack describes it, "Harte was held at gunpoint for two hours while cops combed through his home. The police were looking for a marijuana growing operation. They did not find that or any other evidence of criminal activity in the Hartes' house."

McCormack, on the ACLU website, writes worriedly: "It's also important to understand that these technologies have a way of creeping towards ubiquity. It starts with a camera here or a license plate reader there, but soon they are everywhere."[12]

In China, though, such concerns over civil liberties aren't even considered. What better place to develop surveillance technology than in a "surveillance state." So far, more than forty Chinese cities have installed SenseTime's facial recognition software. *Fortune* reports that this technology "has helped Guangzhou police identify more than 2,000 suspects, arrest more than 800 people, and solve close to 100 cases since it was deployed in the city last year."

Both SenseTime and Megvii act as if they are absolved of any abuses of civil liberties that the government may inflict. Luciano Floridi, a digital ethicist, doesn't believe the companies should get a free pass: "The justification of saying 'Oh, we're just producing a tool' has not worked since we started sharpening stones a long time ago."

The Chinese government maintains, like every government anywhere claims, that the technology is just about stopping violent crime. Maya Wang from Human Rights Watch disagrees: "The intention of these systems is to weave a tighter net of social control that makes it harder for people to plan action or push the government to reform. With ever more intelligent cameras, who will watch the watchers?"[13]

G. Clay Whittaker writes of how China has taken "PreCrime" to a new level: "China has a new strategy in fighting crime, ripped from science fiction and hastily pasted at the top of the list of paranoia-inducing concepts. It's called pre-crime. It goes further than sting operations, counterterrorism, or any other government action to preempt criminal activity ever before."

The China Electronics Technology Group is now gathering and organizing big data on everything they can get their hands on, from employer data to social media data to consumer purchases, all ostensibly to analyze and predict crime or terrorism before it occurs.

Every text or email is retrieved and stored. Every individual's daily travel pattern is captured by GPS and recorded. Critics of the government get special attention. No detail of your life is too insignificant. Do you drink alcohol? How much? Do you smoke? What brand?

As Whittaker puts it: "It's a scary thought, especially when you consider that the main target of Chinese pre-crime efforts wouldn't be 'terrorists,' murderers, rapists, or child molesters, but rather dissidents of every shape and size. By publicly announcing their intention to build an intelligence network that can predict crimes, China just took a step closer to all the thought-policing dystopian nightmare scenarios we've always worried about as members of a modern society. And they want people to know it."[14]

AFTERWORD:
FINDING COMMON GROUND

Freedom brings people together.

—RON PAUL

I don't hate Bernie or Alexandria Ocasio-Cortez. Who wouldn't admire Alexandria's winsome smile and earnestness, however misplaced? And I, for one, am envious, not at all critical, of her spontaneity with dance. That being said, socialism as an economic and political system is an avoidable disaster. It's likely too late to convince Bernie or Ocasio-Cortez of the miracle of Adam Smith's invisible hand or the unparalleled prosperity that comes with the division of labor. But it's never too late to find common ground.

In fact, I've worked many times with Bernie Sanders and other members of the progressive left. While I wouldn't want to characterize my friend Senator Ron Wyden of Oregon as a socialist, I think he would accept the label progressive. He and I have worked together on so many bills protecting privacy and civil liberties that I'm convinced we largely think alike on issues of privacy and the Fourth Amendment. Wyden jokes that he and I make up the Ben Franklin Caucus, the senators who believe that if you trade liberty for security, you may wind up with neither.

I've worked with Senator Kirsten Gillibrand on achieving justice for members of our military who have been the victim of sexual assault. Likewise, I've worked with Senators Booker, Leahy, and Harris on criminal justice reform. The passage of the First Step Act, the first meaningful criminal justice reform law in decades, was a true bipartisan achievement that occurred under President Trump and a Republican-led Congress.

My wife, Kelley, advocated for the First Step Act and was a vocal presence in the media encouraging the majority leader to bring the bill to the Senate floor. Kelley argued for First Step's passage on national and Kentucky television and radio shows, wrote op-eds, gave speeches, and personally lobbied senators, all on a volunteer basis. She was in the media so often in the months leading up to its passage that the president called me to let me know that she was "the real star in the family."

Just a few weeks after it was signed into law, the First Step Act was freeing Americans such as Matthew Charles. In 1996, Charles was sentenced to thirty-five years in prison for selling crack cocaine to an informant—under sentencing laws that penalized one gram of crack as if it were equivalent to 100 grams of powder cocaine. Powder cocaine was the form of the drug predominantly abused by whites, while the cheaper crack was the type abused primarily by blacks. The Clinton crime bill codified this sentencing disparity, resulting in the disproportionate and unjust incarceration of tens of thousands of African Americans.

While incarcerated, Matthew Charles helped other inmates earn their GEDs and organized Bible studies. He completed thirty Bible correspondence classes, as well as college courses. He became a law clerk to help other prisoners understand the legal system, helping read legal documents to those who were illiterate to shield them from humiliation. After serving twenty-one years, he was released in 2016 under the 2010 changes to the sentencing guidelines that reduced the disparity in crack versus powder cocaine.

Upon reentering society, Charles held a steady job, renewed his relationship with his children and grandkids, leased an apartment, and filled it with photos of loved ones. He volunteered every week at a Nashville food pantry called "the Little Pantry That Could," long after his parole required it. He mentored young men who were on probation or parole.

Nevertheless, prosecutors appealed his release on the grounds that the 2010 retroactivity in sentencing guidelines did not apply to him, and he was sent back to prison in 2018—after nearly two years as a productive and contributing member of society. The Sixth Circuit judge even stated that Charles had a record "not only of rehabilitation but of good works" but "her hands were tied." In a profile on Nashville Public Radio, Charles was quoted expressing his disappointment outside the courtroom— disappointment, but not resignation. "I'm just disappointed again," he said. "But I believe that God is still in charge of the situation. He hasn't revealed to me what He's doing yet, but my faith remains the same."

On December 27, 2018, six days after President Trump signed the First Step Act into law, public defenders petitioned for his release. And on January 3, Matthew Charles walked out of prison, once again a free man. Shortly afterward, my political chief of staff, Doug Stafford, sent this note to me and Kelley: "If you ever think this work isn't worth the attacks, if you ever think the results take too long or sometimes are only measured in what doesn't happen, remember there are people getting out of jail and reclaiming their lives because of work we have all done. Not many people get to say that."

The First Step Act is an example of legislation that brought together the left and right. Doug Collins, a conservative Republican from Georgia, and Hakeem Jeffries, a progressive Democrat from

New York, introduced it in the House. Both Van Jones and Jared Kushner advocated tirelessly for its passage. Evangelical Christian conservatives supported it out of their belief in the power of redemption and second chances. Small government advocates and libertarians recognized mass incarceration as more unsustainable government spending, waste, and overreach. Progressives supported the First Step Act out of desire for social justice and an end to the devastating effects of over-incarceration on low-income and minority communities. We all recognized that laws must be applied equally and fairly. We all saw the humanity in each other. We all worked together to make America better.[1]

I suppose the media perpetuates the lie that Democrats and Republicans in Congress hate each other for ratings. After all, conflict, drama, and scandal get more clicks on the Internet. Yet every time the media promotes this falsehood they also inadvertently promote the hate that fills the Internet. Commenters on Twitter are stoked by anonymity and also by the media's misreporting that there is no common ground among the left and the right. Hillary Clinton's attack on Trump voters as "deplorables" has only been amplified by a media and celebrity culture that demonizes Trump and his supporters.

The MAGA hat has become the symbol of intolerance on the left. In my hometown of Bowling Green, a crazy leftist pulled a gun on Terry and Cherrie Pierce for wearing MAGA hats. The gunman flipped them off, then pulled a loaded .40-caliber pistol on them at our local Sam's Club. The gunman stuck the gun in Terry Pierce's face and said, "It is a good day for you to die." Pierce responded: "I told him to pull the trigger or put the gun down and fight me like a man." Fortunately, the police intervened before blood was shed— but how polarized is our country when people are threatened with murder for wearing a MAGA hat?[2]

Consider that actor and activist Alyssa Milano called the MAGA hat "the new white hood."

She and her ilk are so triggered by the election of Donald Trump that they claim the wearing of a hat is a threatening act. Is it any wonder that in the two years since his election we have seen multiple high-profile hoax crimes falsely blamed on Trump supporters? The left wants to be victimized so badly that they are resorting to creating false crimes against themselves.[3]

Not a day goes by that the new media doesn't perpetuate and foment the divide between left and right. While they continually complain about lack of civility they perpetuate incivility by ignoring the bipartisanship that goes on every day in Congress.

The media's obsession with the "Russian collusion" story offers a prime example of how the desire to center every Russia story on Trump distracts us from intelligent debate about real issues. Formerly sane voices on engagement have been silenced to the point that Congress nearly unanimously voted for complete embargoes of Russia and the sanctioning of its legislators; thus diplomacy between our countries is severely weakened.

I'll give you a worrisome example of the media's stoking the flames. I traveled to Russia in 2018 with the Cato Institute, a libertarian-leaning think tank that promotes free market solutions. I and other members of our group met with former president Gorbachev and members of the Russian legislature to discuss engagement on nuclear arms control. I also met with Mikhail Svetov, a young Russian YouTube star and libertarian who is an outspoken critic of Vladimir Putin and his government. A CNN reporter tweeted out a picture of me talking to the former Russian ambassador and current member of the Russian upper house, Sergey Kislyak, which was taken during our nuclear arms control meeting with members of the Russian legislature. The reporter captioned his photo, "Rand Paul meets with Russian spy." The falsehood that I was in Russia meeting with a spy was not only nonsensical and insulting, but it encouraged the Internet haters to pile on.

I've got thick skin. I can take media bias, but the fake news seriously damages our nation's ability to develop a bipartisan coalition to negotiate new and continue old arms treaties, at great cost to all of our futures.

Meeting with Mikhail Gorbachev and hearing him tell of the friendship he developed with President Reagan, in the midst of the Cold War, was a profound experience for me. We all need to remember how close we came to nuclear holocaust due to fear, distrust, and hatred. Statesmanship and communication saved us, not blind refusal to come to the table of diplomacy. We all need to remember that ultimately it is our ability to acknowledge the humanity of our adversaries that is the key to our mutual survival. In the words of Bishop Desmond Tutu, "My humanity is bound up in yours. For we can only be human together."

Since Trump's election, I have seen an increase in media bias in the reporting of foreign policy, and not only related to Russia. After seventeen years in Afghanistan, spending over trillions of dollars, losing over 2,000 soldiers, and over 20,000 more with lifelong injuries and amputations, President Trump stated his objective to end the war. Suddenly even the progressive media outlets, who supported President Obama's stated objective of ending this never-ending war, went ballistic. Because of their overt hatred of our president, they have a reflexive opposition to anything he proposes, even the ending of a grisly war whose stated objective was accomplished years ago. No discussion of the pros and cons—if Trump is for it, they are against it. This reflexive opposition, based on personal animus, is extremely dangerous for our country.

Despite the real debate between foreign policy interventionists like Lindsey Graham and noninterventionists like myself, there is an underreported right-left coalition on foreign policy.

For example, conservative senator Mike Lee and I have worked with Bernie Sanders and Senator Chris Murphy on trying to end our support for the Saudi war on Yemen. Currently, I'm part of a coalition to end the Afghan War that includes Representatives Ted Lieu and Ro Khanna, both leaders of the progressive caucus.

There is a false narrative that compromise always means splitting the difference and giving up on half of what you believe. Another way of looking at compromise is to discount party labels to try to find common ground, which is what happened with criminal justice reform.

But on socialism, or its fellow traveler, welfarism, it is unlikely that we will find common ground. In fact, I'm not inclined to split the difference between socialism and capitalism. I will continue to fight for a free market economy because it is the only system consistent with liberty and the only system that provides greater prosperity and opportunity for all. If your goal is to help the poor become better off, there is no more humanitarian economic system than capitalism.

I continue to find common ground by seeking out, regardless of party label, people on the left who share my steadfast belief that the Constitution demands that Congress authorize war before military action ensues and that the Fourth Amendment does protect not only the papers and effects in your house but also the papers and effects kept by third parties such as the phone company or Internet providers.

I am an equal opportunity critic of unconstitutional government. While I have defended President Trump consistently from attacks that I believe are purely partisan in nature, I have opposed more of his policies and appointments than any other Republican.

While I was a critic of President Obama's economic policy, I was a consistent and loud supporter of his commutation of excessive prison sentences for nonviolent drug offenses.

But I'm not a splitter. I'm not one who wishes America to be half socialist and half capitalist. Any shift in the direction of socialism not only damages economic prosperity but also threatens liberty. Capitalism is synonymous with voluntarism and individual freedom. As long as you refrain from violence and fraud, as long as you honor your contract, government should leave us free to voluntarily interact in the marketplace.

Capitalism, the freedom of voluntary exchange, is what made America great. The pursuit of freedom is a noble quest and one not to be compromised. My hope is that the next generation of American youth will study and reflect on socialism's long history of violence and famine. My hope is that the next generation will understand that free markets and free people have produced better health, longer life expectancy, and reduced poverty and suffering around the world. My hope is that they will choose liberty.

ACKNOWLEDGMENTS

Kelley and I would like to thank the great team at HarperCollins, especially Eric Nelson and Hannah Long, for your insight, professionalism, and commitment to this book. It was a pleasure to work with you.

Thank you to my deputy chief of staff, Sergio Gor, not only for your help with this book but also for your invaluable contributions over the past eight years. I am grateful for your dedication, ideas, and enthusiasm, and also your friendship.

Thanks to all of the excellent conservative and libertarian organizations out there that are working every day to educate young people and amplify the message of liberty. Many of them were sourced in this book, and I encourage readers to follow their social media for further information: mises.org, humanprogress.org, theamericanconservative.com, FEE.org, freedomworks.org, and cato.org.

Finally, we would like to express our gratitude to our family: our parents, Carol and Ron Paul and Lillian and Hilton Ashby; our sons, William, Duncan, and Robert Paul; and our brothers and sisters and their spouses. Kelley and I are grateful for the blessing of your boundless encouragement and love.

NOTES

INTRODUCTION

1. Brian Barrett, "DJI's M600 Drone Is Not for You. Don't Even Look at It," *Wired*, April 19, 2016, https://www.wired.com/2016/04/dji-m600-drone/.

2. Ulrike Franke, "The Caracas Drone Attack Won't Be the Last of Its Kind," *Verge*, August 17, 2018, https://www.theverge.com/2018/8/17/17703570/caracas-drone-attack-venezuela-president-nicolas-maduro.

3. Joe Parkin Daniels, "Venezuela's Nicolás Maduro Survives Apparent Assassination Attempt," *Guardian*, August 4, 2018, https://www.theguardian.com/world/2018/aug/04/nicolas-maduros-speech-cut-short-while-soldiers-scatter.

4. Alexandra Ulmer and Daniel Wallis, "Maduro Says Foes Used Explosive Drones to Try to Kill Him," Reuters, August 4, 2018, https://www.reuters.com/article/us-venezuela-politics-maduro/blast-scattering-soldiers-makes-venezuelas-maduro-look-vulnerable-analysts-idUSKBN1KQ0KL.

5. Megan Janetsky, "Fleeing Venezuela, Migrants Flood Colombia Amid Region's Worst Humanitarian Crisis in Decades," *USA Today*, November 20, 2018, https://www.usatoday.com/story/news/world/2016/05/18/Venezuela.

6. Nicholas Casey, "Dying Infants and No Medicine: Inside Venezuela's Failing Hospitals," *New York Times*, May 16, 2016, https://www.nytimes.com/2016/05/16/world/americas/dying-infants-and-no-medicine-inside-venezuelas-failing-hospitals.html.

7. Dominique Mosbergen, "Trump Knocks Socialism and Bernie Sanders Does Not Look Pleased," *HuffPost*, February 5, 2019, https://www.huffingtonpost.com/entry/trump-bernie-sanders-socialism-state-of-the-union_us_5c5a5d49e4b00187b5562046.

8. Jordan Drischler, "Self-Identified Socialists Don't Know What They're Talking About," *Pitt News*, September 6, 2016, https://pittnews.com/article/110288/opinions/columns/self-identified-socialists-dont-know-theyre-talking/.

9. Geoff Dembicki, "Socialism Is Incredibly Popular but Does Anyone Know What 'Socialism' Is?," *Vice*, October 4, 2018, https://www.vice.com/en_us/article/a3p4y8/what-actual-socialists-think-about-socialism.

10. Joseph Blasi and Douglas L. Kruse, "Today's Youth Reject Capitalism, but What Do They Want to Replace It?," CNBC, April 8, 2018, https://www.cnbc.com/2018/04/08/todays-youth-reject-capitalism-but-what-do-they-want-to-replace-it.html.

11. Esteban Ortiz-Ospina, "Does the Impressive Historical Decline in Poverty Capture Non-Market Transactions?," Our World in Data, January 23, 2017, https://ourworldindata.org/poverty-home-production-and-consumption.

12. Max Roser, "Child Mortality," Our World in Data, https://ourworldindata.org/child-mortality.
13. Frank Newport, "Americans' Views of Socialism, Capitalism Are Little Changed," Gallup, May 6, 2016, https://news.gallup.com/poll/191354/americans-views-socialism-capitalism-little-changed.aspx.
14. Drischler, "Self-Identified Socialists Don't Know What They're Talking About."
15. Dan Ferber, "How Children Outgrow Socialism," *Science Magazine*, May 27, 2010, https://www.sciencemag.org/news/2010/05/how-children-outgrow-socialism.

CHAPTER 1: SOCIALISM DESTROYED VENEZUELA'S ONCE-VIBRANT ECONOMY

1. José Niño, "Venezuela Before Chavez: A Prelude to Socialist Failure," Mises Institute, May 14, 2017, https://mises.org/wire/venezuela-chavez-prelude-socialist-failure.
2. Ibid.
3. Federico Fernández, "The Economist Promoting Austrian Economics in Venezuela," Mises Institute, November 20, 2018, https://mises.org/wire/economist-promoting-austrian-economics-venezuela.
4. John Stossel, "Chomsky's Venezuela Lesson," Creators, May 31, 2017, https://www.creators.com/read/john-stossel/05/17/chomskys-venezuela-lesson.
5. Fernández, "The Economist Promoting Austrian Economics in Venezuela."
6. Niño, "Venezuela Before Chavez."
7. Ibid.
8. Ian Simpson, "Pennsylvania Professor Under Fire for 'White Genocide' Tweet," Reuters, December 26, 2016, https://www.reuters.com/article/us-pennsylvania-professor-idUSKBN14F154.
9. John Phelan, "The Three Phases of Socialism," Foundation for Economic Education, May 8, 2019, https://fee.org/articles/the-three-phases-of-socialism/.
10. "From Riches to Rags," Al Jazeera, February 14, 2018, https://www.aljazeera.com/programmes/the-big-picture/2018/02/riches-rags-venezuela-economic-crisis-180211123942491.html.
11. Kevin Voigt, "Chavez Leaves Venezuelan Economy More Equal, Less Stable," CNN, March 6, 2013, https://www.cnn.com/2013/03/06/business/venezuela-chavez-oil-economy/index.html.
12. Ibid.
13. "From Riches to Rags," Al Jazeera, February 14, 2018, https://www.aljazeera.com/programmes/the-big-picture/2018/02/riches-rags-venezuela-economic-crisis-180211123942491.html.
14. Ibid.
15. Ibid.
16. Ibid.
17. Benjamin Kentish, "Venezuelans Lose Average of 19lb in Weight Due to Nationwide Food Shortages, Study Suggests," *Independent*, February 23, 2017, https://www.independent.co.uk/news/world/americas/venezuela

-weight-loss-average-19lb-pounds-food-shortages-economic-crisis
-a7595081.html.

18. Peter Wilson, "Venezuela Food Shortages Cause Some to Hunt Dogs, Cats, Pigeons," *USA Today*, May 18, 2016, https://www.usatoday.com/story/news /world/2016/05/18/venezuela-food-shortages-cause-some-hunt-dogs-cats -pigeons/84547888/.

19. Kentish, "Venezuelans Lose Average of 19lb."

20. *Caracas Chronicles* Team, "A Staggering Hunger Crisis, in Cold, Hard Numbers," *Caracas Chronicles*, February 21, 2018, https://www.caracaschronicles.com /2018/02/21/encovi-2017/.

CHAPTER 2: SOCIALISM REWARDS CORRUPTION

1. Cory Franklin, "The Deafening Silence of Hollywood's Chavistas," *Washington Examiner*, May 1, 2017, https://www.washingtonexaminer.com/the-deafening -silence-of-hollywoods-chavistas.

2. John Stossel and Maxim Lott, "Stossel: Socialism Fails Every Time," *Reason*, October 1, 2018, https://reason.com/reasontv/2018/10/09/stossel-socialism -fails-every-time.

3. Keith Flamer, "10 Surprises About Fidel Castro's Extravagant Life," *Forbes*, November 26, 2016, https://www.forbes.com/sites/keithflamer/2016/11/26 /10-surprises-about-castros-extravagant-life/#1c6188ed6d76.

4. Carlos Frías, "First He Praised Castro. Now 'Salt Bae' Chef Lavishes Venezuela's Maduro with Steak Dinner," *Miami Herald*, September 17, 2018, https://www .miamiherald.com/entertainment/restaurants/article218581025.html.

5. Eliza Mackintosh and Natalie Gallón, "Maduro Dines on Pricey 'Salt Bae' Steaks as Venezuelans Starve," CNN, September 19, 2018, https://www.cnn .com/2018/09/18/world/venezuela-maduro-salt-bae-steak-intl/index.html.

6. Scott Smith, "Venezuela President Ties Opposition Leader to Drone Attack," AP News, August 7, 2018, https://www.apnews.com/840713b2848142d398266 6c13b487bcf.

7. Glenn Reynolds, "Glenn Reynolds: Don't Be a Sucker for Socialism," *USA Today*, May 16, 2016, https://www.usatoday.com/story/opinion/2016/05/16 /socialism-venezuela-ussr-cuba-sanders-clinton-elections-2016-column /32613393/.

8. Gerard Di Trolio, "Socialist in Name Only," *Jacobin*, December 28, 2014, https:// www.jacobinmag.com/2014/12/socialist-international-capitalism.

9. Susanna Kim, "Egypt's Mubarak Likely to Retain Vast Wealth," ABC News, February 2, 2011, https://abcnews.go.com/Business/egypt-mubarak-family -accumulated-wealth-days-military/story?id=12821073.

10. Ian Birrell, "The Strange and Evil World of Equatorial Guinea," *Guardian*, October 22, 2011, https://www.theguardian.com/world/2011/oct/23 /equatorial-guinea-africa-corruption-kleptocracy.

11. "Equatorial Guinea's VP Obiang's Cars Seized in Switzerland," BBC, November 3, 2016, https://www.bbc.com/news/world-africa-37861795.

12. Birrell, "The Strange and Evil World of Equatorial Guinea."

CHAPTER 3: INTERFERING WITH FREE MARKETS CAUSES SHORTAGES

1. José Niño, "Price Controls Are Disastrous for Venezuela, and Everywhere Else," Mises Institute, August 16, 2016, https://mises.org/wire/price-controls-are-disastrous-venezuela-and-everywhere-else.

2. Hugh Rockoff, "Price Controls," Library of Economics and Liberty, https://www.econlib.org/library/Enc/PriceControls.html.

3. Niño, "Price Controls Are Disastrous for Venezuela, and Everywhere Else."

4. Tibisay Romero and Corina Pons, "With Venezuelan Hyperinflation, Multinationals Buck Price Controls," Reuters, March 8, 2018, https://www.reuters.com/article/us-venezuela-companies/with-venezuelan-hyperinflation-multinationals-buck-price-controls-idUSKCN1GK0IV.

5. Niño, "Price Controls Are Disastrous for Venezuela, and Everywhere Else."

6. George Reisman, "Why Nazism Was Socialism and Why Socialism Is Totalitarian," Mises Institute, November 11, 2005, https://mises.org/library/why-nazism-was-socialism-and-why-socialism-totalitarian.

7. Ibid.

8. Gene Healy, "Remembering Nixon's Wage and Price Controls," *Washington Examiner,* August 15, 2011, https://www.washingtonexaminer.com/remembering-nixons-wage-and-price-controls.

9. Ibid.

10. Slavoj Zizek, "The Problem with Venezuela's Revolution Is That It Didn't Go Far Enough," *Independent,* August 9, 2017, https://www.independent.co.uk/voices/venezuela-socialism-communism-left-didnt-go-far-enough-a7884021.html.

11. Girish Gupta, "Price Controls and Scarcity Force Venezuelans to Turn to the Black Market for Milk and Toilet Paper," *Guardian*, April 16, 2015, https://www.theguardian.com/global-development-professionals-network/2015/apr/16/venezuela-economy-black-market-milk-and-toilet-paper.

12. Stephen Gibbs, "Venezuela's Maduro Imposes Food Price Controls," *Times,* May 29, 2018, https://www.thetimes.co.uk/article/maduro-blames-crisis-on-capitalism-5dkh0td3t.

13. David Brennan, "Venezuela Army Sent to Enforce Food Prices as Currency Crashes," *Newsweek,* June 21, 2018, https://www.newsweek.com/venezuela-army-sent-enforce-food-prices-currency-crashes-989556.

14. John Stossel and Maxim Lott, "Stossel: Socialism Fails Every Time," *Reason,* October 1, 2018, https://reason.com/reasontv/2018/10/09/stossel-socialism-fails-every-time.

15. Marian Tupy, "Venezuelan Price Controls Lead to Predictable Shortages," *Reason,* September 19, 2017, https://reason.com/archives/2017/09/19/venezuelan-price-controls-lead-to-predic.

CHAPTER 4: CAPITALISM IS THE MORE MORAL SYSTEM

1. David Harsanyi, "What Thomas Piketty's Popularity Tells Us About the Liberal Press," *Federalist,* April 23, 2014, http://thefederalist.com/2014/04/23/pundits-of-the-world-unite-what-thomas-pikettys-popularity-tells-us-about-the-liberal-press/.

2. Daniel Shuchman, "Thomas Piketty Revives Marx for the 21st Century," *Wall Street Journal,* April 21, 2014, https://www.wsj.com/articles/book -review-capital-in-the-twenty-first-century-by-thomas-piketty-1398118166.
3. Ben Domenech, "Why Inequality Doesn't Matter," *Federalist,* April 23, 2014, https://thefederalist.com/2014/04/23/why-inequality-doesnt-matter/.
4. Shuchman, "Thomas Piketty Revives Marx for the 21st Century."
5. Ibid.
6. Sam Bowman, "Inequality Doesn't Matter: A Primer," Adam Smith Institute, January 11, 2017, https://www.adamsmith.org/blog/inequality-doesnt-matter -a-primer.
7. Alexander C. R. Hammond, "The World's Poorest People Are Getting Richer Faster," *HumanProgress,* October 27, 2017, https://humanprogress.org/article .php?p=770.
8. Bowman, "Inequality Doesn't Matter: A Primer."
9. Tim Worstall, "Using Homer Simpson to Explain Why Inequality Doesn't Matter," *Forbes,* August 26, 2014, https://www.forbes.com/sites /timworstall/2014/08/26/using-homer-simpson-to-explain-why-inequality -doesnt-matter/#1eda0594407c.
10. Ibid.
11. Dalibor Rohac, "Income Inequality Doesn't Matter," *Washington Times,* May 13, 2011, https://www.washingtontimes.com/news/2011/may/13/income -inequality-doesnt-matter/.
12. Deirdre McCloskey quoted by Worstall, "Using Homer Simpson to Explain Why Inequality Doesn't Matter."

CHAPTER 5: CAPITALISM BENEFITS THE MIDDLE CLASS
1. McCloskey, in Worstall, "Using Homer Simpson to Explain Why Inequality Doesn't Matter."
2. Donald J. Boudreaux, "No Time Like the Present," Mercatus Center, September 14, 2013, https://www.mercatus.org/expert_commentary/no-time -present.
3. Christina Zhao, "NY Rep. Alexandria Ocasio-Cortez Says 'Capitalism Is Irredeemable,'" *Newsweek,* March 10, 2019, https://www.newsweek.com /alexandria-ocasio-cortez-says-capitalism-irredeemable-1357720.
4. Tupy, "Venezuelan Price Controls Lead to Predictable Shortages."
5. Glenn Kessler, "Ocasio-Cortez's Misfired Facts on Living Wage and Minimum Wage," *Washington Post,* January 24, 2019, https://www .washingtonpost.com/politics/2019/01/24/ocasio-cortezs-misfired-facts -living-wage-minimum -wage/?utm_term=.3d81e322f48a.
6. Glenn Kessler, "Rand Paul's Suggestion He Looks to Eisenhower for 'Inspiration and Guidance,'" *Washington Post,* July 24, 2017, https://www.washingtonpost .com/blogs/fact-checker/post/rand-pauls-suggestion-he-looks-to-eisenhower -for-inspiration-and-guidance/2013/07/23/47757076-f3ca-11e2-aa2e -4088616498b4_blog.html?utm_term=.dd76db3e75bd.

7. David Harsanyi, "Millennials Are the Most Prosperous Generation That's Ever Lived," *Federalist,* March 22, 2019, https://thefederalist.com/2019/03/22/stop-whining-millennials-youre-prosperous-generation-thats-ever-lived/#.XOAY_M7MouB.twitter.

8. Phil Gramm and John Early, "The Myth of 'Wage Stagnation,'" *Wall Street Journal,* May 17, 2019, https://www.wsj.com/articles/the-myth-of-wage-stagnation-11558126174.

9. Harsanyi, "Millennials Are the Most Prosperous Generation That's Ever Lived."

10. Jim Geraghty, "Millennials Are Experiencing American Prosperity," *National Review,* March 22, 2019, https://www.nationalreview.com/the-morning-jolt/millennials-are-experiencing-american-prosperity/.

11. Scott Lincicome, "People our age have never experienced," Twitter, March 21, 2019, https://twitter.com/scottlincicome/status/1108858010250678272.

12. Harsanyi, "Millennials Are the Most Prosperous Generation That's Ever Lived."

13. Derek Thompson, "How America Spends Money: 100 Years in the Life of the Family Budget," *Atlantic,* April 5, 2012, https://www.theatlantic.com/business/archive/2012/04/how-america-spends-money-100-years-in-the-life-of-the-family-budget/255475/.

14. Ben Domenech, "Why Inequality Doesn't Matter," *Federalist,* April 23, 2014, https://thefederalist.com/2014/04/23/why-inequality-doesnt-matter/.

15. Ibid.

16. Mark J. Perry, "Some Amazing Findings on Income Mobility in the US," American Enterprise Institute, November 16, 2017, http://www.aei.org/publication/some-amazing-findings-on-income-mobility-in-the-us-including-this-the-image-of-a-static-1-and-99-percent-is-false/.

17. Ibid.

CHAPTER 6: INCOME INEQUALITY DOES NOT RUIN THE ECONOMY OR CORRUPT GOVERNMENT

1. Joseph Stiglitz, "Inequality Is Holding Back the Recovery," *New York Times,* January 19, 2013, https://opinionator.blogs.nytimes.com/2013/01/19/inequality-is-holding-back-the-recovery/?emc=eta1&pagewanted=print&mtrref=undefined&gwh=5DAE51CCD6C1787BC30B65C764F808D0&gwt=pay.

2. Dan Andrews, Christopher Jencks, and Andrew Leigh, "Do Rising Top Incomes Lift All Boats?," *B.E. Journal of Economic Analysis and Policy* 11, no. 1, Article 6 (2011), http://andrewleigh.org/pdf/TopIncomesGrowth.pdf.

3. Alan Reynolds, "Piketty Problems: Top 1% Shares of Income and Wealth Are Nothing Like 1917–28," Cato Institute, May 20, 2014, https://www.cato.org/blog/piketty-problems-top-1-shares-income-wealth-are-nothing-1917-28.

4. Scott Winship, "Overstating the Costs of Inequality," *National Affairs,* Spring 2013, https://nationalaffairs.com/publications/detail/overstating-the-costs-of-inequality.

5. Ibid.

6. Ibid.

7. Ibid.

8. Ibid.
9. Ibid.

CHAPTER 7: UNDER CAPITALISM, THE 1 PERCENT IS ALWAYS CHANGING

1. Gregg Re, "Bernie Sanders, at Combative Fox News Town Hall, Makes No Apologies for Making Millions," Fox News, April 15, 2019.
2. John Phelan, "Bernie Is a Capitalist, Whether He Likes It or Not," Foundation for Economic Freedom, April 19, 2019, https://fee.org/articles/bernie-is-a-capitalist-whether-he-likes-it-or-not/.
3. Perry, "Some Amazing Findings on Income Mobility in the US."
4. Robert Carroll, "Special Report: Income Mobility and the Persistence of Millionaires, 1999 to 2007," Tax Foundation, June 2010, https://files.taxfoundation.org/legacy/docs/sr180.pdf.
5. Andrew Syrios, "A Closer Look at Income Inequality," Mises Institute, March 31, 2014, https://mises.org/library/closer-look-income-inequality.
6. Domenech, "Why Inequality Doesn't Matter."

CHAPTER 8: THE POOR ARE BETTER OFF UNDER CAPITALISM

1. Selwyn Duke, "The Equality Con: Why Income Gaps Don't Matter," *Observer*, February 1, 2017, https://observer.com/2017/02/npr-oxfam-report-eight-richest-men/.
2. Ibid.
3. Ibid.
4. Thomas Sowell, "Socialism for the Uninformed," *Indianapolis Business Journal* 37, no. 16, 15B, https://www.creators.com/read/thomas-sowell/05/16/socialism-for-the-uninformed.
5. Duke, "The Equality Con."
6. Dalibor Rohac, "Income Inequality Doesn't Matter," *Washington Times*, May 13, 2011, https://www.washingtontimes.com/news/2011/may/13/income-inequality-doesnt-matter/.
7. Winston Churchill, "Speech in the House of Commons," UK Parliament, October 22, 1945, https://api.parliament.uk/historic-hansard/commons/1945/oct/22/demobilisation#S5CV0414P0_19451022_HOC_300.
8. Ibid.
9. Harry Frankfurt, "Inequality Isn't Immoral," *Los Angeles Times*, October 9, 2015, https://www.latimes.com/opinion/op-ed/la-oe-1011-frankfurt-inequality-morality-20151011-story.html.
10. Steven Pinker, "Why Income Inequality Is Not the Injustice We Perceive It to Be," Big Think, February 13, 2018, https://bigthink.com/big-think-books/steven-pinker-enlightenment-now-inequality-happiness.
11. Rea Hederman and David Azerrad, "Defending the Dream: Why Income Inequality Doesn't Threaten Opportunity," Heritage Foundation, September 13, 2012, https://www.heritage.org/poverty-and-inequality/report/defending-the-dream-why-income-inequality-doesnt-threaten-opportunity.
12. Ludwig von Mises, "The Inequality of Wealth and Income," Mises Institute,

March 23, 2016, https://mises.org/wire/mises-inequality-wealth-and
-income.

13. Ed Fuelner, "Socialism, the True Gospel of Greed," *Washington Times,* June 10,
2019, https://www.washingtontimes.com/news/2019/jun/10/socialism-is-the
-opposite-of-freedom/.

14. Stuart Dredge, "Facebook Closes Its $2bn Oculus Rift Acquisition. What Next?"
Guardian, July 22, 2014, https://www.theguardian.com/technology/2014
/jul/22/facebook-oculus-rift-acquisition-virtual-reality.

15. The Daily Dish, "Quote for the Day," *Atlantic,* August 12, 2008, https://www
.theatlantic.com/daily-dish/archive/2008/08/quote-for-the-day/213088/.

16. Duke, "The Equality Con."

CHAPTER 9: BERNIE'S SOCIALISM ALSO INCLUDES PRAISE FOR DICTATORS

1. Jonathan Swan, "Sanders Defends Past Praise of Fidel Castro," *Hill,* March 9,
2016, https://thehill.com/blogs/ballot-box/presidential-races/272485-sanders
-defends-past-praise-of-fidel-castro.

2. David Unsworth, "Bernie Sanders' Longtime Hypocritical Infatuation with
Nicaraguan Communism," *Panam Post,* May 3, 2018, https://panampost.com
/david-unsworth/2018/05/03/bernie-sanders-longtime-hypocritical
-infatuation-with-nicaraguan-communism/.

3. Ibid.

4. Michael Moynihan, "When Bernie Sanders Thought Castro and the Sandinistas
Could Teach America a Lesson," *Daily Beast,* February 28, 2016, https://www
.thedailybeast.com/when-bernie-sanders-thought-castro-and-the-sandinistas
-could-teach-america-a-lesson.

5. Ibid.

6. Stephen Kinzer, "Socialist? Yes, Says Sandinista Chief," *New York Times,* July 20,
1988, https://www.nytimes.com/1988/07/20/world/socialist-yes-says
-sandinista-chief.html.

7. Moynihan, "When Bernie Sanders Thought Castro and the Sandinistas Could
Teach America a Lesson."

8. Ibid.

9. Michele Ver Ploeg and Ilya Rahkovsky, "Recent Evidence on the Effects of Food Store
Access on Food Choice and Diet Quality," United States Department of Agriculture,
May 2, 2016, https://www.ers.usda.gov/amber-waves/2016/may/recent-evidence
-on-the-effects-of-food-store-access-on-food-choice-and-diet-quality/.

10. Moynihan, "When Bernie Sanders Thought Castro and the Sandinistas Could
Teach America a Lesson."

11. Jesse M. Plunkett, "Putting an End to the Venezuela vs. Sweden Debate," *Orlando
Sentinel,* October 25, 2018, https://www.orlandosentinel.com/opinion/os-op-us
-democratic-socialists-dont-get-scandinavia-20181025-story.html.

12. Ibid.

13. Moynihan, "When Bernie Sanders Thought Castro and the Sandinistas Could
Teach America a Lesson."

CHAPTER 10: TODAY'S AMERICAN SOCIALISTS DON'T KNOW WHAT
SOCIALISM MEANS

1. Geoff Dembicki, "Socialism Is Incredibly Popular but Does Anyone Know What
    'Socialism' Is?," *Vice*, October 4, 2018, https://www.vice.com/en_us/article
    /a3p4y8/what-actual-socialists-think-about-socialism.
2. Charles Krupa, "What Would a Socialist America Look Like?," *Politico*,
    September 3, 2018, https://www.politico.com/magazine/story/2018/09/03
    /what-would-a-socialist-america-look-like-219626.
3. Dembicki, "Socialism Is Incredibly Popular but Does Anyone Know What
    'Socialism' Is?"
4. Lukas Mikelionis, "Socialist Demo Ocasio-Cortez Laments Coffee Shop's
    Closure—Over Wage Hikes That She Supports," Fox News, August 22, 2018,
    https://www.foxnews.com/politics/socialist-dem-ocasio-cortez-laments
    -coffee-shops-closure-over-wage-hikes-that-she-supports.
5. Jeffrey Dorfman, "Sorry Bernie Bros but Nordic Countries Are Not
    Socialist," *Forbes*, July 8, 2018, https://www.forbes.com/sites
    /jeffreydorfman/2018/07/08/sorry-bernie-bros-but-nordic-countries-are
    -not-socialist/#111e274274ad; Corey Iacono, "The Myth of Scandinavian
    Socialism," Foundation for Economic Education, February 25, 2016, https://
    fee.org/articles/the-myth-of-scandinavian-socialism/, https://www
    .austriancenter.com/shattering-myth-nordic-socialism/; Kai Weiss, "Shattering
    the Myth of Nordic Socialism," Svensk Tidskrift, June 8, 2018, http://www
    .svensktidskrift.se/shattering-the-myth-of-nordic-socialism/; Chris Moody,
    "Bernie Sanders' American Dream Is in Denmark," CNN, February 17, 2016,
    https://www.cnn.com/2016/02/17/politics/bernie-sanders-2016-denmark
    -democratic-socialism/index.html.
6. Dembicki, "Socialism Is Incredibly Popular but Does Anyone Know What
    'Socialism' Is?"
7. Ibid.
8. "What Is Democratic Socialism?," Democratic Socialists of America, https://
    www.dsausa.org/about-us/what-is-democratic-socialism/.
9. "Socialism in America," *Economist*, August 30, 2018, https://www.economist
    .com/united-states/2018/08/30/socialism-in-america.
10. Dembicki, "Socialism Is Incredibly Popular but Does Anyone Know What
    'Socialism' Is?"
11. "Socialism in America," *Economist*, August 30, 2018, https://www.economist
    .com/united-states/2018/08/30/socialism-in-america.
12. Dembicki, "Socialism Is Incredibly Popular but Does Anyone Know What
    'Socialism' Is?"
13. Jack Staples-Butler, "The Falsity of the Sanders Venezuela Meme," Quillette,
    March 10, 2018, https://quillette.com/2018/03/10/sanders-venezuela
    -meme/.
14. Ibid.
15. George Reisman, "Why Nazism Was Socialism and Why Socialism Is
    Totalitarian," Mises Institute, November 11, 2005, https://mises.org/library
    /why-nazism-was-socialism-and-why-socialism-totalitarian.

CHAPTER 11: BERNIE SANDERS IS TOO LIBERAL TO GET ELECTED IN DENMARK

1. Nima Sanandaji, "5 Myths About Nordic Socialism Peddled by the Left," The Stream, September 6, 2016, https://stream.org/5-myths-nordic-socialism -mislead-the-american-left/.
2. Moody, "Bernie Sanders' American Dream Is in Denmark."
3. "Transcript of the Democratic Presidential Debate," New York Times, February 5, 2016, http://www.nytimes.com/2016/02/05/us/politics/transcript-of-the -democratic-presidential-debate.html.
4. Valerie Richardson, "Corporate Taxes Would 'Absolutely' Go Back Up if Democrats Win Senate in 2018," Washington Times, December 17, 2017, https:// www.washingtontimes.com/news/2017/dec/17/sen-bernie-sanders-corporate -taxes-would-absolutel/.
5. Moody, "Bernie Sanders' American Dream Is in Denmark."
6. Ibid.
7. Ibid.

CHAPTER 12: NO, BERNIE, SCANDINAVIA IS NOT SOCIALIST

1. Murray N. Rothbard, "The End of Socialism and the Calculation Debate Revisited," Mises Institute, December 8, 2006, https://mises.org/library/end -socialism-and-calculation-debate-revisited.
2. Giancarlo Sopo, "Debunking Socialist Myths: 90 Percent of Scandinavia's Wealth Is Privately Owned," Federalist, August 17, 2018, http://thefederalist .com/2018/08/17/debunking-socialist-myths-90-percent-scandinavias-wealth -privately-owned/.
3. Corey Iacono, "The Myth of Scandinavian Socialism," Foundation for Economic Education, February 25, 2016, https://fee.org/articles/the-myth -of-scandinavian-socialism/; Weiss, "Shattering the Myth of Nordic Socialism."
4. John Larabell, "Scandinavia: Successful Socialism?," New American, August 10, 2016, https://www.thenewamerican.com/economy/economics/item/23805 -scandinavia-successful-socialism.
5. Sopo, "Debunking Socialist Myths," The Federalist, August 17, 2018.
6. Tyler Cowen, "Denmark's Nice, Yes, but Danes Live Better in U.S.," Mercatus Center, August 16, 2016, https://www.mercatus.org/expert_commentary /denmarks-nice-yes-danes-live-better-us; Tyler Cowen, "The Myth of Scandinavian Socialism," Las Vegas Review Journal, August 20, 2016, https:// www.reviewjournal.com/opinion/the-myth-of-scandinavian-socialism/.
7. Jesse M. Plunkett, "Putting an End to the Venezuela vs. Sweden Debate," Orlando Sentinel, October 25, 2018, https://www.orlandosentinel.com/opinion/os-op-us -democratic-socialists-dont-get-scandinavia-20181025-story.html.
8. Jordan Drischler, "Self-Identified Socialists Don't Know What They're Talking About," Pitt News, September 6, 2016, https://pittnews.com/article/110288 /opinions/columns/self-identified-socialists-dont-know-theyre-talking/.
9. Plunkett, "Putting an End to the Venezuela vs. Sweden Debate."

CHAPTER 13: SWEDEN'S RICHES ACTUALLY CAME FROM CAPITALISM
1. Dorfman, "Sorry Bernie Bros but Nordic Countries Are Not Socialist."
2. Ibid.
3. Matt Palumbo, "Does Socialism Work in Scandinavia?," *The Dan Bongino Show*, July 10, 2018, https://bongino.com/does-socialism-work-in-scandinavia-part-1/.
4. Dorfman, "Sorry Bernie Bros but Nordic Countries Are Not Socialist."
5. Palumbo, "Does Socialism Work in Scandinavia?"
6. Rich Lowry, "Sorry, Bernie—Scandinavia Is No Socialist Paradise After All," *New York Post*, October 19, 2015, https://nypost.com/2015/10/19/sorry-bernie-scandinavia-is-no-socialist-paradise-after-all/.
7. Weiss, "Shattering the Myth of Nordic Socialism"; Drischler, "Self-Identified Socialists Don't Know What They're Talking About."
8. Iacono, "The Myth of Scandinavian Socialism."
9. Dorfman, "Sorry Bernie Bros but Nordic Countries Are Not Socialist."
10. Chris Matthews, "What the Left Gets Wrong About Scandinavia," *Fortune*, January 26, 2016, http://fortune.com/2016/01/26/democrat-bernie-sanders-scandinavia-socialism/.
11. Palumbo, "Does Socialism Work in Scandinavia?"
12. Catherine Boyle, "Clinton and Sanders: Why the Big Deal About Denmark?," CNBC, October 14, 2015, https://www.cnbc.com/2015/10/14/clinton-and-sanders-why-the-big-deal-about-denmark.html.
13. Palumbo, "Does Socialism Work in Scandinavia?"
14. Plunkett, "Putting an End to the Venezuela vs. Sweden Debate."
15. Daniel Lacalle, "Face It, Nordic Counties Aren't Socialist," Mises Institute, June 8, 2018, https://mises.org/wire/face-it-nordic-countries-arent-socialist.
16. Jesús Fernández-Villaverde and Lee E. Ohanian, "How Sweden Overcame Socialism," *Wall Street Journal*, January 9, 2019, https://www.wsj.com/articles/how-sweden-overcame-socialism-11547078767?mod=searchresults&page=1&pos=1.
17. Plunkett, "Putting an End to the Venezuela vs. Sweden Debate."
18. Drischler, "Self-Identified Socialists Don't Know What They're Talking About."
19. Sanandaji, "5 Myths About Nordic Socialism Peddled by the Left."
20. Jeff Jacoby, "No, Bernie Sanders, Scandinavia Is Not a Socialist Utopia," *Boston Globe*, October 15, 2016, https://www.bostonglobe.com/opinion/2015/10/15/bernie-sanders-scandinavia-not-socialist-utopia/lUk9N7dZotJRbvn8PosoIN/story.html.
21. Rich Lowry, "Sorry, Bernie—Scandinavia Is No Socialist Paradise After All," *New York Post*, October 19, 2015, https://nypost.com/2015/10/19/sorry-bernie-scandinavia-is-no-socialist-paradise-after-all/.
22. Sanandaji, "5 Myths About Nordic Socialism Peddled by the Left."
23. Stefan Karlsson, "The Sweden Myth," Mises Institute, August 7, 2006, https://mises.org/library/sweden-myth.
24. Ibid.
25. John Larabell, "Scandinavia: Successful Socialism?," *New American*, August 10, 2016, https://www.thenewamerican.com/economy/economics/item/23805-scandinavia-successful-socialism.

26. Ibid.
27. Karlsson, "The Sweden Myth."
28. Ibid.
29. Sanandaji, "5 Myths About Nordic Socialism Peddled by the Left."
30. Karlsson, "The Sweden Myth."
31. Ibid.

CHAPTER 14: THE NORDIC MODEL IS WELFARISM, NOT SOCIALISM

1. Corey Iacono, "The Myth of Scandinavian Socialism," Foundation for Economic Education, February 25, 2016, https://fee.org/articles/The-Myth-Of -Scandinavian-Socialism/; Kai Weiss, "Shattering the Myth of Nordic Socialism," Svensk Tidskrift, June 8, 2018, http://www.svensktidskrift.se /Shattering-The-Myth-Of-Nordic-Socialism/.
2. Johan Norberg, "Dead Wrong, with Johan Norberg—Swedish Taxes: Squeeze the Poor," Free to Choose Network, September 12, 2018, https://www.youtube .com/watch?v=54gVHx3sbGk.
3. Palumbo, "Does Socialism Work in Scandinavia?"
4. Dorfman, "Sorry Bernie Bros but Nordic Countries Are Not Socialist."
5. Plunkett, "Putting an End to the Venezuela vs. Sweden Debate."
6. Dorfman, "Sorry Bernie Bros but Nordic Countries Are Not Socialist."
7. "Socialism in America," Economist, August 30, 2018, https://www.economist .com/united-states/2018/08/30/socialism-in-america.
8. Barack Obama, "Remarks by President Obama and Prime Minister Reinfeldt of Sweden in Joint Press Conference," White House Archives, September 4, 2013, https://obamawhitehouse.archives.gov/the-press-office/2013/09/04/remarks -president-obama-and-prime-minister-reinfeldt-sweden-joint-press.
9. Nima Sanandaji, "Misreading the Nordic Model," Foreign Affairs, August 17, 2016, https://www.foreignaffairs.com/articles/northern-europe/2016-08-17 /misreading-nordic-model.
10. Moody, "Bernie Sanders' American Dream is in Denmark."
11. Lars Hedegaard, "Denmark as a Model for American Socialists," Gatestone Institute, May 21, 2019, https://www.gatestoneinstitute.org/12881/denmark -welfare-socialism.
12. Peter Levring, "Soon, Cars in Denmark Will Only Be Taxed at 100%," Bloomberg, August 29, 2017, https://www.bloomberg.com/news/articles /2017-08-29/soon-cars-in-denmark-will-only-be-taxed-at-100.
13. Palumbo, "Does Socialism Work in Scandinavia?"
14. Larabell, "Scandinavia: Successful Socialism?"
15. Plunkett, "Putting an End to the Venezuela vs. Sweden Debate."

CHAPTER 15: SWEDEN IS SHRINKING TAXES AND WELFARE

1. "SWEDEN. Something Souring in Utopia," Time, July 19, 1976, http://content .time.com/time/magazine/article/0,9171,914329,00.html.
2. Jeff Jacoby, "No, Bernie Sanders, Scandinavia Is Not a Socialist Utopia," Boston Globe, October 15, 2016, https://www.bostonglobe.com/opinion/2015/10/15

/bernie-sanders-scandinavia-not-socialist-utopia/lUk9N7dZotJRbvn8PosoIN
/story.html.

3. Drischler, "Self-Identified Socialists Don't Know What They're Talking About."

4. Lowry, "Sorry, Bernie—Scandinavia Is No Socialist Paradise After All."

5. Karlsson, "The Sweden Myth."

6. Sanandaji, "5 Myths About Nordic Socialism Peddled by the Left," The Stream, September 6, 2016, https://stream.org/5-myths-nordic-socialism-mislead-the -american-left/. Larabell, "Scandinavia: Successful Socialism?"

7. Karlsson, "The Sweden Myth."

8. Drischler, "Self-Identified Socialists Don't Know What They're Talking About."

9. Sanandaji, "5 Myths About Nordic Socialism Peddled by the Left."

10. Larabell, "Scandinavia: Successful Socialism?"

11. Ibid.

12. Sanandaji, "5 Myths About Nordic Socialism Peddled by the Left."

13. Lowry, "Sorry, Bernie—Scandinavia Is No Socialist Paradise After All."

14. Daniel J. Mitchell, "Sweden Repeals Wealth Tax," Cato Institute, March 31, 2007, https://www.cato.org/blog/sweden-repeals-wealth-tax.

15. Larabell, "Scandinavia: Successful Socialism?"

16. Jacoby, "No, Bernie Sanders, Scandinavia Is Not a Socialist Utopia."

17. Karlsson, "The Sweden Myth."

18. Mitchell, "Sweden Repeals Wealth Tax."

19. Drischler, "Self-Identified Socialists Don't Know What They're Talking About."

20. Mitchell, "Sweden Repeals Wealth Tax."

21. "TV Says Borg Had Tax Waiver Deal in Sweden," Chicago Tribune, January 13, 1998, https://www.chicagotribune.com/news/ct-xpm-1998-01-13-9801140296 -story.html.

22. Lowry, "Sorry, Bernie—Scandinavia Is No Socialist Paradise After All."

23. Sanandaji, "5 Myths About Nordic Socialism Peddled by the Left."

24. Karlsson, "The Sweden Myth."

25. Per Bylund, "Turning Their Backs on Sweden's Welfare State," Mises Institute, January 27, 2014, https://mises.org/wire/turning-their-backs-swedens-welfare -state.

26. Chris Matthews, "What the Left Gets Wrong About Scandinavia," Fortune, January 26, 2016, http://fortune.com/2016/01/26/democrat-bernie-sanders -scandinavia-socialism/.

CHAPTER 16: WELFARISM REQUIRES HIGH MIDDLE-CLASS TAXES

1. Brian Riedl, "Why 70 Percent Tax Rates Cannot Finance Socialism," National Review, January 8, 2019, https://www.nationalreview.com/2019/01/alexandria -ocasio-cortez-70-percent-tax-cannot-finance-socialism/.

2. Ben White, "Soak the Rich? Americans Say Go for It," Politico, February 4, 2019, https://www.politico.com/story/2019/02/04/democrats-taxes-economy -policy-2020-1144874.

3. Robert Bellafiore, "America Already Has a Progressive Tax System," Tax Foundation, January 11, 2019, https://taxfoundation.org/america-progressive -tax-system/.
4. Palumbo, "Does Socialism Work in Scandinavia?"
5. Kai Weiss, "Shattering the Myth of Nordic Socialism," Svensk Tidskrift, June 8, 2018, http://www.svensktidskrift.se/shattering-the-myth-of-nordic -socialism/.
6. José Niño, "Dismantling the Myth of Scandinavian Exceptionalism," American Institute for Economic Research, January 13, 2018, https://www.aier.org/article /dismantling-myth-scandinavian-exceptionalism.
7. Mitchell, "Sweden Repeals Wealth Tax," Cato Institute, March 31, 2007, https:// www.cato.org/blog/sweden-repeals-wealth-tax.
8. Per Bylund, "Turning Their Backs on Sweden's Welfare State," Mises Institute, January 27, 2014, https://mises.org/wire/turning-their-backs-swedens-welfare -state.
9. Jacoby, "No, Bernie Sanders, Scandinavia Is Not a Socialist Utopia."
10. Larabell, "Scandinavia: Successful Socialism?"
11. Plunkett, "Putting an End to the Venezuela vs. Sweden Debate."

CHAPTER 17: AMERICAN SCANDINAVIANS HAVE IT BETTER HERE THAN IN SCANDINAVIA
1. Paul Krugman, "A Lot to Learn from Denmark's Successes and Failures," *Irish Times*, October 20, 2015, https://www.irishtimes.com/business/economy/paul -krugman-a-lot-to-learn-from-denmark-s-successes-and-failures-1.2397860.
2. Ben Shapiro, "America's Left Is Falling in Love with Scandinavian Socialism. So Why Are Scandinavians Moving Right?," *The Daily Wire*, October 19, 2015, https://www.dailywire.com/news/483/americas-left-falling-love-scandinavian -socialism-ben-shapiro.
3. Matthews, "What the Left Gets Wrong About Scandinavia."
4. William L. Anderson, "Sorry, Stiglitz, It's Socialism That's Rigged—Not Capitalism," Mises Institute, November 14, 2018, https://mises.org/wire/sorry -stiglitz-it's-socialism-'s-rigged--not-capita.
5. Lowry, "Sorry, Bernie—Scandinavia Is No Socialist Paradise After All."
6. Sanandaji, "5 Myths About Nordic Socialism Peddled by the Left."
7. Ibid.
8. Rich Lowry, "Sorry, Bernie—Scandinavia Is No Socialist Paradise After All."
9. Ibid.
10. Ibid.
11. Tyler Cowen, "The Myth of Scandinavian Socialism," *Las Vegas Review-Journal*, August 20, 2016, https://www.reviewjournal.com/opinion/the-myth-of -scandinavian-socialism/.
12. Jacoby, "No, Bernie Sanders, Scandinavia Is Not a Socialist Utopia."
13. Nima Sanandaji, *Scandinavian Unexceptionalism* (London: Institute of Economic Affairs, 2015), 62.
14. José Niño, "Dismantling the Myth of Scandinavian Exceptionalism," American

Institute for Economic Research, January 13, 2018, https://www.aier.org/article/dismantling-myth-scandinavian-exceptionalism.
15. Cowen, "The Myth of Scandinavian Socialism."

CHAPTER 18: SWEDISH COLLEGE IS FREE, BUT IT'S NOT CHEAP OR UNIVERSAL

1. Tiffany May, "For Survivors of a 9-Hour Chinese Exam, a Door Opens to America," *New York Times*, June 13, 2018, https://www.nytimes.com/2018/06/13/world/asia/china-gaokao-new-hampshire.html.
2. Larabell, "Scandinavia: Successful Socialism?"
3. Matt Phillips, "College in Sweden Is Free but Students Still Have a Ton of Debt. How Can That Be?," *Quartz*, May 31, 2013, https://qz.com/85017/college-in-sweden-is-free-but-students-still-have-a-ton-of-debt-how-can-that-be/.

CHAPTER 19: SOCIALISM BECOMES AUTHORITARIANISM

1. Tyler Curtis, "George Bernard Shaw Was so Enamored with Socialism He Advocated Genocide to Advance It," Foundation for Economic Education, January 9, 2019, https://fee.org/articles/george-bernard-shaw-was-so-enamored-with-socialism-he-advocated-genocide-to-advance-it/.
2. George Reisman, "Why Nazism Was Socialism and Why Socialism Is Totalitarian," Mises Institute, November 11, 2005, https://mises.org/library/why-nazism-was-socialism-and-why-socialism-totalitarian.
3. Chris Smith, "In Conversation: Bill de Blasio," *New York*, September 4, 2017, http://nymag.com/intelligencer/2017/09/bill-de-blasio-in-conversation.html?gtm=bottom.
4. Ibid.
5. Reisman, "Why Nazism Was Socialism and Why Socialism Is Totalitarian."
6. Nick Givas, "Rubio Leads Bipartisan Backlash After De Blasio Quotes Castro Ally Che Guevara," Fox News, June 27, 2019. https://www.foxnews.com/politics/de-blasio-apologizes-for-che-guevara-quote-seiu.
7. Ibid.
8. Ibid.
9. Ibid.
10. Ibid.
11. Ibid.
12. Ibid.
13. Ibid.
14. Ibid.
15. Ibid.
16. Ibid.
17. Ibid.
18. Ibid.
19. Ibid.
20. Ibid.

CHAPTER 20: HITLER WAS A SOCIALIST

1. George Watson, "Hitler and the Socialist Dream," *Independent*, November 22, 1998, https://www.independent.co.uk/arts-entertainment/hitler-and-the-socialist-dream-1186455.html.
2. Ibid.
3. Nazi Conspiracy and Aggression, vol. 4, 1946. "Translation of Document 1708-PS," Washington, DC: Office of United States Chief of Counsel for Prosecution of Axis Criminality, http://www.loc.gov/rr/frd/Military_Law/pdf/NT_Nazi_Vol-IV.pdf, 208–11.
4. F. A. Hayek, *The Collected Works of F.A. Hayek,* vol. 2, *The Road to Serfdom* (New York: Taylor & Francis, 2008).
5. Jonah Goldberg, "Nazis: *Still* Socialists," *National Review*, February 27, 2014.
6. Ibid.
7. Reisman, "Why Nazism Was Socialism and Why Socialism Is Totalitarian."
8. Peter Drucker, *The End of Economic Man: A Study of the New Totalitarianism* (New York: John Day, 1939), 246.
9. George Watson, "Hitler and the Socialist Dream," *Independent*, November 22, 1998, https://www.independent.co.uk/arts-entertainment/hitler-and-the-socialist-dream-1186455.html.
10. Ibid.
11. George Orwell, "Shopkeepers at War," in *The Lion and the Unicorn: Socialism and the English Genius* (London, 1941), http://orwell.ru/library/essays/lion/english/e_saw.
12. Watson, "Hitler and the Socialist Dream."
13. Ibid.
14. Ibid.
15. Ibid.
16. Ibid.
17. Gregor Strasser, "Thoughts About the Tasks of the Future: The Spirit of the Economy," *Nazi Ideology before 1933,* translated by Barbara Miller Lane and Leila J. Rupp (Manchester, England: Manchester University Press, 1978), 89.
18. Watson, "Hitler and the Socialist Dream."
19. Ibid.
20. Ibid.
21. Ibid.
22. Ibid.
23. Ibid.

CHAPTER 21: THE NAZIS HATED CAPITALISM

1. Chris Calton, "The Myth of 'Nazi Capitalism,'" Mises Institute, October 30, 2017, https://mises.org/library/myth-nazi-capitalism.
2. Ibid.
3. Hayek, *The Road to Serfdom.*
4. Ibid.
5. Ibid.

6. Ibid.
7. Ibid.

CHAPTER 22: THE NAZIS DIDN'T BELIEVE IN PRIVATE PROPERTY

1. Ludwig Von Mises, "Planned Chaos," Mises Institute, April 1, 1961, https://mises.org/library/myth-nazi-capitalism.
2. Reisman, "Why Nazism Was Socialism and Why Socialism Is Totalitarian."
3. Ayn Rand, "The Fascist New Frontier," Ayn Rand Column, http://aynrandlexicon.com/lexicon/fascism-nazism.html.
4. Leonard Peikoff, "The Cause of Nazism," in *The Ominous Parallels* (New York: Stein & Day, 1982), http://aynrandlexicon.com/lexicon/fascism-nazism.html.
5. Chris Calton, "The Myth of 'Nazi Capitalism,'" Mises Institute, October 30, 2017, https://mises.org/library/myth-nazi-capitalism.
6. Adam Young, "Nazism Is Socialism," Mises Institute, September 1, 2001, https://mises.org/library/nazism-socialism.
7. Calton, "The Myth of 'Nazi Capitalism.'"
8. Young, "Nazism Is Socialism."
9. Ibid.
10. Ralph Reiland, "National Socialism," Mises Institute, September 28, 1998, https://mises.org/es/library/national-socialism.
11. Ibid.
12. Ibid.
13. Young, "Nazism Is Socialism."
14. Ibid.
15. Reisman, "Why Nazism Was Socialism and Why Socialism Is Totalitarian."
16. Ibid.
17. Ibid.
18. Young, "Nazism is Socialism."

CHAPTER 23: SOCIALISM ENCOURAGES EUGENICS

1. George Watson, "Hitler and the Socialist Dream," *Independent*, November 22, 1998, https://www.independent.co.uk/arts-entertainment/hitler-and-the-socialist-dream-1186455.html.
2. Ibid.
3. Ibid.
4. Jonathan Freedland, "Eugenics: The Skeleton That Rattles Loudest in the Left's Closet," *Guardian*, February 17, 2012, https://www.theguardian.com/commentisfree/2012/feb/17/eugenics-skeleton-rattles-loudest-closet-left.
5. Ibid.
6. John J. Conley, "Margaret Sanger Was a Eugenicist," *America Magazine*, November 27, 2017, https://www.americamagazine.org/politics-society/2017/11/27/margaret-sanger-was-eugenicist-why-are-we-still-celebrating-her.
7. Ibid.
8. Freedland, "Eugenics: The Skeleton that Rattles Loudest in the Left's Closet."
9. Ibid.

10. Gavan Tredoux, *Comrade Haldane Is Too Busy to Go on Holiday* (New York: Encounter Books, 2018).
11. Ibid.
12. Freedland, "Eugenics: The Skeleton that Rattles Loudest in the Left's Closet."
13. Ibid.
14. Ibid.
15. Matthew McCaffrey, "The Economic Evil of Eugenics," Mises Institute, February 2, 2017, https://mises.org/wire/economic-evil-eugenics.
16. Freedland, "Eugenics: The Skeleton that Rattles Loudest in the Left's Closet."
17. Ibid.
18. Watson, "Hitler and the Socialist Dream."
19. Ibid.

CHAPTER 24: YOUR DEGREE OF ENTHUSIASM FOR SOCIALISM MAY DECIDE WHETHER YOU LIVE OR DIE

1. Alexander Solzhenitsyn, *The Gulag Archipelago* (New York: Harper & Row, 1975), https://archive.org/details/TheGulagArchipelago-Threevolumes/page/n1.
2. Michael Brendan Dougherty, "The Rand Paul Clap Gap," *Week*, March 5, 2015, https://theweek.com/articles/542480/rand-paul-clap-gap-why-gop-afraid-have-real-debate-about-foreign-policy.
3. Seth Lipsky, "Unlike Obama, Rand Paul and Congress Have Israel's Back," *Haaretz*, May 4, 2014, https://www.haaretz.com/opinion/.premium-rand-paul-and-congress-have-israel-s-back-1.5247155.
4. Dougherty, "The Rand Paul Clap Gap."
5. Matt Purple, "Rand Paul Found Guilty of Not Clapping Hard Enough for Bibi Netanyahu," Rare, March 4, 2015, https://rare.us/rare-politics/youre-not-helping/rand-paul-found-guilty-of-not-clapping-hard-enough-for-bibi-netanyahu/.

CHAPTER 25: SOCIALISM PROMISES EQUALITY AND LEADS TO TYRANNY

1. Richard M. Ebeling, "Why Socialism Is Impossible," Foundation for Economic Education, October 1, 2004, https://fee.org/articles/why-socialism-is-impossible/.
2. Ibid.
3. Ibid.
4. Ebeling, "Why Socialism Is Impossible."
5. Mao Tse-tung, *Quotations from Chairman Mao* (Beijing: Foreign Languages Press, 1974).
6. Riazat Butt, "Darwinism, Through a Chinese Lens," *Guardian*, November 16, 2009, https://www.theguardian.com/commentisfree/belief/2009/nov/16/darwin-evolution-china-politics.
7. Maurice Meisner, *Mao's China and After* (New York: Free Press, 1999), 17.
8. James Piereson, "Socialism as a Hate Crime," *New Criterion*, August 21, 2018, https://www.newcriterion.com/blogs/dispatch/socialism-as-a-hate-crime-9746.

9. Nicholas D. Kristof, "China's Rise Goes Beyond Gold Medals," *Spiegel Online*, August 21, 2008, https://www.spiegel.de/international/nicholas-d-kristof -china-s-rise-goes-beyond-gold-medals-a-573436.html.

10. Frank Dikötter, *Mao's Great Famine: The History of China's Most Devastating Catastrophe, 1958–62* (New York: Walker Books, 2010), 333.

11. Frank Dikötter, "Q. & A.: Frank Dikötter on Famine and Mao," interview by Evan Osnos, *New Yorker*, December 15, 2010, https://www.newyorker.com /news/evan-osnos/q-a-frank-diktter-on-famine-and-mao.

12. Frank Dikötter, "Mao's Great Leap to Famine," *New York Times*, December 15, 2010, https://www.nytimes.com/2010/12/16/opinion/16iht-eddikotter16.html.

13. Ibid.

14. Yang Jisheng, *Tombstone: The Great Chinese Famine, 1958–1962* (New York: Farrar, Straus & Giroux, 2013), translated by Edward Friedman, 40.

15. Yang Jisheng, "How Friedrich Hayek Helped Me to Understand China's Economic Tragedy," *Forbes*, May 30, 2013, https://www.forbes.com/sites /realspin/2013/05/30/how-friedrich-hayek-helped-me-to-understand-chinas -economic-tragedy/#6db026f343e0.

16. Dikötter, "Q. & A.: Frank Dikötter on Famine and Mao."

17. Yang Jisheng, "How Friedrich Hayek Helped Me to Understand China's Economic Tragedy."

18. Ibid.

CHAPTER 26: ALL ASPECTS OF CULTURE EVENTUALLY BECOME TARGETS FOR THE PLANNERS

1. Tom Phillips, "The Cultural Revolution: All You Need to Know About China's Political Convulsion," *Guardian*, May 10, 2016, https://www.theguardian.com /world/2016/may/11/the-cultural-revolution-50-years-on-all-you-need-to -know-about-chinas-political-convulsion.

2. Ming Wang, *From Darkness to Sight* ([n.p.]: Dunham Books, 2016).

3. Phillips, "The Cultural Revolution."

4. Alice Shen, "During the Cultural Revolution He Had to Toil in the Fields, Now He's Leading China's Biggest Ever Antarctic Mission," *South China Morning Post*, December 5, 2018, https://www.scmp.com/news/china/science /article/2176362/during-cultural-revolution-he-had-toil-fields-now-hes-leading.

5. Chris Buckley, Didi Kirsten Tatlow, Jane Perlez, and Amy Qin, "Voices from China's Cultural Revolution," *New York Times*, May 16, 2016, https://www .nytimes.com/interactive/2016/05/16/world/asia/17china-cultural-revolution -voices.html.

6. Ibid.

7. Zehao Zhou, "I Survived China's Horrific Cultural Revolution," *York Daily Record*, May 11, 2016, https://www.ydr.com/story/opinion /columnists/2016/05/11/survived-chinas-horrific-cultural-revolution -column/84192734/.

8. Ibid.

9. Ibid.

10. Karoline Kan, "My Uncle Was a Red Guard in China's Cultural Revolution. He Isn't Sorry," *Foreign Policy,* May 16, 2016, https://foreignpolicy.com/2016/05/16/my-uncle-was-a-red-guard-in-chinas-cultural-revolution-he-isnt-sorry/.
11. Ibid.
12. Tania Branigan, "China's Cultural Revolution," *Guardian,* March 27, 2013, https://www.theguardian.com/world/2013/mar/27/china-cultural-revolution-sons-guilt-zhang-hongping.
13. David McKenzie and Steven Jiang, "Murdered for Mao," CNN, June 4, 2014, https://www.cnn.com/2014/06/04/world/asia/china-maoist-scars/index.html.
14. David Segal, "China Brings Its Past to Ping-Pong's Birthplace," *New York Times,* July 29, 2012, https://www.nytimes.com/2012/07/30/sports/olympics/china-brings-its-past-to-ping-pongs-birthplace.html.

CHAPTER 27: IF NO ONE HAS TO WORK, NO ONE WILL

1. David Kestenbaum and Jacob Goldstein, "The Secret Document That Transformed China," NPR, January 20, 2012, http://www.npr.org/sections/money/2012/01/20/145360447/the-secret-document-that-transformed-china.

CHAPTER 28: THE CURE FOR FAILED SOCIALISM IS ALWAYS MORE SOCIALISM

1. Robin McDowell, "Pol Pot: Mistakes Were Made," AP News, October 23, 1997, https://www.apnews.com/2a1128d4b0c52563496f1e296df0a229.
2. Martin Woollacott, "King Norodom Sihanouk Obituary," *Guardian,* October 15, 2012, https://www.theguardian.com/world/2012/oct/15/king-norodom-sihanouk.
3. Andrew Cook, "Lost in Cambodia," *Guardian,* January 9, 2010, https://www.theguardian.com/lifeandstyle/2010/jan/10/malcolm-caldwell-pol-pot-murder.
4. Vincent Cook, "Pol Pot and the Marxist Ideal," Department of Economics and Mercatus Center, George Mason University, http://econfaculty.gmu.edu/bcaplan/museum/cook.htm.
5. Morgan O. Reynolds, "The Cambodian Experiment in Retrospect," Foundation for Economic Education, May 1, 1989, https://fee.org/articles/the-cambodian-experiment-in-retrospect/.
6. Ibid.
7. Cook, "Pol Pot and the Marxist Ideal."
8. Meg Sullivan, "UCLA Demographer Produces Best Estimate Yet of Cambodia's Death Toll Under Pol Pot," UCLA Newsroom, April 16, 2015, https://newsroom.ucla.edu/releases/ucla-demographer-produces-best-estimate-yet-of-cambodias-death-toll-under-pol-pot.
9. Reynolds, "The Cambodian Experiment in Retrospect."
10. James Piereson, "Socialism as a Hate Crime," *New Criterion,* August 21, 2018, https://www.newcriterion.com/blogs/dispatch/socialism-as-a-hate-crime-9746.
11. Reynolds, "The Cambodian Experiment in Retrospect."
12. Elaine McArdle, "Killing Fields of Choeung Ek, Phnom Penh, Cambodia: The Saddest Sight of All," The Whole World Is a Playground, June 13, 2014, https://

www.thewholeworldisaplayground.com/killing-fields-choeung-ek-phnom
-penh-cambodia/.

13. Ibid.
14. Georgie Anne Geyer, "French Marxism and Young Cambodians Were a Deadly Mix," *Chicago Tribune*, June 27, 1997, https://www.chicagotribune.com/news /ct-xpm-1997-06-27-9706270087-story.html.
15. Ibid.
16. Ibid.
17. Ibid.
18. "'Killing Fields' Death Toll May Be Closer to 2 Million," *Washington Post*, https://www.washingtonpost.com/archive/politics/1997/01/26/killing -fields-death-toll-may-be-closer-to-2-million/755b1cd0-f09e-4b11-98c8 -cef6e11be45e/?utm_term=.02324da35779.
19. Aleksandr Solzhenitsyn, *The Gulag Archipelago, 1918–1956* (New York: Basic Books, 1997), 173.
20. Geyer, "French Marxism and Young Cambodians Were a Deadly Mix."
21. McArdle, "Killing Fields of Choeung Ek, Phnom Penh, Cambodia: The Saddest Sight of All."
22. Reynolds, "The Cambodian Experiment in Retrospect."
23. Cook, "Pol Pot and the Marxist Ideal."
24. Reynolds, "The Cambodian Experiment in Retrospect."

CHAPTER 29: POETRY CAN BE DANGEROUS UNDER SOCIALISM

1. Osip Mandelstam, "The Stalin Epigram," Poets.org, translated by W. S. Merwin and Clarence Brown, 1989, https://www.poets.org/poetsorg/poem/stalin -epigram.
2. Viv Groskop, *The Anna Karenina Fix* (New York: Abrams, 2005).
3. Eimear McBride, "'It Gets People Killed': Osip Mandelstam and the Perils of Writing Poetry Under Stalin," *New Statesman*, May 9, 2017, https://www .newstatesman.com/culture/poetry/2017/05/it-gets-people-killed-osip -mandelstam-and-perils-writing-poetry-under-stalin.
4. Ibid.
5. Nadezha Mandelstam, *Hope Against Hope: A Memoir*, translated by Max Hayward (London: Modern Library, 1999), 83.
6. Carl Schreck and Nikita Tatarsky, "Tortured Past," Radio Free Europe, December 27, 2018, https://www.rferl.org/a/russian-memorial-victims-and -perpetrators-of-stalin-s-purges-stand-side-by-side/29679174.html.
7. John Crowfoot, "Witness to the Persecution," *Guardian*, April 16, 2004, https:// www.theguardian.com/books/2004/apr/17/featuresreviews.guardianreview9; Anonymous Writers, "Mandelstam's 'Ode' to Stalin," Cambridge University Press, https://www.cambridge.org/core/services/aop-cambridge-core/content /view/EEE7E9FF664CE46C4FE8F8E25E12AC5D/S0037677900068066a .pdf/div-class-title-mandelstam-s-ode-to-stalin-div.pdf.
8. Milan Kundera, *The Book of Laughter and Forgetting* (New York: Harper Perennial, 1999), 3–4.

9. George Orwell, *1984* (New York: Signet Classics, 1961), 75.
10. Schreck and Tatarsky, "Tortured Past."
11. Ibid.
12. Ibid.
13. "'Whisperers' of Stalin's Russia Find Their Voice," NPR, *Weekend Edition*, December 22, 2007, https://www.npr.org/templates/story/story.php?storyId=17376494.
14. Ibid.
15. Ibid.
16. Eugenia Semyonovna Ginzburg, *Journey into the Whirlwind*, translated by Paul Stevenson and Max Hayward (New York: Harcourt, 1967), 174.

CHAPTER 30: IT'S NOT SOCIALISM WITHOUT PURGES
1. "Jon Basil Utley," Fitzgerald Griffin Foundation, http://www.fgfbooks.com/Utley/Utley-bio.html.
2. Georgie Anne Geyer, "Son Solves Mystery of Father's Death in Soviet Gulag," *UExpress*, September 24, 2007, https://www.uexpress.com/georgie-anne-geyer/2007/9/24/son-solves-mystery-of-fathers-death.
3. Alexander Solzhenitsyn, *One Day in the Life of Ivan Denisovich* (New York: Bantam Books, 1990), 18.
4. Jon Basil Utley, "Vorkuta to Perm," Foundation for Economic Education, July 1, 2005, https://fee.org/articles/vorkuta-to-perm-russias-concentration-camp-museums-and-my-fathers-story/.
5. Geyer, "Son Solves Mystery of Father's Death in Soviet Gulag."
6. James Piereson, "Socialism as a Hate Crime," *New Criterion*, August 21, 2018, https://www.newcriterion.com/blogs/dispatch/socialism-as-a-hate-crime-9746.

CHAPTER 31: SOCIALISM EXPECTS SELFLESS RULERS AND CITIZENS
1. Richard Kilminster, "The Debate About Utopias from a Sociological Perspective," Human Figurations, June 2014, https://quod.lib.umich.edu/h/humfig/11217607.0003.203/--debate-about-utopias-from-a-sociological-perspective?rgn=main;view=fulltext.
2. Merijn Oudenampsen, "In Defence of Utopia," *Krisis,* no. 1 (2016), https://krisis.eu/in-defence-of-utopia/.
3. Ludwig von Mises, *Omnipotent Government* (New Haven, CT: Yale University Press, 1945), v.
4. Karl R. Popper, "Science as Falsification," University of Washington, September 21, 2016, https://staff.washington.edu/lynnhank/Popper-1.pdf.
5. Oudenampsen, "In Defence of Utopia."
6. William Gorton, "Karl Popper: Political Philosophy," *Internet Encyclopedia of Philosophy,* https://www.iep.utm.edu/popp-pol/.
7. Leo Tolstoy, *War and Peace* (Mineola, NY: Dover, 2017), 570.
8. Roger Kimball, "Francis Fukuyama and the End of History," *New Criterion*, February 1992, https://www.newcriterion.com/issues/1992/2/francis-fukuyama-and-the-end-of-history.

9. Leon Trotsky, "Revolutionary and Socialist Art," *Literature and Revolution,* Marxists.org, June 1, 2007, https://www.marxists.org/archive/trotsky/1924/lit_revo/ch08.htm.
10. Murray N. Rothbard, "Marx as Utopian," Mises Institute, November 8, 2012, https://mises.org/library/marx-utopian.
11. Adam B. Ulam, *The Bolsheviks* (Cambridge, MA: Harvard University Press, 1998).

CHAPTER 32: PROGRESS COMES FROM REBELS AND DREAMERS

1. Editors of *Encyclopaedia Britannica,* "Crystal Palace," Britannica.com, May 29, 2019, https://www.britannica.com/topic/Crystal-Palace-building-London.
2. David Patterson, *Exile: The Sense of Alienation in Modern Russian Letters* (Lexington: University Press of Kentucky, 1995), 31.
3. Fyodor Dostoyevsky, "Notes from Underground: Chapter VII," Adelaide University, March 27, 2016, https://ebooks.adelaide.edu.au/d/dostoyevsky/d72n/chapter8.html.
4. Fyodor Dostoyevsky, "Notes from Underground: Chapter IX," Adelaide University, March 27, 2016, https://ebooks.adelaide.edu.au/d/dostoyevsky/d72n/chapter10.html.
5. Dostoyevsky, "Notes from Underground: Chapter VII."
6. Yevgeny Zamyatin, *We* (New York: HarperCollins, 1972), 3.
7. Evgeny Zamyatin, *A Soviet Heretic: Essays by Yevgeny Zamyatin* (Chicago: University of Chicago Press, 1970).
8. Matthew Rothschild, "Margaret Atwood Interview," *Progressive,* December 2, 2010, https://progressive.org/magazine/margaret-atwood-interview/.
9. Evgeny Zamyatin, *We: New Edition* (New York: Penguin, 1993), 65–66.
10. Adrian Wanner, "The Underground Man as Big Brother," *Utopian Studies,* Winter 1997, https://www.questia.com/library/journal/1G1-19535193/the-underground-man-as-big-brother-dostoevsky-s-and.
11. Fyodor Dostoyevsky, *Short Novels of the Masters: Notes from Underground,* edited by Charles Neider (New York: Cooper Square Press, 2001), 146.
12. Sarah J. Young, "Russian Thought Lecture 5," SarahJYoung.com, December 10, 2012, http://sarahjyoung.com/site/2012/12/10/russian-thought-lecture-5-dostoevsky-and-the-anti-rationalist-argument/; Ulam, *The Bolsheviks*; Adrian Wanner, "The Underground Man as Big Brother: Dostoevsky's and Orwell's Anti-Utopia," *Utopian Studies* 8, no. 1 (1997): 77–88 (handout).

CHAPTER 33: FREEDOM IS NOT THE INEVITABLE OUTCOME OF HISTORY AND MUST BE PROTECTED

1. William Gorton, "Karl Popper: Political Philosophy," *Internet Encyclopedia of Philosophy,* https://www.iep.utm.edu/popp-pol/.
2. Eliane Glaser, "Bring Back Ideology," *Guardian,* March 21, 2014, https://www.theguardian.com/books/2014/mar/21/bring-back-ideology-fukuyama-end-history-25-years-on.
3. Timothy Stanley and Alexander Lee, "It's Still Not the End of History," *Atlantic,*

September 1, 2014, https://www.theatlantic.com/politics/archive/2014/09/its
-still-not-the-end-of-history-francis-fukuyama/379394/.
4. Ibid.
5. Kimball, "Francis Fukuyama and the End of History."
6. Ibid.
7. Francis Fukuyama, *The End of History and the Last Man* (New York: Simon & Schuster, 2006), xii.
8. Ibid.
9. Ibid., xx.
10. Isaac Ben-Israel, "Beware of Rule by Dreamers," *Haaretz*, August 1, 2003, https://www.haaretz.com/life/books/1.5354195.
11. Kimball, "Francis Fukuyama and the End of History."
12. Stanley and Lee, "It's Still Not the End of History"; Glaser, "Bring Back Ideology."

CHAPTER 34: SOCIALISM LEADS TO CRONYISM
1. Byron Schlomach, "Crony Capitalism Is Just Socialism Lite," *Hill*, July 24, 2018, https://thehill.com/opinion/finance/398593-crony-capitalism-is-just-socialism-lite.
2. Ibid.
3. Robert Bellafiore, "America Already Has a Progressive Tax System," Tax Foundation, January 11, 2019, https://taxfoundation.org/america-progressive-tax-system/.
4. Adam Brandon, "Are You a Multimillionaire Who Wants to Pay Your 'Fair Share'? Just Donate to the Government," *Washington Examiner,* April 9, 2019, https://www.washingtonexaminer.com/opinion/are-you-a-multimillionaire-who-wants-to-pay-your-fair-share-just-donate-to-the-government.

CHAPTER 35: IF SOCIALISTS CAN'T FIND A CRISIS, THEY WILL CREATE ONE
1. Yaron Steinbuch, "AOC Explains Why 'Farting Cows' Were Considered in Green New Deal," *New York Post*, February 22, 2019, https://nypost.com/2019/02/22/aoc-explains-why-farting-cows-were-considered-in-green-new-deal/.
2. Miguel Bustillo, "In San Joaquin Valley, Cows Pass Cars as Polluters," *Los Angeles Times*, August 2, 2005, https://www.latimes.com/archives/la-xpm-2005-aug-02-me-cows2-story.html.
3. Diane Francis, "The Real Inconvenient Truth," *Financial Post*, December 14, 2009, http://www.financialpost.com/story.html?id=2314438.
4. Jeff Cox, "Ocasio-Cortez's Green New Deal Offers 'Economic Security' for Those 'Unwilling to Work,'" CNBC, February 7, 2019, https://www.cnbc.com/2019/02/07/ocasio-cortezs-green-new-deal-offers-economic-security-for-those-unwilling-to-work.html.
5. Robert Bellafiore, "A Growing Percentage of Americans Have Zero Income Tax Liability," Tax Foundation, March 14, 2019, https://taxfoundation.org/america-progressive-tax-system/.

6. "Earned Income Tax Credit: Small Benefits, Large Costs," Cato Institute.
7. José Niño, "A 'Universal Basic Income' Costs More Than You Think," Mises Institute, June 21, 2018, https://mises.org/wire/universal-basic-income-costs -more-you-think.
8. David Williams, "Solar Energy Delivers Too Little Bang for Billions Invested," *Forbes,* February 25, 2015, https://www.forbes.com/sites/realspin/2015/02/25 /solar-energy-delivers-too-little-bang-for-billions-invested/#3651fa6349f3.
9. "Climate Change Investment Totals USD $359 Billion Worldwide," Climate Policy Initiative, October 22, 2013, https://climatepolicyinitiative.org/press -release/climate-change-investment-totals-usd-359-billion-worldwide/.
10. Stephen Moore, "Follow the (Climate Change) Money," Heritage Foundation, December 18, 2018.
11. "Klimapolitik verteilt das Weltvermögen neu," *Neue Zürcher Zeitung,* November 14, 2010.
12. Barbara Hollingsworth, "UN's Top Climate Official: Goal is to 'Intentionally Transform the Economic Development Model,'" *CNS News,* February 18, 2015; Benjamin Zycher, "The Climate Comintern Speaks," *Hill,* February 10, 2015, https://thehill.com/blogs/pundits-blog/energy-environment/232229-the -climate-comintern-speaks.
13. "Klimapolitik verteilt das Weltvermögen neu," *Neue Zürcher Zeitung,* November 14, 2010.
14. Robert Rapier, "Yes, the U.S. Leads All Countries in Reducing Carbon Emissions," *Forbes,* October 24, 2017, https://www.forbes.com/sites/rrapier /2017/10/24/yes-the-u-s-leads-all-countries-in-reducing-carbon-emissions /#111ea2b35355.
15. Stephen Moore, "Who's the Cleanest of them All," *Washington Times,* August 19, 2018, https://www.washingtontimes.com/news/2018/aug/19/the-united-states -didnt-sign-the-paris-climate-acc/.

CHAPTER 36: SOCIALISM AND CLIMATE CHANGE ALARMISM GO TOGETHER

1. Eric Holthaus (@EricHolthaus), "If you are wondering," Twitter, October 8, 2015, https://twitter.com/ericholthaus/status/1049339997827084295?lang=en.
2. Matthew Huber, "Five Principles of a Socialist Climate Politics," The Trouble, August 16, 2018, https://www.the-trouble.com/content/2018/8/16/five -principals-of-a-socialist-climate-politics.
3. Ian Schwartz, "Chuck Todd: We're Not Going to Give Time to Climate Deniers," *Real Clear Politics,* January 2, 2019, https://www.realclearpolitics.com/video /2019/01/02/chuck_todd_im_not_going_to_give_time_to_climate _deniers.html.
4. Michael Guillen, "Physicist: Don't Fall for the Argument About 'Settled Science,'" Fox News, January 21, 2019, https://www.foxnews.com/opinion /physicist-dont-fall-for-the-argument-about-settled-science.
5. Susan Crockford and Patrick Moore, "What David Attenborough and Netflix's 'Our Planet' Get Wrong About Climate Change," *Townhall,* April 14, 2019,

https://townhall.com/columnists/drpatrickmoore/2019/04/14/what-netflixs
-our-planet-gets-wrong-about-climate-change-n2544726.

6. Adam Popescu, "A Greenland Glacier Is Growing. That Doesn't Mean Melting Is
Over," *National Geographic*, March 25, 2019, https://www.nationalgeographic
.com/environment/2019/03/one-part-of-greenland-ice-growing/.

7. John Bowden, "Ocasio-Cortez: 'World Will End in 12 Years' if Climate Change
Not Addressed," *Hill*, January 22, 2019, https://thehill.com/policy/energy
-environment/426353-ocasio-cortez-the-world-will-end-in-12-years-if-we
-dont-address.

8. Coral Davenport, "Major Climate Report Describes a Strong Risk of Crisis as
Early as 2040," *New York Times*, October 7, 2018, https://www.nytimes.com
/2018/10/07/climate/ipcc-climate-report-2040.html.

9. Tamar Lapin, "Scientists Admit Errors in Study Showing Oceans are Warming,"
New York Post, November 15, 2018, https://nypost.com/2018/11/15/scientists
-admit-errors-in-study-showing-oceans-are-warming/.

10. Chris Mooney and Bray Dennis, "Scientists Acknowledge Key Errors in Study
of How Fast the Oceans are Warming," *Washington Post*, November 13, 2018,
https://www.washingtonpost.com/energy-environment/2018/11/14
/scientists-acknowledge-key-errors-study-how-fast-oceans-are-warming
/?utm_term=.37e695cd62fd.

11. Ben Shapiro, "No, Global Warming Isn't the End of the World. Here's Why,"
Daily Wire, October 11, 2018, https://www.dailywire.com/news/37021
/no-global-warming-isnt-end-world-heres-why-ben-shapiro.

12. "IPCC Third Assessment Report, Chapter 14, Section 14.2.2.2," IPCC, 2001,
https://archive.ipcc.ch/ipccreports/tar/wg1/505.htm.

13. Joshua K. Willis, Andrew Kemp, and Benjamin H. Strauss, "Sea Level Rise:
Introduction," *Smithsonian*, April 2018, https://ocean.si.edu/through-time
/ancient-seas/sea-level-rise.

14. "Global Warming Is Only Part Human Caused," Open Source Systems, Science,
Solutions, http://ossfoundation.us/projects/environment/global-warming
/myths/global-warming-is-only-part-human-caused.

CHAPTER 37: SOCIALIST GREEN NEW DEAL ALLOWS FOR NO DISSENT

1. Robert Conquest, *Reflections on a Ravaged Century* (London: Norton, 2000), 111.
2. Ibid.
3. Megan Murphy, "Twitter Wants Me to Shut Up and the Right Wants Me
to Join Them; I Don't Think I Should Have to Do Either," *Feminist Current*,
November 20, 2018.
4. Nicole Russell, "Twitter Permanently Bans Feminist for Writing That 'Men Aren't
Women,'" *Federalist*, November 25, 2018, https://thefederalist.com/2018/11/25
/twitter-permanently-bans-feminist-writing-men-arent-women/.
5. Ibid.
6. Jack Shafer, "The Conservative Revolt Against Twitter," *Politico*, November 26,
2018, https://www.politico.com/magazine/story/2018/11/26/the-conservative
-revolt-against-twitter-222688.

7. Russell, "Twitter Permanently Bans Feminist for Writing That 'Men Aren't Women.'"

8. Michael Nunez, "Former Facebook Workers: We Routinely Suppressed Conservative News," Gizmodo, May 9, 2016, https://gizmodo.com/former -facebook-workers-we-routinely-suppressed-conser-1775461006.

9. Ibid.

10. Jason Pye and Daniel Savickas, "Pingree, Ocasio-Cortez Pressure Big-Tech CEOs for Sponsoring LibertyCon," Federalist, February 11, 2019, https:// thefederalist.com/2019/02/11/pingree-ocasio-cortez-pressure-big-tech -ceos-sponsoring-libertycon/.

11. Andy Ngo, "Hate-Crime Hoaxes Reflect America's Sickness," National Review, February 18, 2019, https://www.nationalreview.com/2019/02/hate-crime -hoaxes-reflect-americas-sickness/.

12. "Organist Spray Painted 'Heil Trump,' Swastika, Gay Slur on Brown County Church," Fox 59, May 3, 2017, https://fox59.com/2017/05/03/police-organist -spray-painted-heil-trump-swastika-gay-slur-on-brown-county-church/; WWL Staff, "Lafayette woman faces criminal charges after falsely claiming Trump supporters robbed her," 4WWL, November 11, 2016; "Police: Threat to burn UM student wearing hijab did not happen," Fox 2, December 21, 2016.

CHAPTER 38: FAKE NEWS AND PROPAGANDA ON THE RISE IN AMERICA

1. Andrew Sullivan "The Abyss of Hate Versus Hate," New York, January 25, 2019, http://nymag.com/intelligencer/amp/2019/01/andrew-sullivan-the-abyss-of -hate-versus-hate.html?utm_source=tw&__twitter_impression=true.

2. Caitlin Flanagan, "The Media Botched the Covington Catholic Story," Atlantic, January 23, 2019, https://www.theatlantic.com/ideas/archive/2019/01/media -must-learn-covington-catholic-story/581035/.

3. Joseph A. Wulfsohn, "CNN's Chris Cuomo, Don Lemon Pile on Covington Students over MAGA Hats," Fox News, January 23, 2019, https://www.foxnews .com/entertainment/cnns-chris-cuomo-don-lemon-pile-on-covington-students -over-maga-hats.

4. Paul Bedard, "68% Say the Media are Biased, Just 21% Trust 'a Lot,'" Washington Examiner, September 25, 2018, https://www.washingtonexaminer.com /washington-secrets/pew-68-say-the-media-are-biased-just-21-trust-a-lot.

5. Dionne Gleaton, "Bakari Sellers Says Tweet Not Promoting Violence, Students Symbolize Bigotry, Division," Times and Democrat, January 22, 2019, https:// thetandd.com/bakari-sellers-says-tweet-not-promoting-violence-students -symbolize-bigotry/article_6b5cf25d-bb55-5ed1-abd0-7cf5487eede3.html.

6. Marlon James, "Here's the Thing About Covington Catholic School Boy," Facebook, January 20, 2019, https://www.facebook.com/marlon.james1 /posts/10157054513240850.

7. John Kass, "Thought Crimes, Media Abuse and Those Catholic High School Boys from Covington," Chicago Tribune, January 23, 2019, https://www .chicagotribune.com/news/columnists/kass/ct-met-covington-catholic-dc -video-kass-20190122-story.html; Kyle Smith, "Hatcrime and Facecrime,"

National Review, January 23, 2019, https://www.nationalreview.com/2019/01
/covington-catholic-maga-hatcrime-facecrime/; Sarah Mervosh, "Viral Video
Shows Boys in 'Make America Great Again' Hats Surrounding Native Elder,"
New York Times, January 19, 2019, https://www.nytimes.com/2019/01/19/us
/covington-catholic-high-school-nathan-phillips.html?login=email&auth=login
-email; Jon Levine, "GQ Writer Regrets Tweet Calling for Covington Students
to Be Doxxed," *Wrap,* January 21, 2019, https://www.thewrap.com/gq-writer
-regrets-call-for-doxxing-covington-catholic-high-school-students/; Dionne
Gleaton, "Bakari Sellers Says Tweet Not Promoting Violence, Students
Symbolize Bigotry, Division," *Times and Democrat,* January 22, 2019, https://
thetandd.com/bakari-sellers-says-tweet-not-promoting-violence-students
-symbolize-bigotry/article_6b5cf25d-bb55-5ed1-abd0-7cf5487eede3.html;
Tucker Carlson, "Covington Story Was Not About Race but About People in
Power Attacking People They've Failed," Fox News, January 22, 2019, https://
www.foxnews.com/opinion/tucker-carlson-covington-story-was-not
-about-race-but-about-people-in-power-attacking-people-theyve-failed; Steve
Cortes, "Buzzfeed, the Covington Teens and the Harm of False Witness,"
Real Clear Politics, January 22, 2019, https://www.realclearpolitics.com
/articles/2019/01/22/buzzfeed_the_covington_teens_and_the_harms
_of_false_witness_139247.html; Tucker Carlson, "There's No Sympathy for
Covington Catholic Teens in America's Newsrooms," Fox News, January 23,
2019, https://www.foxnews.com/opinion/tucker-carlson-theres-no-sympathy
-for-covington-catholic-teens-in-americas-newsrooms.

CHAPTER 39: WELCOME TO THE PANOPTICON: FACECRIME, PRECRIME,
AND THE SURVEILLANCE STATE

1. Harry Cockburn, "China Blacklists Millions of People from Booking Flights as
   'Social Credit' System Introduced," *Independent,* November 22, 2018, https://
   www.independent.co.uk/news/world/asia/china-social-credit-system-flight
   -booking-blacklisted-beijing-points-a8646316.html.
2. James O'Malley, "China's Social Credit System: The Big Experiment to Turn
   Real Life into a Video Game," *National,* November 20, 2018, https://www
   .thenational.ae/arts-culture/comment/china-s-social-credit-system-the-big
   -experiment-to-turn-real-life-into-a-video-game-1.793732.
3. Anders Corr, "China's Surveillance State: Using Technology to Shape Behavior,"
   La Croix International, February 1, 2019, https://international.la-croix.com
   /news/chinas-surveillance-state-using-technology-to-shape-behavior/9374#.
4. Alex Linder, "Facial Recognition Toiler Paper Dispenser Rolled Out at
   Shanghai Public Bathroom!," *Shanghaiist,* June 8, 2018, http://shanghaiist
   .com/2018/06/08/facial-recognition-toilet-paper-dispenser-rolled-out-at
   -shanghai-public-bathroom/.
5. Nicole Kobie, "The Complicated Truth about China's Social Credit System,"
   Wired, January 21, 2019, https://www.wired.co.uk/article/china-social-credit
   -system-explained.
6. Eamon Barrett, "In China, Facial Recognition Tech Is Watching You," *Fortune,*

October 28, 2018, http://fortune.com/2018/10/28/in-china-facial-recognition-tech-is-watching-you/.

7. David Edelstein, "Blame Runner," *Slate,* May 22, 2019, http://www.slate.com/articles/arts/movies/2002/06/blame_runner.html.

8. Alex Peak, "Minority Report: The Security State and Civil Liberties," AlexPeak.com, http://alexpeak.com/art/films/mr/statism/; John Powers, "Majority Report," *LA Weekly,* June 19, 2002, http://www.laweekly.com/news/majority-report-2134959.

9. Stephen Carson, "Films on Liberty and the State," Mises Institute, November 13, 2006, https://mises.org/library/films-liberty-and-state-1.

10. James Wilkinson, "Civil Liberties Union Horrified by Chicago PD's 'Minority Report' Computer Algorithm That Can Predict Who Might Be a Victim of Crime—or Commit One," *Daily Mail,* May 27, 2016, http://www.dailymail.co.uk/news/article-3613708/Civil-liberties-union-horrified-Chicago-PD-s-Minority-Report-computer-algorithm-predict-victim-crime-commit-one.html#ixzz4wiSTcreR.

11. Simon McCormack, "When Minority Report Becomes New Yorkers' Reality," ACLU, October 11, 2016, https://www.aclu.org/blog/national-security/discriminatory-profiling/when-minority-report-becomes-new-yorkers-reality.

12. Ibid.

13. Barrett, "In China, Facial Recognition Tech is Watching You."

14. G. Clay Whittaker, "China Wants to Make 'Minority Report' a Reality," *Daily Beast,* March 18, 2016, https://www.thedailybeast.com/china-wants-to-make-minority-report-a-reality.

AFTERWORD: FINDING COMMON GROUND

1. Mark Joseph Stern, "The New Criminal Justice Reform Law Has Already Righted One Outrageous Injustice," *Slate,* January 3, 2019, https://slate.com/news-and-politics/2019/01/matthew-charles-released-under-first-step-act.html; Julieta Martinelli, "As He Heads Back to Prison, a Nashville Man Says 'Goodbye' to the New Life He Hoped to Build," Nashville Public Radio, May 25, 2018, https://www.nashvillepublicradio.org/post/he-heads-back-prison-nashville-man-says-goodbye-new-life-he-hoped-build#stream/0.

2. Mary Ann Georgantopoulos, "A Man Was Charged with Pulling a Gun on a Kentucky Couple for Wearing MAGA Hats," BuzzFeed News, February 19, 2019, https://www.buzzfeednews.com/article/maryanngeorgantopoulos/gun-allegedly-pulled-couple-maga-hat-trump-supporters.

3. Heather Mac Donald, "The Frenzied Search for Racism," *City Journal,* February 18, 2019, https://www.city-journal.org/jussie-smollett-bigotry.

INDEX

ABOUT THE AUTHORS

U.S. senator Rand Paul, M.D., is one of the nation's leading advocates for liberty. Elected to the United States Senate in 2010, he has proven to be an outspoken champion for constitutional liberties and fiscal responsibility. As a fierce advocate against government overreach, Senator Paul has fought tirelessly to return government to its limited, constitutional scope. A graduate of Duke University School of Medicine, Dr. Paul completed his residency in ophthalmology at Duke University Medical Center. Since his election to the U.S. Senate, Dr. Paul has continued to perform eye surgery pro bono in his home state of Kentucky and on medical mission trips to countries around the world.

Kelley Ashby Paul serves as Kentucky co-chair of Helping a Hero, a wounded veterans charity that has built over one hundred fully adapted homes for soldiers who have suffered severe injuries. Kelley also serves on the board of the Coalition for Public Safety, a bipartisan organization dedicated to criminal justice reform. She is a frequent speaker and panelist for groups advocating for reduced incarceration rates, alternative drug policy solutions, and better employment opportunities for returning citizens. A writer and former corporate communications manager, Kelley is the author of *True and Constant Friends*, which was published in 2015.

Rand and Kelley have been married since 1990 and are the parents of three sons.